The End of Knowledge in Higher Education

Also available in the Institute of Education series:

THE END OF KNOWLEDGE IN HIGHER EDUCATION

Ronald Barnett and Anne Griffin

Cassell

Wellington House, 125 Strand, London WC2R 0BB

P O Box 605, Herndon, VA 21072

First published 1997

British Library Cataloguing-in-Publication Data

A catalogue record for this book is available from the British Library.

Library of Congress Cataloging-in-Publication Data

ISBN   0-304-33705-6 (hardback)
           0-304-33706-4 (paperback)

Designed and typeset by Kim Allen at Bowling Green Cottages, Oxfordshire.
Printed and bound in Great Britain by Redwood Books, Trowbridge, Wiltshire

Contents

Dedication

For Marjorie Reeves

Acknowledgements

This collection had its beginnings in a conference organized by Anne Griffin on behalf of the Higher Education Foundation at St John's College Oxford, in April 1993. Six of the original conference speakers are represented here: Peter Abbs, Ronald Barnett, Nigel Blake, Sonia Greger, Kate Soper and Anne Seller. Two other of our contributors, John Haldane and Stephen McNair, were also present at the conference. The late Ernest Gellner presented the keynote address, and his powerful views on rationality stimulated many discussions out of which this book grew.

We would like to thank the Trustees of the Foundation for allowing those presenting papers to adapt their material for our book, and for their sympathetic discussions with the editors on the topics raised throughout.

We are grateful to the following publishers for permission to reprint material in this collection:

- Nigel Blake's chapter has appeared in a modified version entitled 'Truth, Identity and Community in the University' in *Curriculum Studies*, Vol. 3 No. 3, 1995.
- Some passages from Anne Seller's chapter also appeared in *Knowing Feminism: on Academic Borders, Territory, and Tribe*' Liz Stanley (ed.), Sage, 1996.
- Mary Midgley's chapter is a modified version of the chapter in *Science Today: A Problem or Crisis*, Ralph Levinson and Jeff Thomas (eds.), Routledge, 1997.

List of Contributors

Ronald Barnett is Professor of Higher Education, Institute of Education, University of London, where he is also Dean of Professional Development. His books include *The Idea of Higher Education* (winner of the SCSE book prize, 1991), *Improving Higher Education* and *The Limits of Competence*.

Anne Griffin was formerly Principal Lecturer at the School of Post-Compulsory Education and Training, University of Greenwich. She has had an extensive involvement in post-16 teacher education and has published in educational journals, mainly on the philosophy of vocational teacher education.

Peter Abbs is Reader in Education at the University of Sussex, where he directs the MA in Language, Arts and Education. He is a poet and author, most recently of *Personal and Other Selected Poems* (1994) and *The Polemics of Imagination: Selected Essays on Art, Culture and Society* (1995).

Nigel Blake lectures at the Institute of Educational Technology, the Open University. He publishes in educational journals on Critical Theory and postmodernism. He is currently Vice-Chair of the Philosophy of Education Society of Great Britain.

Sonia Greger is an Honorary Research Fellow, Department of Social Anthropology at Manchester University. She has published in educational journals on philosophy, aesthetics and social anthropology, which is the perspective of her book *Village on the Plateau* (1985).

John Haldane is Professor of Philosophy and Director of the Centre for Philosophy and Public Affairs, at the University of St Andrews. He has published widely in social and political philosophy and the philosophy of education.

Stephen McNair is Associate Director (HE) at the National Institute for Adult and Continuing Education. He is principal author of the NIACE Policy Discussion paper *An Adult Higher Education: A Vision* (1993).

Mary Midgley was until 1980 Senior Lecturer in Philosophy at the University of Newcastle-upon-Tyne. Her most recent books are *The Ethical Primate: Humans, Freedom amd Morality* (1994) and *Utopias, Dolphins and Computers: Problems in Philosophical Plumbing* (1996).

George Myerson is Reader in English, King's College London. He is the author of *Rhetoric, Reason and Society: Rationality as Dialogue* (1994).

Peter Scott is Professor of Education and Director of the Centre for Policy Studies in Education at the University of Leeds. His most recent book is *The Meanings of Mass Higher Education* (1995).

Anne Seller lectures in Philosophy and Women's Studies at the University of Kent. She has published on philosophy and feminism, most recently in *Knowing the Difference: Feminist Perspectives in Epistemology* (1994) K. Lennon and M. Whitford (eds.), and *Women Review Philosophy: New Writings by Women in Philosophy* (1996) M. Griffiths and M. Whitford (eds.).

Kate Soper is Senior Lecturer in Philosophy at the University of North London. She has published widely on philosophy and feminism. Her writings include *Troubled Pleasures* (1990) and, most recently, *What is Nature? Culture, Politics and the Non-Human* (1995).

Robin Usher is Reader in Post-Compulsory Education and Head of the School of Education at the University of Southampton. He is the author with R. Edwards of *Postmodernism and Education: Different Voices, Different Worlds* (1994).

PART I
Introduction

ONE

Knowledge under Attack: Consumption, Diversity and the Need for Values

Anne Griffin

INTRODUCTION

1993

Higher education in the United Kingdom is in crisis. Few would disagree, although different voices would identify different crises. The crisis in funding resulting from the provision of a mass system to meet demands for access is self-evident, as the government reduces its financial support to higher education. A Robbins-style committee of inquiry into the future of higher education under the chairmanship of Sir Ron Dearing is currently reporting on its 'shape, structure, size and funding' to meet the needs of the next twenty years.

Then, more students with increasingly varied backgrounds and attainments, have precipitated a crisis in how the teaching and learning process should be both conceived and managed, mass enrolment having coincided with both a reduction in staff and a heavier teaching and administrative workload for academics. At the same time the latter on tighter, less often permanent contracts are pressured to publish scholarly work regularly, so that their institutions may gain high ratings in the cyclical national research assessment exercises.

To these escalating pressures have to be added the widespread perception of higher education staff that the academic community is itself under threat in that collegiality is being lost as institutions are more firmly managed along business lines.

Universities have become organizations adopting a more explicit market ethos which dominates working conditions, academic activities and the very character of higher education.

However, none of these crises concern us directly in the book. The crisis that concerns us here relates directly to the purposes and the legitimacy of higher education. Higher education is deeply and intrinsically bound up with knowledge and with values. The higher education student seeks the knowledge, skills and attitudes which will provide a transformative experience in developing the understanding needed for his/her personal and professional life. The teacher *qua* teacher will learn too, and the teacher as researcher will gain knowledge and insights of use and value to the academic community, as well as to serve the needs of a wider public. If society were to attack higher education knowledge as irrelevant, useless or of transient value, or if academics were to reject the knowledge taught as meaningless, then we would confront a crisis arguably more serious than those of finance, organization and structure. For then we would be faced with a crisis in values, especially in moral values.

But this is indeed the crisis we face in higher education today: that knowledge, as we have known it in the academy, is coming to an end. The aim in this introductory chapter is to sketch a general framework within which the arguments of our contributors can be considered. Three main strands of the end of knowledge can be identified, with implications for the values we continue to hold in a pluralistic democratic society.

First, there is a loss of faith in what is called 'the Enlightenment project', with consequent implications for the values of a liberal democracy. Second, there is the market-dominated consumer society which has come to influence knowledge and the learning individual. Third, the group of ideas loosely-termed postmodernism, offer a host of critiques which (I shall argue) both undermine and at the same time give practical support towards the survival and health of knowledge and values in higher education.

Finally, I shall discuss the need for values in higher education: in particular its need to reassert and reinvigorate concepts of rationality and truth, of individual and community, as higher education mounts replies to the attacks on knowledge just indicated.

THE ENLIGHTENMENT PROJECT AND ITS LOST MEANING

The basic metaphor of the Enlightenment in eighteenth-century Western Europe, that of light: 'was intended to convey the message that the progressive development of human reason will illuminate the darkness of ignorance and superstition created by the religious and political institutions of the old despotic social order' (Carr 1995*a*: 121).

Thus freed by reason, human beings would autonomously order and develop their individual lives, building social practices to meet their needs and aspirations; an emancipatory ideal which also sustains a democratic form of society, governed by rational principles. It was the task of education to develop this rationality. This vision of human and social progress was critically linked to science: indeed rationality was centrally construed as the development and application of scientific principles.

The yoking of science and rationality, now partially but by no means wholly disentangled, has had severe consequences for the status, support and development of other disciplines (a term itself under dispute as this book shows). Even today some scientists believe that science is the only way to understand the world, and to contribute to human development (see the chapters in this volume by Midgley, Blake, Scott). Not just science, but scientific *man*: the enlightenment stereotype of the man of reason persists despite powerful feminist rebuttals (see the chapters by Seller, Soper, Greger).

But today this belief in the emancipatory power of the Enlightenment project is rejected as a utopian fiction. The great Enlightenment texts from Rousseau and Kant to Dewey and Freire still survive, but greater peace, democracy, equality or respect for this planet and those living on it have demonstrably not been achieved.

Alongside the scientific take-over of rationality there is its 'transformation ... in so many places into instrumental rationality, its neglect of self-reflectiveness, its setting aside of value considerations' (Greene 1995: 6).

Instrumental rationally legitimizes bureaucracies and underpins, for instance, the working of a market-driven economy such as our own. The market economy in turn has a growing influence on all sectors of education: utilitarian pragmatic thinking increasingly dominates educational thought, policy and practice. Our market-led consumer society is a major factor in undermining knowledge in higher education.

UTILITARIAN KNOWLEDGE, THE CONSUMER AND TECHNOLOGY

British society has long been beset by the issue of how far our education system should serve the needs of industry and commerce, as well as the community and the individual. Notwithstanding the traditional prestige accorded to 'key' professions such as law and medicine in higher education, vocational education has always been a poor relation in the UK education system with sad resonances from Aristotle (concerned with the liberal education of a gentleman): 'the useful arts are considered mean'.

But in the last thirty years, particularly since the Great Debate (1965), when the then Prime Minister, James Callaghan, argued for a dramatically increased focus on vocational education, to prevent the UK from slipping further behind the rest of the Western world in economic performance, vocational programmes designed to increase workforce skills at all levels have been given prominence. These initiatives are described elsewhere (see the chapter by Usher), in particular the idea of competence whose major thrust has been to identify and assess the skills necessary for competent performance in the workplace.

Competence is usually defined in terms of narrow, predominantly behavioural skills which downplay, (and in some cases eliminate) the need for learners to understand and have mastery of those skills they are to perform confidently in specific contexts. Ironically, this means that employees who have attained competence-based

National Vocational Qualifications often still lack the broader skills employers seek and which the programmes were allegedly designed to develop (Hyland 1994).

A 'competency' element which exists in the General National Vocational Qualification, increasingly offered by students as an entry qualification for higher education, must cast doubt in the same way on the adequacy of understanding achieved. The utilitarian ethos of competency has thus begun to find a grip on higher education, with its emphasis on skills, performance criteria and measurable outcomes (Barnett 1994). This threatens the achievement by the learner of broader intellectual qualities, knowledge and understanding which has some potential for use in a variety of contexts.

This learner is not the reasoning individual of the Enlightenment: he or she is a consuming individual, consuming education as one product among others in the market economy. Just as the consumer can accept or reject goods available on the market, secure in the rule that the customer is always right, so the 'consuming' student can reject the knowledge and expertise higher education has to offer at will, without a need to justify such choice.

The individual consumes information made widely available by the technology which is a major tool of the market economy. The effect of technology on higher education is profound. Taking the case of information technology, individuals can interact with machinery, and via their machines with other information users, consuming information derived from the proliferating networks available. Learning need not be a development of mind, but an extraction of relevant information for a given utilitarian purpose, thus blocking possibilities for intrinsic achievement. Not only this, but higher education institutions may be by-passed in the process, as consumers avail themselves of national and international networks available outside.

The take-over by technology in our academic, social, business and individual lives is so complete, that social debate on its use and value hardly exists. Nevertheless it is acknowledged that the stress on manipulative techniques, ready-made structures, impoverished language, and delight in surface appearance can destroy a learner's powers of reception and perception, and capacity to think and judge. Conceptualization is downgraded in favour of information gathering: the consumer is free to reject the demand to think.

THE POSTMODERN CHALLENGE TO HIGHER EDUCATION KNOWLEDGE

The individual consumer of higher education lives out his/her choices in a postmodern society where a postmodernist outlook allies with the market ethos to reject Enlightenment thinking. But what is postmodernism? The term resists full definition since its major thrust is to recognize that all knowledge claims are partial, local and specific:

there is a rejection of universal and transcendental foundations of knowledge and thought, and a heightened awareness of the significance of language, discourse and social-cultural locatedness in the making of any knowledge claim. (Usher and Edwards 1994: 10)

'Objective reality' is made problematic: postmodernists claim that a sign does not (as was hitherto claimed by modernist thinking) *represent* reality: it *is* one of many realities. Put very simply, a word or image is no more than our representation of it at a given point to set alongside multiple other possible representations. Meanings thus multiply and become richer, and hierarchies of meaning are hard if not impossible to identify. As postmodernist readers we are open and more sensitive to muted meanings arising in discourse. When we make a decision we 'close' a meaning; but 'closure' should only be temporary (a resting place). 'Closure' can be partly due to the desire to dominate and control (others, ourselves, the world). Keeping 'open' means openness to *difference*, perhaps the most famous of postmodern terms. Difference, multiplicity, variety, diversity within and between human beings and the social practices they engage in: these are what postmodernists celebrate. By recognizing difference, our own ways of thinking are opened up; the new understandings achieved might help us see what we want or need to change.

POSTMODERNISM AND HUMAN 'NATURE'

The lack of fixity and endless provisionality postmodernists point to have necessary implications for human 'nature' which now becomes more fluid. Our multiple identities are to be characterized without fixed goals or fixed means of achieving them: whether one or another way of being human is better or worse, or whether there is an 'authentic self' are impermissible questions. This has implications for teachers and learners: what would be a teacher's authority and purpose in an interaction where the development of a student's 'nature' (personhood, identity) is not a coherent goal?

This postmodern fluidity profitably forces us to question anew deterministic views of a fixed nature which ignore the social construction and locatedness of the individual self.

For instance, Usher and Edwards (1994), discussing Lacan's contribution to psychoanalysis show how the discourse of the analyst offers a means of recognizing how an identity is constructed. It is not unified, autonomous, self-aware as we habitually fancy. The unconscious, Lacan claims, is a place of *knowledge* not instincts: this knowledge is gained in a discontinuous way with diversions and breakthroughs, not as a linear progression towards maturity. Lacan compares the teacher–student relationship to that between analyst and analysand: the teacher, as with the analyst, is a learner too, with a self to construct and a need to hold up the grounds of his/her authority to continual inspection.

POSTMODERNISM, POWER AND RESISTANCE

Whilst postmodernism allows temporary representations (meanings), it is a central tenet most forcefully addressed by Foucault that representation is inescapably linked with power. As a result, many postmodernists emphasize a role for resistance. However, if we reject what the French postmodernist Lyotard calls 'grand narratives' (the Enlightenment project), do we not deprive ourselves of the necessary ammunition to resist oppression? (Squires 1993: 4). But if we reject only abstract universalizing 'grand narratives' and focus instead on 'small narratives', in Lyotard's phrase, we can challenge dominant forms of power, uncovering oppressive practices hiding behind confident affirmations of progress.

Blake argues, for instance that those who are excluded or silenced (the nurse, the inmate) may come to have their voices heard and taken account of. We have a long way to go before this happens. Seller remarks: 'You can deconstruct the university all you like – it's still a boys' club.' The experience of women in universities, she argues, has shown up the connection between knowledge and power: the legitimization of knowledge-claims is intimately tied to networks of domination and exclusion.

Those defending the Enlightenment humanist argument as Soper argues, had their attention drawn by postmodernist challenges to those groups or communities who were excluded or marginalized: 'by its supposedly universalist but at times decidedly partial forms of representation ... without a deconstruction of the humanist subject we would not have had the feminist, anti-racist and gay movements' (Soper this volume p. 42).

Usher gives a postmodernist interpretation of the literature ('text') of the National Council for Vocational Qualifications (NCVQ). He argues that it is a rhetorical achievement where we are seduced by appeal to our rationality, by belief in 'relevant, useful practice' to accept the 'liberating' access-friendly claims of competence-based education and training. We are even encouraged to feel guilty about the 'mess' (a jungle of unorganized provision) which preceded it. By characterizing Jessup's representation of NCVQ as 'seductive', the implication (Usher does not choose to make it) is that the NCVQ misrepresentation disguises an alternative, submerged, more emancipatory approach with which we might choose to align ourselves. Similar critiques (as Usher and Edwards 1994 show), demonstrate how the two all-pervasive learned-centred concepts – experiential learning and empowerment – could be given either an emancipatory reading (as liberals do, pointing up autonomy, openness, individual rights), or one which exposes their repressive potential in which experience can collapse into individual consumption.

POSTMODERNIST VALUE POSITIONS

The above examples illustrate how postmodernists have vigorously engaged in criticism of social and educational practices. Yet there is also a postmodernist ambiguity and equivocation about values, and a self-subverting reliance on values which they at the same time profess to scorn in others. For instance, a postmodern critique of 'competency' literature can reveal how a text may act as surveillance and exclusion, while at the same time postmodernism is celebrating the individual consumer who plays with lifestyles, a full participant in the market economy.

There is also an ambiguity in the reverential position postmodernists accord to the idea of difference. There is a failure to distinguish the grounds on which some differences matter and others do not. For instance, to be a member of a neo-Nazi group is 'different' from being a member of a gardening club: difference itself is not the relevant respect which distinguishes them. (The same might be said about the postmodern espousal of 'openness'; there are limits: we are not open to being deprived or abused.) But as Soper argues, underlying the prominence postmodernists give to 'difference', there is clearly a value commitment to social justice: 'Why should we "respect" or "preserve" the plurality of social actors unless we think it right that they should be represented and that in treating different persons or groups as different, we are treating them more equally' (Soper this volume p. 45).

Postmodern readings of the arts sharply illustrate these ambiguities and equivocations. In emancipatory guise postmodernists point out that a work of art whether deliberately or unconsciously can be a site of gender or ethnic oppression, elitist and excluding. But postmodernists *also* want to say that there is nothing outside the text to refer to: the reader may draw provisional meanings always mindful that the work of art is 'playful'. The denial of value in this case is self-subverting since a postmodernist would presumably want his/her own account of aesthetic value to prevail. And why indeed bother to deconstruct the canon, rather than enlarge or diversify it unless it were recognized that works of cultural production can enlarge, excite and illuminate our lives in an intrinsic sense which transcends their potential to oppress? (Greger and Soper, this volume).

Postmodernism has been subject to stronger attacks on its value position than equivocation and ambiguity. Norris, for example, heartily condemns the postmodern move that 'truth-seeking' enquiry is off limits (Norris 1994: chapter 10). Others have rejected its pessimistic view of human possibility and its inhibiting effect on alternative concepts and practices of justice. The disablement of judgement consequent on adopting postmodernism positions is found distressing and abhorrent: the fervour of such denunciations perhaps indicates fear at what would be lost by such adoption.

In the light of such powerful criticisms, it remains an open question whether the emancipatory strands of postmodernist thought can energize the reconceptualization and reconstruction of value positions and social practices, and be seen as an indispensable aid to critical educational inquiry as Carr, for instance, hopes (Carr 1995a: 128). Some writers have suggested that postmodernism should be 'downgraded' by capitalizing on its potential as a heuristic device, alongside its emancipatory purposes. Seller argues that: 'the crisis in knowledge in higher education is less about *what* texts to read, as right-wing critics in the States seem to think, more about *how* to read' (Seller this volume p. 91).

Certainly it is a damaging and undermining experience for higher education to be sustaining attacks on the status and value of knowledge at the very time it is also shaken by the increasing domination of market-led thinking, as discussed earlier. How can higher education meet these challenges in reasserting the values upon which its intrinsic purposes depend?

HIGHER EDUCATION AND ITS NEED FOR VALUES

The undeniably emancipatory purposes of postmodernism just discussed can only be explained in the light of *some* forms of truth, ethical value and political principle. Some postmodernists would deny this (though not any of the contributors showing sympathy with postmodern positions in this book), despite the self-defeating consequences of avoiding all principled positions in theory.

There is a growing and robust come-back from a variety of writers on education and culture (for instance in philosophy of education, and by cultural theorists such as Norris), who reject the strongest claim of discourse theorists that there is nothing beyond the text, maintaining that a sturdy sense of historical and social realities be held to, but that meanwhile postmodernists are cleaning up old concepts in a useful and sometimes creative way.

Carr, for instance has argued that the real challenge of postmodernism has been to reconceptualize the relationship between education and democracy in a way that takes into account postmodern insights (Carr 1995*b*: 79). Democracy enshrines moral values such as freedom, a belief in the autonomy and worth of the individual and the community, and has equality and justice at its heart. Education for a democratic society also entails commitment to some conception of rationality, truth and objectivity.

The authors here show how these values cannot be dislodged, but their engagement in the discourses of higher education must be conducted in a way that brings out individual, social and practical realities which give point to education. How then might rationality, truth and objectivity be reinvigorated and the old concepts of individual and community be seen afresh?

TRUTH, RATIONALITY AND OBJECTIVITY

To give up on the Enlightenment 'grand narrative', and its idea of a single truth which transcends social, cultural or institutional situations does not mean abandoning truth as a regulative ideal which governs our actions and critical responses (Soper 1993: 29). Greger's 'truth concern' (Greger this volume p. 113), is to interpret her anthropological material with a growing understanding and insight. Blake shows us that though rationality may be deconstructed, it can be reconstructed again: that cultural pluralism is not the same as what Midgley calls 'goofy relativism'.

Given that we cannot entirely escape from the perspective of our own conceptual schemes, themselves related in complex ways to the historical, social and cultural circumstances in which we live, this in itself does not condemn us to the making of merely local judgements. We always need logical and ethical space in which to comment on the (outrageous) practices of others, and to intervene when our principles tell us to. The postmodern insistence that we respect the differences of others needs elaboration here: it is not just that *some* differences must never be respected, but that to respect an alternative view or practice does not commit one to *agreeing* with that view, or letting it swamp one's own once alternatives have been carefully considered (Siegel 1995: 42).

The same point may be made in relation to objectivity. First, the traditional gap between 'how I see it' and 'how it is' can be narrowed by what postmodernists call our reflexive efforts to reduce partiality by being sensitive to our own assumptions, prejudices and ideological standpoints. Further, our interactions with others, as Burbules has argued (Burbules 1995: 92), are crucial to the intersubjective negotiation of knowledge and value claims. Burbules quotes Donna Haraway:

> The alternative to relativism is not totalitarianism and single vision ... [it] is practical, locatable, critical knowledge sustaining the possibility of webs of connections called solidarity in politics and shared conversations in epistemology. (Burbules 1995: 92)

The role that this democratic dialogue has to play in working together to substantiate knowledge claims and increase intersubjective understanding is a particular theme in this book (see the chapters by Seller, Greger, Soper and Myerson). It is supported by a gathering body of academic opinion.

INDIVIDUAL AUTONOMY AND COMMUNITY REVALUED

The individual participant in such dialogues – as postmodernists have shown – has a socially constructed and located nature, is aware of multiple differences and partial vantage points, and of struggling identity. (This allows a reconceptualization of the responsibilities of teacher and learner as discussed, for instance, in relation to Lacan earlier.) This somewhat daunting picture of the self does not however give us leave to sink into fragmented despair. Belief in the self is still a necessity, for without the self whose freedom are we trying to protect?

The great American philosopher of education Maxine Greene asks whether we can construct, and deconstruct and still preserve (Greene 1995: 12). She celebrates the role of the individual in creating values: 'Values may be groundless; but an act of rebellion, a taking of initiative, a repairing of a lack can create values' (Greene 1995: 14).

She goes on to say:

> It can be said that if teaching is our project, and if teaching responds to a need or a lack (absence of literacy, susceptibility to indoctrination, inarticulacy), the *praxis* created by the teacher builds a kind of wall against meaninglessness; it brings value into the world. (Greene 1995: 14)

Both learner and teacher are involved in a reconceptualization of values, including the value of autonomy. Autonomy is not a 'one-off' achievement, but develops in dynamic relation to the social practices and values which may inhibit or develop it, and the individual needs and desires which fuel it. It is not to be gained from an abstract Enlightenment form of reason but could come about through the kind of reasoning Dewey calls social intelligence, and Aristotle called phronesis: a form of practical reasoning which requires collective deliberation about the relative attractions of various courses of action.

Dewey's vision of individual and community continues to have resonance for many philosophers of education and others: 'A freeing of individual capacity in a progressive growth directed to social aims' (Dewey 1916: 115).

In various ways, the writers here show how community is what is needed. For instance, Greger, invites us to consider how 'communitas' may help us to find a way out of inappropriate social structures such as confrontational modes of behaviour inherited from patriarchy, through understanding more localized meaning negotiations. Seller argues that 'we should aim for a postmodern sensibility or practice: a recognition of the variety of constituencies or communities that the university should serve, the variety of languages it must be able to speak.' At the same time, she says we should keep the dream of a common language, or of a common multi-lingual community: a further point where we would all understand each other without any particular language dominating.

The need to reassert the values discussed here, at a time when academics are threatened by the knowledge crisis in its several aspects (as well as those other crises not the subject of this book), calls on reserves of courage and persistence as well as imagination. Iris Murdoch requires a character in one of her novels, an author, to have the courage to go beyond his best formulation. That courage is also needed to argue for an alternative vision of higher education, which gives due weight to its intrinsic purposes, while encompassing a more enlightened conception of the needs of the society we all belong to.

PART II

Crisis: What Crisis?

TWO

The Crisis of Knowledge and the Massification of Higher Education

Peter Scott

DISSOLUTION AND EXPANSION

In the late twentieth century the signs of intellectual dissolution are everywhere. All semblance of a shared academic culture rooted in supposedly universal cognitive values, unified subjects that transcend the particularities of disciplinary traditions or transient market exchanges, has disappeared. The common coinage of the late-modern world is the images of global life-styles fleetingly but addictively glimpsed through the mass media, world-wide advertising brands and the global leisure/entertainment industries. The men-of-letters, supremely self-confident in their intellectual culture however beleaguered in terms of their social position, have been succeeded by the 'chattering classes', socially privileged but culturally febrile. Within the academy, broadly constituted, truth has been reduced to mere discourses incommensurably jostling for academic attention. The idea of 'science', robust theoretical frameworks built on sustained empirical inquiry, has been remorselessly deconstructed. The very methodologies of truth-seeking have been called into question, as well as their revisable results. Rigorous critique has been replaced by lax reflexivity.

Yet, alongside this evidence of intellectual ruination, higher education systems, the cutting-edge institutions of the knowledge industry, have flourished as never before. The advance of higher education and the retreat of high academic culture have been synchronized – paradoxically so, it seems, in the light of the university's customary identification with that culture. The coincidence – if it is coincidence? – is uncanny. Higher education, once marginal, has become socially pervasive at the very time when traditional intellectual structures have been dismantled or allowed to decay. Most higher education systems, and many institutions that comprise them, are post-1960 creations; yet it was during the 1960s that 'the relative primacy of cognitive interests and functions' within universities was first questioned (Parsons and Platt 1973: 387). Since that decade both processes have accelerated. Mass, even universal, populations are now encompassed by higher education, directly as students or indirectly through the effects of its research, consultancy, technology transfer and the impact of its intellectualoid interventions in public policy. But the academic hegemonies, on which the social prestige and utility of higher education ultimately seemed to depend, have been progressively overthrown. Or, rather, not progressively because that suggests a stately succession of superior paradigms or improving hypotheses, when it is the very notion of hegemony that (apparently) has been abandoned.

This dualism, the decay of the old academic culture and the growth of mass higher education systems, is not the only available account of the present articulation between the intellectual and institutional domains, superstructure and structure in Marxist terminology or the 'private' and 'public' worlds of higher education, to adopt a more recent sociological *schema*. Theories of the 'knowledge' society, and of 'learning' organizations, have been substituted for traditional concepts of academic culture or, more bluntly, donnish values. While there appears to be an unavoidable friction, even an antithetical dialectic, between the mass university and the latter, between it and the former there may be a natural synergy. In other words modern higher education systems make sense in the context of the 'learning society' where knowledge has been brought within market and political exchanges, real-time knowledge that is now a primary resource; they make much less sense in the context of traditional academic values that continue to reflect, however dimly, the 'otherness' of knowledge.

The aim of this chapter is to explore these articulations between, on the one hand, the crisis of knowledge and, on the other, the growth of mass higher education. These are far from straightforward, not least because neither – crisis or massification – is itself an unambiguous phenomenon. The first part of the chapter, therefore, will be devoted to a discussion of the crisis of knowledge. Is there such a crisis – or is our experience of intellectual stress merely evidence of a process of, undoubtedly painful, transition such as has been experienced in several earlier epochs? If there is a crisis, what are its components? The second part will attempt to align the answers with the experience of massification in higher education. How is any crisis reflected in new organizational structures within (and between) universities; new approaches to teaching, learning and the curriculum; and novel conceptions of research?

CRISIS OR CONJUNCTURE?

The starting point must be the nature of the crisis that is the subject of this chapter, and book. What kind of crisis -- of what kind of knowledge? According to one account there is an ever-present risk that the cognitive values first made manifest in the scientific revolution of the seventeenth century are being un-bundled, rather as the dominant cultural values of Western civilization were reconstituted in the mid-nineteenth century. Darwin, and Comte, assaulted the sense of divine transcendence that sustained both individual morality and the social order, by substituting universal (and amorally 'objective') principles of scientific inquiry. Arnold struggled manfully to contain the consequences of that assault by seeking new representations of 'culture'. Nietzsche and later Heidegger clutched at darker and more obscure consolations. But all had to contend with the collapse of the old cultural order and of the social arrangements and moral parameters which depended on it.

Similarly, so the argument goes, at the end of the twentieth century those cognitive values that served as a fall-back from, or safety-net for, that old order face similar extinction. The culture of disciplined reflection and orderly rationality, which offered substitute social arrangements and moral parameters for those anachronistically linked to high culture and religion, is at risk. But it is important to be clear. Science, whether its operational procedures or specific results, is in good rude health. More scientific experiments are being conducted, more research papers written, more technology transferred than ever before. It is the culture of science, its universalism rather than its particularities, that is called into question. Its disaggregated pieces remain. For this reason it is better to talk of reconstitution rather than extinction.

A rival account of the 'crisis' of knowledge emphasizes transition rather than dissolution. We have been here before. In the last years of the nineteenth century and the first decade of the twentieth a new kind of culture, generally labelled modernism, emerged. Its effects could be observed not simply in the intellectual, scientific and aesthetic arenas (Freud, Einstein, Wittgenstein on the one hand and Dada and Schoenberg on the other) but in society, politics, industry, technology. It could even be observed in a curious popular restlessness as old habits and routines were sloughed off. Perhaps the turning of the century contributed powerfully to this creative unease. In his novel *A Man Without Qualities* the Austrian author Robert Musil described it in these terms:

> Suddenly, out of the becalmed mentality of the nineteenth century's last two decades, an invigorating fever rose all over Europe. No one knew exactly what was in the making; nobody could have said whether it was to be a new art, a new humanity, a new morality, or perhaps a reshuffling of society. So everyone said what he pleased about it. ... This illusion, embodied in the magical date of the turn of the century, was so powerful that it made some people hurl themselves with zeal at the new, still-unused century, while others chose one last quick fling in the old one, as one runs riot in a house one absolutely has to move out of, without anyone feeling much a difference between these new attitudes. (Musil 1995: 53)

This may be happening again in the late twentieth-century world, a similar conflu-
ence of intellectual, aesthetic and cultural currents on the one hand and political, socio-economic, institutional and organizational flows on the other – and, this time, as
the millennium turns, not just another century. Again a new kind of culture seems to
be emerging, labelled confusingly as postmodernism in the boutique of ideas, post-
industrialism or post-Fordism in the socio-economic arena, the 'end of history' in the
domain of ideology. The growth of mass higher education is implicated in this new
culture; indeed it is among its most distinctive formations (Scott 1995).

This second account, the pain of transition, offers more hope than the first, the
collapse of core cognitive values. The latter implies a decline-and-fall without hope
of restoration, and from which higher education systems, however weakly cognitively grounded, cannot ultimately escape; the former a permanent, although uneven,
revolution in the world of ideas perfectly consistent with the progressive development of society (and its key institutions, including the universities). Similar conjunctures of social-economic, technological, political and ideological change leading to
seismic shifts in intellectual culture have occurred in the past – in the sixteenth and
seventeenth century when national states first began to replace the universalism and
localism of medieval Europe, when Reformation and Counter-Reformation reworked
man's relationship with God and truth, when Europe coiled its commercial grip
round the world; in the eighteenth and nineteenth centuries when Enlightenment
sensibility, revolutionary ideas, and the industrial revolution produced a new kind of
society – scientific, secular, modern; in the early twentieth century, the age of Einstein and Joyce (and Musil), Freud and Picasso, Ford and Hitler. Contained within
all three earlier conjunctures have been radical transformations of higher education –
political roles, social positioning and cultural responsibilities. The present 'crisis'
may simply be a fourth such conjuncture.

But this reformulation of 'crisis' as 'conjuncture' limits the available interpretations of the relationship between a shifting intellectual culture and the massification
of higher education. The first, the descent into Spenglerian gloom implied by talk of
the un-bundling of cognitive values, is perhaps ruled out. But the alleged association
between epistemological volatility (all too readily misinterpreted–interpreted as the
chaotic collapse of academic standards) and the growth of a mass system (again, too
easily glossed as 'over-expansion') may continue to be an influential, even irreducible, element in debates about the future of higher education.

A second interpretation, Marxoid in the sense that it stresses the subordination of
shifts in intellectual culture to changes in the material base of higher education, is
also undermined by the emphasis on 'conjuncture' rather than 'crisis'. But again, although a crude cause-and-effect structure-and-superstructure model has become more
difficult to defend, this second interpretation cannot be discarded entirely. Clearly
there are important affinities between the opening-up of higher education systems in
sociological terms and the epistemological wobble, in terms of the proliferation of
discourses, that can easily be mistaken for a full-blown crisis of knowledge. These
affinities are complex and multi-directional rather than simple and linear, but the

emergence of open intellectual systems and the development of open higher education systems are contingent not simply coincidental phenomena (Barnett 1990).

A third interpretation, derived from Kuhn's distinction between the continuity of 'normal' science and the irregularity of paradigm shifts, appears to fit more readily with the replacement of 'crisis' by 'conjuncture' as an explanation of the current turmoil in the intellectual arena (Kuhn 1970). Each 'conjuncture' can plausibly be regarded as producing a new paradigm. But there are two main difficulties with this interpretation. First, Kuhn, although he emphasizes the incommensurability of successive paradigms, does not entirely reject the idea of a progressive science. Einstein's physics offer a better account than Aristotle's, although the latter cannot be blamed for not thinking like the former. This inherent progressivism, which survives the jerky succession of normal science and new paradigms, is difficult to reconcile with contemporary evidence of the dissolution (or, at any rate, de-construction) of intellectual culture. An anti-paradigmatic mentality appears to be dominant; there are few signs yet of a new paradigm cohering.

Second, Kuhn's own account of intellectual change is essentially internalist, even intimate, although his acolytes have offered more ambitious (but unauthorized) interpretations of his ideas. His focus is on scientific communities which, to act as such, must have clear boundaries and shared values. Paradigms shift because these communities, impressed by the accumulation of anomalous data, demand better overall explanations. Changes in the material base, to relapse into Marxist vocabulary, only matter if they are mediated through these scientific communities. Within the settled territory of academic disciplines this may make good sense. But in interdisciplinary spaces or the contested borderlands between higher education and society, culture and the economy where there are no cohesive scientific communities, and at a time when the primacy of cognitive values is increasingly questioned inhibiting the development and undermining the legitimacy of such communities, this 'Kuhn-esque' interpretation is less persuasive. Perhaps, after all, 'crisis' is a better word than 'conjuncture'.

HISTORICAL AND THEORETICAL INTERPRETATIONS

Crisis or conjuncture, contingent or coincidental, the dislocation of intellectual culture is undoubtedly a component of the late twentieth-century condition. Yet an authoritative analysis eludes us. (That is the point postmodern anti-analysts argue, if argument is part of their repertoire.) Trust has been replaced by risk, as surely in the intellectual as in the political arena. Or, in Marx's memorable phrase, 'all that is solid melts into air'. Even labels are contested. Postmodernism, or rupture, to some; high modernity, or culmination, to others. Nevertheless some attempt must be made to represent the unrepresentable, to make sense of intellectual movements that deny themselves the solace of settled forms. Two broad approaches are possible, to describe this dislocation in the context of intellectual history or to define it in terms of its primary attributes.

The historical approach tends to diminish its exceptionalism. First, the novelty of the present dislocation is moderated by earlier examples of equal or greater intellectual turbulence. Is postmodernism's playfulness, or the peremptory demands of 'political correctness', really a more radical disjuncture than the personal, and awful, responsibilities placed on the seventeenth-century puritan to seek God and the truth, unmediated by priest and universal church; than the century-long erosion of religious belief beginning with Hume and culminating with Darwin, Arnold's 'melancholy, long, withdrawing roar'; than the technologizing of scientific culture in the age of the industrial revolution; than modernism's 'shock of the new'? History is a great leveller of supposedly unique experience.

Second, this approach emphasizes the ideological and methodological continuities running through scientific and intellectual cultures alike. Innovation has always depended upon permanent revolution, the un-picking of old orthodoxies. The institutionalization of doubt, in Anthony Giddens' phrase, has been its engine (Giddens 1990: 176). Utopian and totalizing systems have frequently been regarded as antithetical to the open orientation of a secular scientific tradition. Postmodernism's antipathy to meta-discourses, therefore, is merely a restatement of this established prejudice. From Socrates/Plato to Popper fallibility and falsification have been key instruments of intellectual change. Paradigm shifts and multiple 'discourses' can be regarded as continuing, rather than, interrupting, this sceptical flow. Always present too has been what E. P. Thompson called a 'polarised tension', between antinomian affirmation and secular critique (Thompson 1993: 228). On the one hand the desire to reach beyond, and behind, reason; on the other the urge to exclude all non-cognitive considerations in the bracing search for truth. Also the tension between the (relative) autonomy of 'unified subjects', in knowledge or education, and their incorporation in, and subordination to, market exchanges is hardly new, although the encroachment of the latter may have increased.

A more theoretical approach to understanding the present crisis of knowledge may lead to a more radical interpretation. A number of primary attributes of the late-modern world is felt with special intensity in the intellectual domain. The first is acceleration, as fundamental a characteristic of scientific and cultural exchanges as it is of technical innovation and market behaviour. Velocity breeds volatility. According to Jean-François Lyotard: 'The temporary contract is in practice supplanting permanent institutions in the professional, emotional, sexual, cultural and family domains, as well as in political affairs' (Lyotard 1984: 66). He could well have added 'intellectual' to his list of volatile domains. It is not simply volume, although every year 30,000 doctoral theses on modern literature are completed in American and European universities and in one single city, New York, art works are being produced at the staggering rate of 15 million a decade (Gibbons *et al.*, 1994: 94–5). It is also turnover. Ideas, data, theories have shorter and shorter shelf-lives. This has two effects. First, only the most ephemeral 'discourses' can flourish. Second, secondary literatures explode; in George Steiner's caustic phrase, 'Commentary is without end. ... The mechanics of interminability are those of the locust' (Steiner 1989: 39).

(993!

The second attribute is simultaneity, the radical compression (and expansion) of time–space. The concept of standardized time was modern society's most powerful weapon in the war between universalism, innovation, becoming against particularism, stasis, being. The separate regulation of space, through a dynamic but orderly globalization, played a similar role. Now both have collapsed, time into the extended present or u-chronia (Nowotny 1994) and space into 'glocalisation', an ugly but eloquent coinage. As a result there are new drives towards simultaneity, a more intense realization of the moment; towards, paradoxically, a less intense 'ecology' of time to combat its relentless economy; and towards a delight in spontaneity and vicissitude, again to resist the mechanization of time–space. The implications for intellectual culture are immense and complex, extending far beyond a fashionable addiction for an Internet world to the definition, and validation, of knowledge.

The third attribute is risk. At its simplest risks are accumulating, and threaten to overwhelm the progressive effects of innovation (Beck 1992). Risk can no longer be regarded as 'external' to progress. Under conditions of reflexive modernization (a concept which Ulrich Beck borrows from Giddens) unintended consequences are as influential as deliberate intentions in shaping social action. More subtly, risk is replacing the trust on which intellectual Fordism, the reductionism and division of scientific labour, has depended for its creativity.

The fourth attribute is non-linearity, complexity, chaos. Hardly novel concepts: the human and social sciences have always rejected, formally at any rate, linear interpretations whilst complex systems, even chaos theory, can be crunched by the immense computational power available to scientists. But a radical intensification of their application has occurred undermining the cumulative character of routine scholarship and 'normal science'. These concepts have been further radicalized by a growing emphasis on the circularity of knowledge, not simply in the sense that it is revisable (an inherent characteristic of progressive science) but in the more disturbing sense that it is in fact ceaselessly revised through interaction with its environment, including its ostensible creators.

The fifth attribute is reflexivity. This takes several forms. The first has just been mentioned. Once-sharp demarcations between 'producers' and 'users' of knowledge have become much fuzzier. Creative acts have been both collectivized, among multiple producers, and distributed, among both 'producers' and 'users'. Second, ideas and values no longer develop out of stable milieus, whether 'local knowledge' or disciplinary traditions. Instead they must be constructed, and frequently reconstructed, in the light of interaction between abstract and expert systems (which individuals must take 'on trust') and actual environments. In the process they become reflexive. Third, in industrial society, and under the rules of the modern project, progress, whether technical or intellectual, had an 'other' – the traditional world it was modernizing. The post-industrial postmodern world has only itself to interrogate. It too becomes reflexive. Finally, as collective identifications weaken, the individual himself (or herself) becomes, in Beck's phrase, 'the reproduction unit of the social'. Society is defined through aggregated individualization. We construct our own reflexive biographies.

The accumulation of these attributes produces an apparently much more radical context for the dislocation of intellectual culture, or knowledge crisis that is the subject of this book. In this context the broth of 'cultural literacy', or the reassertion of a traditional canon, and anti-canon of so-called political correctness becomes less murky. The former is an attempt to defend a culture of cognitive rationality, an objective science and a universal culture, against the centrifugal pressures of reductionist expertise on the one hand and playful postmodernism on the other; the latter is a confused attempt to rewrite the canon, to embrace the experience and perspectives of groups that have suffered condescension or exclusion in the past (and present?), whilst questioning the objectivity and universalism implicit, if not explicit, in the very notion of a canon. Their combined effect is to problematize the privileged knowledge claimed by the university.

But it is the status, prestige even, rather than the organization of such knowledge that is called into question. Its cognitive unity, if it ever existed outside our utopian imagining, was splintered long ago. It is not immediately clear why its fragmentation into postmodern 'discourses' is a greater threat to the integrity of intellectual culture than the proliferation of disciplines, sub-disciplines and finer-grain specialties. Their practical effects are the same. Perhaps we are merely witnessing a sophisticated form of name-calling. If so, the reasons for our unease and discontents are perhaps to be found not in a supposed crisis of knowledge, but a threatened disruption of the all-too-familiar links between particular forms of knowledge and power, whether material or symbolic, in Western societies.

Even if this second more theoretical approach were adopted, the evidence of crisis is ambiguous. Perhaps a better, and more modest, description of what is happening to knowledge (and so a more suggestive and accurate account of the links between these changes and the evolution of mass higher education systems) emphasizes its wider social distribution rather than epistemological dislocation. This distribution takes two main forms. The first is the re-emergence of 'local knowledge', both inherited and contextualized norms and actual lived experiences, as opposed to expert or abstract knowledge. Many key university notions continue to privilege the latter – Bacon's centuries-old claim that knowledge is a form of power, that prefigured both the dominance of 'objective' science and 'expert' technology and the role played by higher education systems in promoting upward social mobility and élite formation, so creating and mobilizing cultural capital; Leavis' assertion that the purpose of a university education is to enable students to discriminate between the authenticity of high culture and the crassness of its populist rivals; the conviction that a culture of critical rationality, disembedded from 'the immediacies of context', is as necessary to individual and social improvement as a progressive theoretical science is to material improvement. All these notions imply boundaries between the cognitively worthy and less (or un-) worthy that have become difficult to identify.

The term 'local knowledge' is taken from the title of a book by the anthropologist Clifford Geertz who argued that in pre-modern cultures traditional knowledge was rich, varied and well adapted to local milieus (Geertz 1983). But most social analysts and intellectual historians, until recently, have regarded 'local knowledge' as an anachronism. Giddens, for example, defines modernity as the disembedding of social relations and knowledge 'from local contexts of interaction and their restructuring across indefinite spans of time–space' (Giddens 1990: 21). U-chronia and glocalization may cast this process of expert disembedding in a new light, and Giddens himself qualifies its scope:

> Yet, although 'local knowledge' cannot be of the same order as it once was, the sieving-off of knowledge and skill from everyday life is not a one-way process. Nor are individuals in modern contexts less knowledgeable about their local milieus than their counter-parts in pre-modern cultures. Modern social life is a complex affair, and there are many 'filter-back' processes whereby technical knowledge, in one shape or another, is reappropriated by lay persons and routinely applied in the course of their day-to-day activities. (Giddens 1990: 145)

This reappropriation, of course, is of expert knowledge already disembedded from local contexts and codified in abstract systems, not of Geertz's traditional 'local knowledge'. But the extent to which social, as opposed to technical, knowledge has ever been disembedded (rather than a particular type of élite 'local knowledge' being privileged) is open to doubt. In recent years there has been an intriguing re-legitimization of 'social memory', a powerful form of 'local knowledge' well known to cultural historians. For example, Simon Schama has written of 'the knowledge we already have, but knowledge which somehow eludes our recognition and appreciation' (Schama 1995). The renewed interest in oral and popular history, celebrated among others by Raphael Samuel, may also be significant in this context, although critics argue this significance is vitiated by its alignment with the heritage industry (Samuel 1994). The importance of 'local knowledge' in mass higher education is discussed later in this chapter.

The second form taken by the social distribution of knowledge is an important shift in the science, technology and innovation systems. This has been described by Gibbons and his fellow authors as a shift from Mode 1 science to Mode 2 knowledge production. Mode 1 they define in the following terms:

> For many, Mode 1 is identical to what is meant as science. Its cognitive and social norms determine what shall count as significant problems, who shall be allowed to practise science and what constitutes good science. Forms of practice which adhere to these rules are by definition scientific while those that violate them are not. (Gibbons et al., 1994: 2–3)

In place of Mode 1 they see a new form of knowledge production emerging. Whilst Mode 1 is dominated by closed scientific communities, Mode 2 knowledge production is an open system in which 'producers', 'users', 'brokers' and others mingle promiscuously. In addition Mode 2 is eclectic rather than reductionist, and interpenetrated by markets rather than being an autonomous space. It has five key characteristics that differentiate it from Mode 1. First, it is generated within a context of application (this is not the same as applied science, because often there is no pre-existing science to apply). Second, it is transdisciplinary (also to be distinguished from inter-disciplinary behaviour where constituted disciplines collaborate). Third, it is hetero-geneous and diverse. Not only is knowledge produced on many sites, but there are new actors such as think-tanks, consultancies and small and medium-sized enter-prises, 'researching' as well as 'learning organizations' of all kinds. Fourth, Mode 2 knowledge production is accountable to society and the market, in the sense that it is highly reflexive. Fifth, it requires a new definition of quality. Peer review is super-seded by new ways of defining 'good' science that are both more democratic and more market-oriented.

It has been suggested that Mode 2 is not a new phenomenon. Rather it describes how many disciplines originally developed (applications first, theory afterwards) and how much of industrial research and development has traditionally been organized. Modes 1 and 2 have always coexisted. Moreover scientists, generally trained is disciplinary contexts, often worked in more applied environments, and oscillate be-tween the two during their careers. All this is true. But it fails to take account of the breadth of Mode 2 knowledge production that extends far beyond the domains of re-search and development into market and political arenas, or to recognize that the bal-ance between Modes 1 and 2 appears to be undergoing a radical shift. Research council grants, bid for by Mode 1 scientists on the basis of peer review, are being squeezed out by programmes and initiatives, generated in complex negotiations be-tween scientific communities and putative 'users'. The 1995 *Forward Look*, and its associated Technology Foresight exercise, were an organized attempt to transform these negotiations into conversations (Office of Science and Technology 1995*a*). As such they offered clear evidence of the advance of Mode 2.

THE DEVELOPMENT OF MASS HIGHER EDUCATION

The relationship between this crisis of knowledge and the development of mass higher education takes two main forms, their general articulation and the specific impacts of the former on the latter. First, the knowledge industry is a key sector within the post-Fordist economy, and higher education systems are a key component of that industry. Post-Fordism, of course, remains a contested category, both as a theoretical formulation and an empirical account. There is no room to enter into that debate here. In any case there is sufficient agreement on two points. The first is that 'knowledge' in its myriad forms – fundamental research, Mode 2 science, the endless data streams of the information revolution, the pervasive images of the mass media and advertising, new-style human and old-style cultural capital – has become a key commodity in this new kind of economy. The second is that a decisive shift is under way in the pattern of production – away from capital and consumer durable goods that depend on the efficient deployment of financial, energy, labour and other re-sources, towards high value-added symbolic goods that are often encoded in abstract data and ephemeral goods, characterized by an accelerating turnover of instantaneous images and fleeting life-styles.

These changes impact on higher education in many ways. The primacy of 'knowledge' means that higher education systems have become an arena in which the new high-tech wars of economic advantage are waged and the flexible workforces of the information economy are formed. But the knowledge industry is now crowded with rivals to the universities, often operating in its most dynamic sectors. In the process higher education's autonomous space has been invaded, even abolished. The rise of symbolic goods production means that higher education itself has become a commodity, the subject of immediate consumer gratification as much as (or more than) the object of long-term capital investment. It must offer an attractive range of 'products' to attract 'customers'. Its claim to be treated as a unified subject, distinct from the turmoil of the market, and, by extension, the claim of academic knowledge to be similarly treated are diminished. The result is a fundamental shift in its cognitive ecology, of which both the playfulness of postmodernism and the tighter embrace of industry, in its widest sense, may be examples.

But it is misleading to present the university solely as victim. It is accomplice too. The development of extended systems of higher education is among the most distinctive features of post-Fordism. Elite universities, and analogous research establishments, are still the main sources of the technological innovations that have made the fundamental restructuring of production possible. All institutions, especially mass ones, contribute powerfully to the social mobilization that has created the market for new symbolic and ephemeral goods. The expansion of higher education has helped to dissolve older social configurations rooted in the material base of industrial society. Although the university may now have powerful scientific rivals, higher education dominates representations of contemporary intellectual culture more thoroughly than ever. Its epistemological doubts are its own. And it is through higher education that these doubts have gained popular currency.

Second, the crisis of knowledge has influenced the practice of teaching and research in higher education more directly, the detailed impact of the mass university's new cognitive ecology. Four components of its influence can be identified. The first is the revival of 'local knowledge' both because the proliferation of postmodern discourses has tended to undermine the authority of abstract and/or expert systems of thought and because the broadening of higher education's social base has brought new students into the system whose prior acquaintance with academic culture, through school or family influences, has been limited. A recent study of further/higher education partnerships found that students on franchized degree programmes in colleges relied on 'local knowledge' in two ways – first, in the eclecticism of their personal experiences, reminiscences and reflections; and second, in their reluctance to discriminate between 'personal' and 'academic' discourses (Bocock and Scott 1995). According to one view they exhibited a lamentable incapacity for conceptual rigour; according to a rival view their 'local knowledge', potentially at any rate, represents a valid, and creative, alternative to standard academic norms. Either way, there is no reason to believe that there are many such students in mass higher education systems – not simply Access and other 'non-standard' entrants but also post-experience part-time postgraduates.

The second component comprises the increasing emphasis on personal transferable skills and generic competences (Barnett 1992: 1994). This has taken many forms – experimental, such as the Enterprise in Higher Education initiative; hortatory, such the Education for Capability movement; and structural, such as the development of higher-level National Vocational Qualifications and General National Vocational Qualifications. In one sense this trend can be interpreted as a strategy to combat the negative effects of academic reductionism and enhance vocationalism and employability. But, in the larger context of the crisis of knowledge, it is perhaps better interpreted as the substitution of instrumental practices for cognitive norms. The former fill the vacuum left by the latter.

The third component is represented by the spread of modular course structures, credit accumulation and transfer schemes, new patterns of assessment (including self-assessment). Again, this can be interpreted as the systematization of teaching and learning in higher education, produced by the economizing imperatives of mass higher education and also encouraged by external policies such as academic audit and teaching quality assessment. But, in the context of the concerns raised in this chapter about the erosion of traditional academic culture, this trend can also be seen as a reflection of the proliferation of postmodern discourses and, more generally, of the 'marketization' of intellectual culture in a mass system.

The fourth component is the reconfiguration of research. This takes many forms. One is the systematization of research outputs exemplified by the research assessment exercise. Although more an exercise in Fordist control than post-Fordist flexibility, its instrumentality can be interpreted as further evidence of the collapse of a common, but tacit, intellectual culture. A second is the shift from bottom-up research funding, research councils and other funders reacting to the proposals of researchers and charged with safeguarding the integrity (generally described as the 'base') of the disciplines for which they have responsibility, to top-down funding, pre-determined programmes and initiatives steered by research councils with user-oriented mission statements.

A third is the rise of Mode 2 knowledge production discussed earlier. A fourth is the elision within the wider knowledge industry of traditional demarcations between scientific research (and academic scholarship) and other forms of knowledge production and information and image generation. The bracketing together of leisure (which incorporated the mass media) and learning, including the university as a common industrial sector in the Technology Foresight exercise is suggestive evidence of this elision (Office of Science and Technology 1995b).

Clearly there are important links between the epistemological unravelling that can be observed across many, but not all, academic sectors and the erosion of any clear sense of a common intellectual culture (in actuality it may never have existed outside an élite redoubt) on the one hand and the growth of mass higher education systems on the other. But these links suggest affinity, perhaps synergy, more powerfully than cause-and-effect. Two reasons can be suggested for this fuzziness. The first is that, in line with the primary attributes of the emerging society discussed earlier in this chapter, both intellectual culture and mass higher education are phenomena characterized by ambiguity and recession. Neither is a regular formation.

The second is that the 'fit' between the knowledge crisis and the massification of the universities is inexact. In many respects the crisis is felt most intensely in those parts of higher education least affected by the pressures of massification, while in mass institutions epistemological wobbles are less pronounced. However, neither reason is sufficiently strong to cast doubt on the significance of the larger conjuncture – the coincidence, and contingency, of radical, even destabilizing, change in both intellectual and higher education systems.

THREE

Is There a Crisis? Does it Matter?

Stephen McNair

IS THERE A CRISIS?

Policymakers in higher education – vice chancellors, quality and funding bodies, government and leaders of disciplines and professions – have many things to worry about. Informed that there is a crisis in knowledge for higher education a vice chancellor might want to know about its scale and urgency before taking action. How, for example, does it compare in significance with a decline in applications for science courses, a 5 per cent efficiency saving imposed by the Funding council, or a poor result in Research Assessment. If she or he were to consult some of the academic leaders of the institution s/he might well be told that the crisis is only in the overheated imaginations of a small inward-looking minority in the humanities and social sciences: a crisis of legitimacy in fields whose academic standing has always been weaker.

This might be true, but I wish to argue that there is a crisis, of legitimacy for the university, related specifically to its role in creating, managing and disseminating knowledge, and that it may only survive as an institution if it comes to terms with a new, or perhaps revived, role within a much larger and more diffuse learning community.

Whilst information and data may be the product of individual effort, knowledge is essentially social. It is not, in any real sense, knowledge until someone other than its creator has validated it, and in most cases it is the product of collective effort. This collective effort may be simultaneous, as with a team of researchers, or learners working together, or may be spread over time, as with much academic discourse in which scholars engage with their predecessors in writing and continuing debate, over years (or millennia: people are still arguing with Plato). If this is the case, the question of who defines the boundaries and membership of the relevant community, and hence who the knowledge 'belongs to' is a critical issue. One of the most substantial challenges to the university lies here, in the forces which are undermining its traditional ownership of the rules of intellectual discourse. If the university is to confirm its position in this territory, it must find a way of establishing a new legitimacy in relation to the creation and validation of knowledge.

A CHANGING HIGHER EDUCATION

It is not very long ago that the value of higher education to society was widely seen as self-evident. The settlement for the higher education system created in the early 1960s by the Robbins Committee (Robbins 1963) survived relatively unchallenged until it met the iconoclastic public mood of the late 1980s.

The challenge came as something of a shock since Government had continued to press, until the early 1990s, for expansion in participation, in the belief that British economic competitiveness would be strengthened if higher education participation rates matched those of other developed countries. However, expansion changed who participated, and what they participated in, and created increasing resource pressures for institutions, while politicians began to argue that public investment would be more effectively directed at the earliest stages of education. The expansion also undermined one of the traditional roles of the university, of defining and maintaining a social élite, and calls began to be heard for the recreation of some grouping or hierarchy of universities. After the uncritical enthusiasm for expansion of the late 1980s came a new enthusiasm for accountability, for 'consolidation', and for a tightening of resources, whose rationale was strengthened by a steep rise in graduate unemployment.

At the same time, the university was being increasingly challenged by competition for its traditional core activities. A CVCP review of research in 1994 confirmed the large volume of traditional forms of research being conducted in the private sector; there was a steady expansion of higher level learning outside the universities (sometimes, but by no means always, validated by universities); government was beginning to support the development of high level National Vocational Qualifications which might not be awarded by universities; and graduates and teachers were beginning to recognize that graduate employment would depend less on traditional 'academic' knowledge, and more on high level generic, core and 'personal transferable' skills.

These changes produced a growing anxiety about purpose. In 1994, Williams and Fry, writing for the Committee of Vice Chancellors and Principals themselves, commented that, 'even amongst people who are well informed there is disagreement and confusion about what higher education is doing and what it ought to be doing' (Williams and Fry 1994). A number of answers were offered. Importantly, Barnett argued that the higher education system had been encouraged to transfer its allegiance from the academic to the operational, but within a limited notion of knowledge itself, which paid inadequate attention to the process of reflection and of dialogue. The National Institute for Adult Continuing Education (NIACE) argued a related case, that the arrival of mature learners as a majority in the system, called for a fundamental change in its nature (McNair 1994). The government launched a review of higher education, and then, recognizing the political sensitivity of the questions and especially of the central question of funding, created a committee of enquiry to make recommendations (after a General Election) about the purposes and operation of British higher education.

FOUR CHALLENGES

For most of this century the university has been able to claim a monopoly of the ownership of particular forms of knowledge, based on a linear notion of knowledge creation, ownership and transmission. This monopoly is now rapidly being undermined, and I wish to argue that the successful survival of the university as an institution will rest on its ability to address four major challenges, which are all undermining its position. All have risen to prominence in national policy debate in the last decade, and each is influencing what policymakers, at institutional, national and international levels, think is important, and is helping to shape their understanding of the purposes and structures of higher education. The success of the university in meeting the challenges will, I believe, rest more on its traditions of collegiality and individual commitment to the pursuit of knowledge, than on its unsustainable monopoly over that knowledge or its transmission.

The knowledge based economy

A knowledge based economy can mean several things. At its simplest, it suggests that the growing complexity of technology means that most productive activity will require higher levels of skills and knowledge. Every job in the economy of the future will involve more 'knowledge', since products will be more complex; and everyone will need to be a better learner, because accelerating change will call for constant updating of skills and knowledge. This is the basis of the argument for the expansion of higher education which rests on the need to raise the educational levels of the workforce.

However, there is a more profound notion of a knowledge based economy, which implies that knowledge itself is what is bought and sold, and that trade in intellectual property, a traditional product of higher education, will represent a growing proportion of economic activity. The case is argued by Reich (1993), who argues that the developed countries are developing a new three tier class system, with globally mobile knowledge workers – 'symbolic analysts' – at the top, supported by a second service class who run restaurants, theatres and galleries, phone systems, computers and maintain cars and gardens. Below them will be the remnants of the old physical labouring classes, semi-skilled and unskilled, in insecure or no employment, and with increasingly little part to play in the economy and society.

In defining 'symbolic analysts' as the new class Reich (1993) identifies three areas of growing skills demand in the American economy 'problem solving skills to put things together in unique ways', 'the skills required to help customers understand their needs, and how those needs can be met by customised products', and 'the skills required to link problem solvers and problem identifiers'. He lists a plethora of occupational areas which fall into these categories, from the familiar, like engineers, doctors, lawyers, historians and novelists, through management consultants and information scientists, to marketing strategists, corporate headhunters and university professors. He describes their common features:

> Symbolic analysts solve, identify, and broker problems by manipulating symbols. They simplify reality into abstract images that can be rearranged, juggled, experimented with, communicated to other specialists and then, eventually, transformed back into reality. The manipulations are done with analytic tools, sharpened by experience. ... Some reveal how to more efficiently deploy resources save time and energy. Other manipulations yield new inventions – technological marvels, innovative legal arguments, new advertising ploys. ... Still other manipulations – of sounds, words, pictures – serve to entertain their recipients, or cause them to reflect more deeply. (Reich 1993: 178)

This is not unlike one of the traditional notions of the university, albeit translated into an unfamiliar language, and it has clear implications for higher education, where knowledge has traditionally been created and transmitted. Some of the knowledge which the consultant sells is academic in the traditional sense – propositional knowledge about electronics, mathematics, logic and so on. Much more is knowledge of how to analyse situations and contexts, and skills of questioning, listening, interpreting, and a body of experiential knowledge developed over time in many contexts. This knowledge is no less real than the academic, and is as subject to debate and theorizing. It is made, however, outside the academy, and starts not from academic theory, but from problem solving.

There are areas of higher education where the implications of this are beginning to be recognized. Medical education is one, where a curriculum which used to begin exclusively with formal delivery of theory, is adopting 'problem based' approaches, where students work in teams on case studies. What students learn first from such an approach is that medicine is about exploring problems and finding the best solution in imperfect circumstances. They also learn how to work with others to solve problems, and to create 'new' knowledge. The focus of the learning becomes the primary purpose of understanding and curing patients, not the secondary one of absorbing volumes of propositional knowledge or pleasing the teacher. By focusing on the underlying purpose students are learning the process of knowledge creation, and developing deep, rather than surface, learning skills. Thus they become good doctors, rather than good examination candidates.

There is no denying the excitement which such approaches to learning generate, but the 'knowledge market' model is not unproblematic. Not only does it shift our notions of what kinds of knowledge are valuable, it also makes knowledge itself the subject of commercial transactions. Universities in some countries have accepted this for many years, but the model is still often perceived as inimical to the culture of collegiality and free exchange of knowledge, which dominates the rhetoric (if not always the practice), of the academic world. The scale and political sensitivity of the issues involved can be seen in the developing international debates about intellectual property law.

Any market model also faces a critical problem, that unless the customer has some practical means of recognizing quality, the market will tend to drive it down in order to compete on price. Unlike supermarkets, where customers are generally well informed about the differences between products, and can make rational choices about balancing price and quality, the product of higher education is knowledge it-self, generated and embedded in the learner through a dynamic relationship with teacher and knowledge base, and the outcomes are always unpredictable. To add to the difficulty, the simplest measure of output – the qualification – is only a proxy for much more complex and nebulous qualities, and is traded in a market where at least one consumer – the potential graduate employer – is often equally ill informed.

This poses two problems: who defines quality, and who helps the 'customer' to make wise choices for her or his particular circumstances? Traditionally both have been done, simultaneously, by the university. However, the university's principal loyalty was ultimately to the knowledge, conceived within a particular academic framework, rather than to the learner, or to the wider community where the knowledge was to be used. If it is to take this role in a new context it will need new authority and skills, based not on the traditional knowledge base, but upon a close understanding of the context in which the individual is operating, and skills in helping him or her to reflect on that context.

Reich's vision implies that knowledge is itself becoming a form of wealth, it is what individuals have to sell, in a world where physical labour and simple technical skill have become largely redundant. The world is dividing into 'knowledge rich' and 'knowledge poor', and the university becomes a major player in the direct distribution of such wealth. It also implies that a much larger group of people will be spending their lives in the kind of activities which used to characterize higher education – creating, manipulating and transmitting knowledge. Society is becoming a kind of university, without the intellectual and institutional frameworks which sustained the old institutions.

The learning organization

Like the 'knowledge based economy', the 'learning organization' is a term with multiple meanings. It has risen to prominence in the literature of management in the late 1980s, led notably by Peter Senge who presented the idea as one which could transform the management of organizations by recognizing the role which learning plays within them (Senge 1994) The argument has many layers but essentially it proposes that a culture which sees problems as challenges to learn, rather than matters of blame, is likely to be more successful. From this flows the idea that the organization must encourage all its members to engage in continuous and collaborative learning.

There are two distinct operational forms of this philosophy. The first can be seen in the government's 'Investors in People' initiative, which stimulates organizations to look systematically at their own skill needs and relate these to the learning of their employees. The second, and much more radical, model is that adopted by a small but influential group of employers who run 'Employee Development Programmes' (EDPs), which offer support to employees to undertake systematic learning related to personal ambitions and interests. The underpinning idea is that employees with positive experiences of learning (of any kind) are more likely to be flexible and confident workers, and able to contribute to the overall productivity of the organization.

Unlike the instrumental approach of Investors in People, which assumes that the needs and mission of the organization can be predetermined, and tidily matched, the Employee Development approach takes a more creative approach to the learning process, in which individual and organizational needs and goals interact dynamically. Employees who develop new skills, and perhaps particularly learning skills, can not only contribute more to the firm, but they have greater personal resources to fall back on if the firm encounters a crisis, either of growth or of collapse. For the individual this makes industrial restructuring less threatening, and for the firm less disruptive. It also makes learning a normal part of the life of the workplace and its members.

A second, and much less debated, dimension of the 'learning organization' is the notion of an organization which itself learns. Like individuals, organizations have experiences, which they reflect on and respond to. With varying degrees of efficiency they remember the lessons and use them to plan their futures. The individuals within them contribute, store and process information, and like the parts of the brain, interchange information and adapt. Organizations have 'personalities' which affect the way they respond to events and look to the future, and they own bodies of knowledge which can be expanded, developed and used. Like individuals, organizations can be very poor learners, bad at absorbing and sharing incoming information, and bad at reflecting on, or remembering the lessons of their experience. One reason for this is that they fail to hear messages from all their constituent parts. Hierarchical notions of knowledge ownership and transmission serve such organizations badly, because they often prevent the organization from learning from those closest to the customers (who are often the most junior). An efficient learning organization is one in which all members are seen as both learners and teachers, with skills, insights and knowledge to share and to acquire.

This model is already well known in some professions. Whereas, in the traditional manufacturing firm, seniority is associated with detachment from the customer, and from the practical production process, in the professions, as within the academic world, the process is reversed. Here, the energies of the most senior people are concentrated on the relationship with client or learner, or with the knowledge creation process, and the organization exists to support this direct relationship with the client, rather than the reverse. Such communities – professional bodies, disciplines, departments and schools – have traditionally clustered around sets of ideas and practices, and have found ways of drawing boundaries around themselves to define their identity. Critically, they have also been the communities which defined and owned the knowledge base of their profession or discipline.

What is happening now is that the model is extending into a much wider range of organizations. More economic activity is focused on the creation and management of knowledge, and organizations are coming to resemble the traditional academic forms, clustered around the ideas in which they trade, rather than physical facilities and manufacturing processes.

Globalization

My third theme is globalization, whose profound significance is only beginning to be understood. Until recently, the interaction of cultures in general was a relatively slow process, except at specific boundary points. While international debate was restricted to small élite groups in many countries it posed only modest and gradual threats to traditional cultural values. Global broadcasting has been challenging this for years, but recent developments in telecommunications, including e-mail and the Internet offer a far more radical test, because they are not controlled by anyone (no one 'owns' or 'manages' the Internet, and it cannot be censored without massive intervention by multinational firms and international government agencies working in concert).

Many academic communities have always been global. However, such communities have generally been based around a common set of cultural values, mostly deriving from northern European roots. Furthermore, the concentration on theory enabled such communities to detach themselves from those aspects of practice where cultural difference is most problematic. Thus globalization compounds the challenge to increased interaction between theory and practice by requiring it to face much more profound and complex areas of difference in values, and notions of knowledge.

Nations wish to trade in knowledge, but the technologies which enable them to do so also undermine their own identities. In theory these developments could lead to a continuing, but refined, plurality of cultural values within a global knowledge economy. The alternative is the gradual imposition of a 'cultural monoculture' in which difference is gradually suppressed in the interests of a more efficient knowledge market. Of the two the second seems the more likely, because of the association of a set of cultural values with economic power. However, even if the outcome is inevitable, the process is unlikely to be smooth, and may be violent, and it is only of small comfort to English speaking societies that the likely language of such a monoculture is English.

In understanding this issue the small body of work on international culture in organizations may be particularly helpful. Hofstede (1991) and Hampden Turner and

Trompenaars (1993) have examined organizational management in a global context, and they have identified dimensions on which cultures differ within the developed world, which are very important to our understanding of how knowledge is created and owned, as well as of why some cultures will adapt to this new world more readily. By studying the values of people carrying out similar roles in different cultures (like IBM managers across many countries), they have developed profiles of the ways in which different national cultures differ. The differences are significant within relatively similar countries (France and Germany, the UK and USA), but much more so when European and Far Eastern cultures interact.

Trompenaars and Hampden Turner identify seven dimensions on which major capitalist cultures differ (Hampden Turner and Trompenaars 1993). For our purposes four are particularly relevant: (i) individualism/communalism, where communal cultures may place more emphasis on agreement than on originality; (ii) integrating/analytical, where some cultures are much more positive about patterns of analytical thinking characteristic of European scientific method; (iii) achieved status/ascribed status, where cultures which value ascribed status will be more respectful of established knowledge, and more sympathetic to the idea that it is owned by an élite; and (iv) inner/outer which reflects the extent to which truth is perceived to be something inside the individual or organization, or to be found through interaction with others. Each of these dimensions of difference will have a profound influence on how people understand the role of knowledge and its application.

Trompenaars and Hampden Turner identified these characteristics primarily in developed, capitalist cultures with European roots (which they contrasted with Japan). Hofstede looks more widely and describes attempts to develop similar scales by researchers from the Far East, pointing out that social scientists from a different cultural background produce scales with different dimensions (Hampden Turner and Trompenaars 1993). He describes the work of Bond, who worked with Chinese social scientists to produce a 'Chinese Values Scale' which produced a set of scales from a 'Confucian' perspective. A comparison of the two sets of scales shows considerable overlap, but two significant differences. The first is what Hofstede (1991) calls 'long term orientation', a quality prominent in the Chinese lists and absent in the Western ones, and 'uncertainty avoidance' for which the reverse is true, and which correlates with the need to identify a single exclusive truth. Thus, he argues, Confucian cultures seek long-term stability but are uninterested in finding 'the truth', while Western ones do the reverse. He comments:

> The three western religions belong to the same thought family; historically they grew from the same roots. ... All three are based on the existence of a Truth which is accessible to all true believers. All three have a Book. In the East neither Confucianism ... nor any major religion is based on the assumption that there is a Truth which a human community can embrace. They offer various ways in which an individual can improve him/herself, however these do not consist in believing, but in ritual, meditation or ways of living.
>
> The Western concern with Truth is supported by an axiom of Western logic that a statement excludes its opposite: if A is true, B, which is the opposite of A, must be false.

Eastern logic does not have such an axiom. If A is true, its opposite B may also be true, and together they produce a wisdom which is superior to either A or B. ... Human truth is always partial. (Hofstede 1994: 171)

These conflicts are, in a sense, a demonstration in concrete form of the relativism which postmodernism focuses attention on. How, and by whom, will decisions be made about the value of knowledge, in a world where there are dramatically different notions of knowledge, truth and its place in society, and where particular value systems support different kinds of knowledge?

Lifelong learning

Lifelong learning has a long history in educational debate. Since the 1960s, one of the more important driving forces in its promotion has been the Organisation for Economic Cooperation and Development (OECD), which has argued for a lifelong perspective on education on economic grounds (OECD 1994). (The argument, at its simplest, is that in a rapidly changing economy the school system is incapable of renewing the human capital of society with adequate speed. Only about 3 per cent of the workforce enters the workplace each year from schools with new knowledge and skills, and any manufacturer who renewed his capital equipment at that rate would rapidly go out of business. The argument is that more resources should be devoted to formal learning for those who have already left the initial education system, and also that more serious recognition should be given to the learning which individuals do in the course of their everyday lives, in and out of employment. This is why the recognition of prior experiential learning has been a major plank of the NVQ enterprise in Britain. The arguments were prominently revived in the OECD *Jobs Study* in 1994, and have been followed up in White Papers from the European Union (European Commission 1995) and the UK Government (Department for Education and Employment 1995).

In the United States, where the notion of lifelong learning is more firmly embedded in popular attitudes and experience, it is common to talk about adults 'going back to school'. If the answer to the problem was simply to provide more schooling to meet higher skill needs, or the opportunity to repeat the same processes as technology and individual circumstances change, lifelong learning would not have major implications for universities: they might be required to expand, but not to change. However, I would argue that the changes taking place are more radical. Precisely because adult learners are members of society not 'apprentices' preparing for entry to it, they have a different status, they have the right to challenge what is offered in the light of their experience in the world, and of their rights as citizens. Alongside this, the speed of change, the growth of knowledge, and its greater accessibility all place greater emphasis on the assembly of a coherent body of personal knowledge, drawn from many traditional fields, but tested against a personal experience of the world beyond the walls of the university.

The implications of this for the university extend far beyond the provision of more courses, for students of different ages. In Europe since the seventeenth century the process of knowledge creation and transmission has been seen as linear: researchers observe the real world, define legitimate knowledge and formulate theory, which teachers then transmit to students. The knowledge is created and owned by this small community of 'experts', whose monopoly of validated knowledge brings high status. The result is that research and theory are more highly valued than learning and practice; and abstraction is more highly valued than solutions to problems. Lifelong learning, by placing the learner, rather than the discipline, at the centre, and by constantly testing academic knowledge against experience in the world outside will change the power relations between learners and teachers, and increasingly challenge the university's monopoly over the validation of knowledge and of individuals' learning. This will be difficult for all cultures, but especially to those which have traditionally given a high status to theoretical knowledge, and those which have drawn sharp dividing lines between vocational and academic knowledge, since skills and knowledge will increasingly flow across such boundaries.

Furthermore, in a knowledge based economy and society learning is not something 'added on' to stable social and economic processes: it changes those processes, and is one of the ways in which a society reflects on and redefines itself. Learners are engaged in the processes about which they are learning, they take their learning out and try it in the world, testing that learning against concrete experience. They will also bring their own problems to that learning, seeking solutions to problems whose parameters are set not by academics but by their own lives. Thus universities, if they are to continue to play a significant role, are likely to find themselves more frequently drawn into political and economic processes in ways which used to be the preserve of specialized units or departments.

WHAT IS TO BE DONE?

The answer to the question, 'is there a crisis?' is yes. The traditional near monopoly of the university over ownership and transmission of established knowledge, and validation of new knowledge is under threat. As knowledge becomes more economically significant, and more immediately marketable, these roles are more widely and frequently contested. A growing number of other agencies are creating new knowledge, and seeking to become learning communities of the same kind. The example of government's intervention to create 'Lead Bodies' which define competence, and hence legitimate knowledge, in specific fields is only one example. At the same time, globalization is challenging its particular notions of value and knowledge, and lifelong learning is forcing it to ask questions about relevance.

Some would see the way out of the crisis in a redefinition of the roles of institutions in terms of distinct processes of 'teaching' and 'research', seeking to draw a conceptual and institutional distinction between the process of knowledge creation and transmission. I would argue that to do this is fundamentally to misconceive the essential nature of higher education, which is the creation of knowledge, in a wide range of forms and levels. 'Higher education' is, I suggest, defined not by the 'difficulty' of the knowledge, but by this interlock of creation and transmission. Without it what is being offered is not 'higher' in any real sense, nor is it what a learning society or a knowledge based economy need from a higher education system.

Rather, I would suggest a reshaping of our notion of the university, not as a place of teaching and research, but as a place whose essential function is the creation of knowledge, which is carried out through many processes, including forms of teaching and research which regularly interact and merge. To view it in this way gives a new salience and focus to two very old elements of the European idea of the university, each of which has been significantly weakened in recent years. They are the notions of academic community, and of personal knowledge.

The notion of academic community reflects the view that knowledge is socially constructed, and is thus the product of groups of people talking to each other, testing and refining their understanding of reality and truth. The university was once the most convenient way of doing this, but the pressures which I have examined above suggest that this model is no longer adequate, because too much new knowledge is being created outside the walls, and the knowledge itself is too dynamic. When most knowledge was conceived of as relatively static, a matter of laborious discovery of eternal truths or natural laws, it made sense to create special spaces where the work could be done. Once discovered, it could then be transmitted to the world outside for application, and since it did not change rapidly, it did not need a two way relationship with that world. The world outside the walls was a place to be examined, theorized about and informed of the conclusions, it was not an active partner in the process. The inadequacy of that model has become increasingly clear in recent years, when the processes which used to be exclusive to the university are also taking place outside, and that world has as much claim to membership of the community as those within.

The implications of lifelong learning and a knowledge based society are that we must redefine the nature of the academic community, as one which embraces all of Reich's symbolic analysts, all engaged throughout our lives (as academics and a few researchers outside always have been) in a lifelong pursuit of knowledge. We have yet to understand what this means for the university as an institution.

In doing this, however, we must recognize the challenge of globalization. The rules of the European academic community have been built on the Enlightenment project. Even in the 'softest' fields, where physical evidence is hardest to find, there remains a notion of a truth to be pursued, even if it can only be established by tentative agreement among 'experts'. The implication of the new academic community is that that community will be much larger, and perhaps less likely to agree, but the implication of globalization may be that there are whole cultures which do not accept the fundamental principles. In the attempt to avoid this dilemma it is tempting to shift focus to instrumental values – the test of 'does it work' seems easier to transfer across cultures than 'is it true'. However, at any level beyond the trivial, this notion of 'working' remains problematic, as has been demonstrated by the attempts of government through NCVQ to produce clear and objective definitions of competence. One implication of this might be that the new higher education will need to give more, rather than less, attention to issues of value, and to ways of recognizing a diversity of systems and truths.

This leads me to my second theme, of personal knowledge. In the classical model, bodies of knowledge exist, academic disciplines seek to understand them, and individuals seek to learn as much as possible of them. The individual is apprenticed to the discipline, which itself rests on a body of natural or social law, not yet fully discovered. The implications of the expansion and increased volatility of many forms of knowledge, the development of new forms, and new ways of validating them, and of the new, much larger, learning community all suggest that this vision is no longer adequate. Bodies of knowledge are inevitably personal, and individuals will assemble what is relevant to their personal situation, developing different parts as their circumstances change. This matches the models of new individualized workforce, of 'portfolio careers' and the growth of symbolic analysts, whose economic wealth rests in their ability to build on unique bodies of knowledge to tailor solutions to individual problems.

It is also a vision with good historical precedent in the classical tutorial model, where the continuing dialogue between tutor and student guides the learner through a process of reflection and negotiation, building on that student's individual knowledge, rather than imposing a predetermined body of knowledge. It also, of course, underlies the apprenticeship tradition, and the models of professional education in the creative arts, to which it is closely related, where the apprentice moves through a process whose aim is to build on individual talent and acquired knowledge with the assistance of more experienced masters, in order to become a master craftsman, with unique style and skills recognized by his peers. The aim is the unique talent, based on knowledge, skill and intellectual rigour.

CONCLUSION

To conclude, then, a crisis exists, rooted in the loss of monopoly. However, the values on which the notion of the university rests, of the communal search for knowledge, by students and teachers together, and the development of individual knowledge and skill remain critical to a developed society. The difference is that the community is becoming much larger and more diffuse and the creation and ownership of knowledge is becoming more politically and economically contested. The challenge for the university is to redefine itself within this new and larger frame.

FOUR

Realism, Postmodernism and Cultural Values

Kate Soper

It is a commonplace of postmodernist cultural criticism in higher education today that the forms of interpretation associated with liberal humanism are guilty of a `cultural imperialism` which denies or marginalizes key differences of ethnicity, gender and sexuality, and too readily judges the values of non-Western cultures in the light of ethical and aesthetic conceptions associated with the Enlightenment project. Postmodernist theory, by contrast, it is claimed, recognizes and seeks to respect the diversity of cultures and social actors, and resists the imposition of universalist values and conceptions of human needs.

Yet clearly, as the opponents of the postmodernist position have in turn pointed out, there are many forms of bigotry, fanaticism and intolerance that can take comfort from this type of argument, and there is thus a real danger that the very liberal values to which appeal is implicitly made in legitimating the postmodernist stance fall victim to the critique itself. Moreover, some would argue that it is now the Enlightenment values themselves that have been placed on the defensive and are in need of protection against the global ascendancy of non-Western forms of cultural expansion. One might cite in this connection a recent *Guardian* article by John Gray on the electoral successes in December 1995 of the radical Islamic Rifah party in Turkey, in which it is argued that this is but one of many current indices of the illusory nature of the belief that modernization and Westernization are one and the same. The epoch we are entering, Gray claims, will not be one of universal Westernization, but rather the opposite – an epoch in which Western models are rejected throughout much of the world:

> The deeper lesson of Islamist advance in Turkey is that the conflicts by which the world will be riven in the coming century will not be between different Western ideologies. They will be conflicts fuelled by militant religions, resurgent ethnicities and – not least – by the pressures of expanding populations on scarce natural resources. In such a world we should not expect liberal values to spread. A sufficiently demanding objective for liberal cultures will be their survival. (Gray 1996)

Obviously one may dispute this assessment, and I do not refer to these predictions here because I think they are necessarily entirely accurate. I do think, however, that Gray here touches on issues which ought to figure prominently in any discussion around the issue of cultural values, and serve to concentrate the minds of those postmodernist critics in the academy who have been calling upon us to reject the familiar credos of Enlightenment humanism in favour of a less ethnocentric commitment to cultural difference and plurality. For if there is indeed a risk that the coming 'modernity' will eclipse liberal values, then we should certainly be giving careful consideration to the implications of current assaults upon them within contemporary Western culture.

In what follows, I shall not deny the relevance and importance of certain criticisms associated with the postmodernist rejection of Enlightenment. But I do want to argue that the approach of the postmodernist critics to questions of ethical and aesthetic values is rather more equivocal than is commonly acknowledged by them; and that insofar as they refuse to confront these tensions in their argument, they are theoretically colluding in the marginalization of those same democratic values they professedly espouse.

Let me begin by referring to an anecdote related in a recent article by Martha Nussbaum (1992) concerning events at an American conference on anthropology. In the course of the conference a paper is given by an American economist long considered a radical in which he urges the preservation of traditional ways of life in a rural area of India. It is defended against audience objections by a French anthropologist who herself thereafter gives a paper in which she expressed regret that the introduction of smallpox vaccinations to India by the British had eradicated the cult of Sittala Devi, the goddess to whom the local community had used to pray in order to avert smallpox. When someone objected that it was surely better to be healthy rather than ill, to live rather than die, the answer was returned that Western essentialist medicine could conceive of things only in terms of binary oppositions: life as opposed to death, health to disease, and was therefore incapable of comprehending the radical otherness of Indian traditions. Another participant at the conference, one Eric Hobsbawm, thereupon rose to deliver a blistering indictment of such traditionalism and relativism. 'He lists examples,' writes Nussbaum, 'of how the appeal to tradition has been used in history to defend various types of oppression and violence. His final example is that of National Socialism. In the chaos that ensues, most of the traditionalist social scientists (above all the ones from abroad, who do not know who Hobsbawm is) demand that Hobsbawm be asked to leave the conference room. The radical American economist, covered with embarrassment at this evidence of a split between his relativism and his left-wing affiliations, convinces them, with much difficulty, to let Hobsbawm remain' (Nussbaum 1992: 203–4).

This is an incident which not only brings out the quality of the intellectual opposition between so-called 'foundationalists' and 'anti-foundationalists', but also points directly to the nature and sources of the equivocation in the postmodernist stance on values. For here clearly the suggestion is that either anti-essentialists are deeply confused in supposing their position to be consistent with their professed leftish commitments; or they are not so confused, but should accept that, for example, in presenting the distinction between life and death as a product of Western discourse, they are committed to an anti-realism which will inevitably find them condoning political agendas radically opposed to those of the left.

In other words, either the postmodernist thinkers are less resistant to every form of metaphysical anchorage than they claim, or they are indeed committed to an anti-foundationalism whose ontological commitments are such as to lead inevitably to an explosive confrontation around values – where what is exposed is the very divergent programmes that are being pursued in the name of a common vocabulary of 'democracy' or 'emancipation', a disagreement, in short, about the very definition to be placed on these ends. Thus what the one side sees as an absolute progress (the eradication of disease), the opposing party views as the unwarranted imposition of a culturally specific norm of 'progress'.

Now it seems to me very doubtful whether in practice all, or even most, professed anti-foundationalists would opt for the preservation of a religious cult over the eradication of typhus, but they should certainly accept that they are arguing in ways that might logically require them to do so. For it is of the essence of their argument that values are normatively constituted and cannot be grounded in any transcendent, extra-discursive qualities or experiences. Anti-foundationalists are not idealists: they do not deny extra-discursive reality, but they certainly deny its determinacy, and would have us believe that because there can be no representation of reality which is not discursive, then there are no pre-given, natural features of reality which govern the truth or falsity of what can be said about it. But if that is the case, then they must, it would seem, also have to accept that even those distinctions which might seem fundamental to ethical judgement – the distinctions, for example, between life and death, suffering and its absence – are to be viewed as culturally specific discursive constructs, and there is thus no reason to jib at the argument of the French anthropologist.

THE CRITIQUE OF ENLIGHTENMENT AND SOCIAL MOVEMENT POLITICS

But having said that, I think one also has to acknowledge that the postmodernists have opened up some necessary debates about what constitutes a progressive politics, and that what is not sufficiently registered in this anecdote is the vulnerability of the left-wing essentialist position to some of the political arguments which have been promoted – however ultimately inconsistently – from within the anti-foundationalist camp.[1] It was important to question the Enlightenment rationality, the faith in science and technology and the conceptions of the 'good life' which it has inspired, not least because it has encouraged a paternalist and technical-fix approach to human welfare and stimulated patterns of growth and consumption which are fast becoming ecologically unsustainable and generating ever more explosive global divisions of wealth. It was equally important that those defending its humanist argument were alerted to the groups and communities which had been excluded or marginalized by its supposedly universalist but at times decidedly partial forms of representation. Indeed, these challenges have been the condition of the emergence of some of the more enlightened social movements of our times: without a deconstruction of the humanist subject we would not have had the feminist, anti-racist and gay movements; without a subversion of the modernist commitment to science and its productivist and technocratic rhetoric (including that of Marxist Prometheanism) we would not have the green movement and ecological rethinking on the left.

At the same time, the influence of post-structuralist theory and the attention it has directed to the 'plurality' of subject places and experiences, has contributed in important ways to the development of these movements. The feminisms, for example, which have come in response to it have justly questioned the easy recourse to a universal category of 'woman', the readiness to speak to a common set of interests or desires, and the resulting confidence in a single 'totalizing' political strategy. They have also, in drawing attention to the role of language and symbolization in the construction of sexual identities, made us more aware of the ways in which the oppressions of gender and sexuality have conceptual underpinnings which can persist across significant changes in socio-economic conditions and are not necessarily dismantled by changes of a legal or institutional character. Though this focus on linguistic considerations may fairly be charged with inviting abstraction from the specific forms of constraint exercised at that level, including their constraints on the possibilities of discourse itself, they have also revealed the limitations of analysing power relations without reference to the discursive dimension.

Relatedly, in the realm of aesthetics and cultural studies, postmodernist critiques have been important in exposing the ways in which conventional critical approaches which focused on the isolated text or art work and defended it as the locus of a pure aesthetic value served as a cover under which literature and art were spared the scrutiny of other value considerations and allowed to pretend to a political neutrality which in reality they never possessed. There is no doubt that the appeal to intrinsic literary and artistic value has served legitimating functions of a dubious kind: allowed 'high' art to deflect engagements with those who challenged its canon and interpretative methods on the grounds that it is improper to confuse questions concerning the aesthetic merit of cultural production with questions concerning its ideological function or political messaging; and fostered critical approaches which distracted attention from the history of literary and art criticism itself, and from the differential values which have been brought over time even to the interpretation of a relatively stable body of canonical works.

In all these respects, the impulse to assert difference over identity, to expose the colonizing tendencies of humanist discourse, to raise the problem of the 'totalitarianism' inherent in totalizing theory, to alert us to the problem of seeing language simply as a medium for expressing a reality 'out there' rather than as playing an active role in the creation of our social and cultural universe: all this has been significant, relevant to our times and politically admirable.

All the same, I think we must recognize that the postmodernist impulse is possessed of a dynamic which has propelled it into theoretical positions which now place its argument at loggerheads with many of the cultural developments it first helped to promote; and that the arguments of the movements it initially inspired have come to look pretty dated from the perspective of the theoretical positions it has now come to embrace. What I am suggesting here is that, if we are associating the 'postmodernist' turn in thinking with the 'new social movement' politics which emerged in the wake of the convulsions of 1968, then I think we would have to recognize that it has proceeded to undermine many of the arguments by which it was originally sustained. Thus while the 'new social movements' might reasonably be said to have initiated the challenge to the 'grand narratives' of science and Marxism, they none the less remained committed to modes of thinking of a kind which have now been thoroughly subverted by the full-blown anti-foundationalism of the 1980s. Their argument was decidedly existentialist–libertarian in cast, with power conceptualized very much in terms of the repressive model, and located essentially at the level of the State and its apparatuses. The talk was of consciousness raising, self-realization, of reclaiming the body, of rescuing the authentic self from the distortion of cultural stereotypes. 'Nature' and the 'natural' self could still be evoked in blissful unawareness of the slippage of the signifieds beneath their cultural signifiers. The subject had yet to be fragmented in any serious sense, the body remained relatively unreconstructed, we were yet to learn that our innermost desires and erotic promptings were themselves the product of our culture rather than a primary Dionysian force that would sweep away its oppressions.

Of course, with the ascendancy of the structuralist programme in the early 1970s, all this had begun to look much more problematic. But we might note that even as the existentialist expression of the 1960s ceded to the structuralist–Althusserian emphasis on ideological interpolation, the political analysis retained realist commitments – as the very vocabulary of 'ideology' rather than of 'discourse' indicates. For 'ideology', as it came through from classical Marxism, necessarily carried with it the implication of reality which it did not so much construct as distortedly represent, and to which we might have access at least in principle – which was precisely why Foucault saw fit to counter this vocabulary with that of the discourse of 'discourse', which breaks with any representational conception of the relations between 'consciousness' and 'social being'.

There is discernible, then, a continuity of some sorts, but also a very definite rupture between these phases of the challenge to socialist orthodoxy and its modernist or realist metaphysics. It is a rupture we may associate with a kind of overdrive through which the logic which challenged certain kinds of identity thinking and deconstructed specific notions of truth, progress, humanism and the like, has pushed on to question the very possibility of objectivity or making reference in language to what is not the effect of discourse. This is a logic which asks us not only to renounce glib assumptions of solidarity and common interests, but to view any ascription of solidarity as suspect. To attempt to offer any general political diagnosis or remedy is supposedly to be caught up in 'totalizing' theory and hence to be lending itself to totalitarian practice. In other words, we have a 'theoretical' overdrive which pulls the political rug from under the original insistence embodied in the new social movements, that we think in terms of new 'identities'. Pushed to its uttermost, the logic of differences rules out any holistic and objective analysis of a kind which allows us to define them as 'capitalist', 'patriarchal' or indeed 'totalitarian', together with the transformative projects such analyses advocate. The philosophical correlate of this is a relativism, which invites us to disown the very aspiration to truth as something unattainable in principle, not even a regulative idea. Theories are after all only narratives and between narratives you choose subjectively what seems most useful or gives you most comfort. In cultural theory this has gone together with a repression of all reference to intuitive, phenomenological response, or to relatively persisting and trans-cultural forms of sensibility as that which ground aesthetic judgements and account for their discriminations. This has led in turn to a reluctance to engage with value questions in the field of cultural studies and a tendency, in fact, to collapse cultural criticism into cultural history and sociology. The result, it is argued, is that postmodernist theory has now deconstructed the possibility of remaining in any kind of critical engagement with our times; that it has flipped over into a validation of the existing plurality, or collapsed into an undiscriminating celebration of the actual. Some critics of the postmodernist turn in cultural theory have therefore rejected it out of hand as the by-product of the consumer society, and deeply collusive with the commodification and neo-libertarian ethos of contemporary capitalism. Yet the fact remains that it is difficult to open any text written from a postmodernist perspective which is not denouncing the modern industrial juggernaut and the insidious processes of commodification, in other words, offering critiques which clearly rely for their force on the appeal to certain values – the elimination of poverty, injustice and domination – as obviously morally preferable, and which are rooted, it would seem, in a humanist assumption of universal needs for precisely those kinds of goods and conditions of self-realization which so-called 'development' has denied to the larger part of humanity. Self-styled postmodernists or anti-foundationalists are in this sense frequently found articulating precisely those forms of critique of the effects of the global market and capitalist imperialism which have been constantly expressed by the left-wing realists.

THE RHETORIC OF DIFFERENCE AND THE
LOGIC OF DEMOCRACY

This inevitably raises the question of the consistency of the political rhetoric of postmodernist argument with its ontological anti-realism: the question of the extent to which it can coherently sustain its professedly humanist and egalitarian commitments while refusing to recognize any extra-discursive, non-normative, features of the world and ourselves which might explain and justify the moral option in their favour. This, moreover, is a charge which can be pressed from a number of differing angles. Thus, in its deconstruction of 'identity' thinking and its binary grid of oppositional concepts, it directs us to a future in which we might be freed from the tyranny of constructed identities – and thus invokes the autonomy of persons even as it argues for their constructed subjectivity. It has challenged truth but only in the name of truth – in other words with a view to revealing the manipulative powers or distortions of the discourses attaining to the status of knowledge. It questions a repressive conception of power but yet invites us to conceive its workings in terms of the manipulation of desire, the co-option of souls, the working over of the body, and other moves which at the very least gesture to the idea of the subject as an autonomous site of resistance. It has presented us as decentred and fragmented subjects the validity of whose conscious experience must always be called in question – but only in that process to submit us to conscious forms of self-scrutiny in the light of which we are supposed to cast off various forms of blindness about ourselves, reorganize our desires and adjust our behavioural responses. It has criticized élitist cultural practice but precisely in the name of the forms of freedom and self-expression to which it has been blinded – in other words to expose the limitations of its liberal pretences rather than to capsize liberal values in themselves.

In sum, in all these forms of argument it has committed itself to a logic of difference which is theoretically incompatible with the logic of democracy whilst all the time implicitly relying on the latter for the force of its political critique. For why should we 'respect' or 'preserve' the plurality of social actors unless we think it right that they should be represented, and that in treating different persons or groups as different we are treating them more equally? If we are obedient only to the logic of difference, we remove the grounds for any claims that different identities come with equal entitlements to the same forms of recognition: we deconstruct the grounds upon which any political values can conceivably be promoted.

Clearly it is an implication of my argument here that postmodernist strategies can only consistently sustain their critical charge by surreptitiously invoking the foundationalist positions in social theory which they have explicitly rejected; in other words, that they are covert or shame-faced realists who ought to acknowledge the ultimate dependency of their critique on value commitments which are actually in alliance with the theoretical perspective they wish to disown. They offer us procedures or methodologies which are critically pointed, but refuse to articulate the values by which they are impelled or by reference to which they might be justified.

One line of response to these charges, however, might be that it mistakes the strategic purposes of the emphasis on 'difference' and in the process takes too literally an anti-foundationalist argument which was never intended to be construed as a denial of a minimal human identity of needs and aspirations. The advocates of difference have the edge over their opponents, it might be said, because they have recognized more clearly than they that there can be no politics which does not invoke an identity of needs in its very attempt to represent the 'other' – and have become that much more cautious about the act of representation as a consequence of this recognition. Their greater sensitivity resides in the fact that they have recognized the risks of assimilation in the very act of empathy with victims of oppression which is indispensable to the pursuit of emancipatory politics. Such, for example, is the position from which Gayatri Spivak has defended the Derridean admonition against hailing the 'other' in the language of the self:

> Contrary to the received assumption, it seems to me that the non-foundationalist thinkers are suggesting that you cannot have any kind of emancipatory project *without* some notion of the ways in which human beings are similar, but that there are practical–philosophical problems that attend on that assumption. Historically, the people who have been involved in emancipatory projects from above – slave-holders and proponents of Christianizing the natives and so on – are the ones who have produced the discourse. This contradiction can be avoided only if the principles of a universal humanism – the place where indeed all human beings are similar – is seen to be lodged in their being different. So that difference itself becomes a name for the place where we are all the same – a *'name for'*, because difference is not something that can be articulated, as a monolithic concept. But if difference becomes a name for the place where we are all the same – if difference becomes the name for that – then it stands as a kind of warning against the fact that we *cannot not* propose identity when we engage in actual emancipatory projects. No more than that. But it is a great deal, no more than that, but also no less than that. (Spivak 1991: 227–8)

Yet there is surely something a touch sophistical about this argument, which begins by acknowledging the reliance of 'emancipatory politics' on the assumption of the sameness of human beings only to end by translating that notion of sameness into that of absolute difference. For is this not to evade the key problem of how we could begin to discriminate between what is or is not 'emancipatory' without invoking those ways in which human beings are similar not in their difference but precisely in their sameness -- the sameness or similarity, for example, of the pain or humiliation they will experience when subjected to similar kinds of maltreatment? Remaining alert to the political and philosophical assumptions of speaking on behalf of the other's needs – being sensitive, as it were, to the risk of 'cultural imperialist' or 'ethnocentric' perspectives that attend on all political acts, must include remaining alert to the humanist presumptions which make sense of the charge of ethnocentrism in the first place.

One can certainly accept the Derridean point that since all attempts to speak to the experience of the 'other' will necessarily be made in the light of one's own identity, one should exercise some caution about any act of representation. But one should note that to exercise indefinite caution would be to disarm oneself of the possibility of acting at all: even one's empathy with the victims of fascism might be seen to be tainted with cultural imperialism. In this sense, one might argue that what is presented as a form of political hyper-sensitivity is really a retreat into theoreticist quietism. It indulges in a political innocence which anyone seriously concerned to promote the cause of oppressed constituencies knows they cannot themselves afford. Take, for example, the Derridean line on the historical 'event' as evidenced in a recent interview on the politics of deconstruction:

> The happening of the event is what cannot and should not be prevented: it is another name for the future itself. Not that it is good – good in itself – that everything or anything should happen; nor that we should give up trying to prevent certain things from coming to pass (in that case there would be no choice, no responsibility, no ethics or politics). But you do not try to oppose events unless you think they shut off the future or carry the threat of death; events which would end the possibility of events, which would end any affirmative opening towards the arrival of the other. (Derrida 1994: 32)

Whilst having all the appearance of a profound respect for ethical value, pieties of this order, one may argue, remain so non-specific in their rhetoric as to constitute its actual evasion. Is it the gnat's death or global holocaust we should be opposing, and if the latter, did we need deconstruction to inform us of it?

For similar reasons I think it is difficult finally to come to rest where Steve Connor has recommended we should when he says it is enough for relativism to accept the paradoxes of its own position, and argues that there is no kind of bottom line of value, no final choice to be made between the retrieval and the critique of values, and therefore no commitment to such ideals as beauty, freedom, equality and justice which would not in principle be vulnerable to the relativist critique (Connor 1993: 31–49). This is in part because the position recommended here contains its own internal paradox – that it promotes as more absolutely valuable a position on value which is neither relativist nor absolutist; but more seriously, I think, because it evades the point about realism. Certainly we have and will continue to re-think our ideas of beauty, freedom , justice, etc., but it is impossible to see how we could justify the forms of rethinking except by reference to a certain base-line of values of a more absolute kind to do with the human predicament – our vulnerability, for example, to physical and mental suffering and our capacity to be moved by empathy for others afflicted by it. How could we rethink the limits of our previous conceptions of equality or justice without referring to the hyper-goods of avoiding pain or humiliation? (Taylor 1989: 63–73). At any rate, I think we should accept that there is a difference between recognizing the relativity of values in the sense of recognizing that discourses about value are historically specific and that we are constantly reviewing the particular content given to core ideals of justice, equality, and so on; and suggesting that values must be analysed as entirely relativist products of discourse. It is one thing to point out that feminist discourse forced a supersession of previous conceptions of the 'just' or 'equal' society, another to suppose that prior to its discourse there was only a difference of status between men and women and not a condition of oppression. In other words, we need to distinguish between the position in epistemological and moral theory which would hold that it is only in virtue of the discourse of 'rights' or 'oppression', that differences of experience emerge as differences which matter and are endowed with normative charge, and the position I want to defend here which insists that it is precisely such differences of experience (as between suffering and its absence) that provide the meaning of moral discourse and distinguish its claims from those of arbitrary whim and subjective preference.

RELATIVISM AND CULTURAL CRITICISM

These points have their relevance even in the area of cultural criticism, where I would readily admit how problematic it is to defend the notion of aesthetic value, and where modes of interpretation which treated works of art and literature as if they were the repository of eternal verities whose meaning could be appreciated quite independently of any reference to their social context, now strike us as extraordinarily blind to the issues of representation and ideology of critical concern today. But insofar as contemporary critical moves are motivated by a concern with representations of class, gender and ethnicity that were previously ignored, they are inevitably also caught up in these questions about essentialist versus relative approaches to the subject, and cannot avoid the problems posed in the debate between humanist and anti-humanist accounts of agency and self-expression.

I am far from suggesting here that cultural critics are conscious advocates of the philosophical positions I have been criticizing, or directly lending themselves to the forms of theoreticism or ethical quietism I have associated with them. On the contrary, the challenge to traditional approaches – the general shift from an Englit to a cultural studies focus – is plainly motivated by a concern to expose the ways in which cultural production, and its modes of criticism, figure in the creation and perpetuation of various forms of sexual, gender or racial oppression, and must be viewed in the light of their potential for prejudicial representation. My point is only that when one is drawing on anti-foundationalist theories in the pursuit of that programme – and Derridean and Foucauldian argument clearly figures very largely in it – one should proceed in some awareness of their implications for its ultimate coherence. If, for example, we proceed as if subjects were always adequately accounted for as 'constructs' of discourse, then it is not clear that we can really avail ourselves of a critical perspective which always relies for its force on a gesture towards that which is inauthentic or distorting or stereotypical in the representation: we disarm ourselves of the basis from which we could coherently expose the literary text as a vehicle of, say, colonial or patriarchal perceptions, or, alternatively, explore its significance as a site of contestation around such partial constructions, since in both cases the force of the critique relies on the assumption that human beings are in a position to negotiate their identity by reference to discursive formations rather than exhaustively constituted by them. If we insist that everything which is presented as a determination of nature, is to be viewed as a culturally imposed norm, then we risk undermining the basis from which we can contest the representation of specific forms of social or sexual practice as 'perverse'. If we deny that there are any universal, essential features of being human, then we cannot really make sense of critical strategies which seek to reveal the illegitimacy of certain forms of essentialist discourse. If we are indefinitely obedient to the strictures about always observing 'difference', then, I have suggested, we may have removed the ground from which we can defend any form of political reading over any other. If there is nothing which is not the effect of difference, then there is no presence of the self to be expressed, realized, fulfilled, redeemed or rescued from its cultural construction.

We might note, moreover, that any account of power relations which severs these from extra-discursive conditions of existence, licences an indefinite and uncontrollable play of meaning which has very problematic implications for any attempt to defend a particular cultural interpretation or textual analysis as inherently 'emancipatory'. If we accept the perspectivist argument then it becomes difficult to say what it means to bring, say, a feminist reading to bear. For on what criteria do we decide whether a given discourse, or literary work or piece of art is 'feminist' or friendly to feminism once we have committed ourselves to the idea that the 'oppression of women' is discursively constructed, a function itself of the ways in which biological sex comes to be perceived, spoken of and evaluated? Do we argue that the discourse/text is 'feminist' because it applauds, or shows sympathy for, or argues for the politically regenerative powers of those dispositions and sensibilities traditionally deemed to be 'feminine'? Or do we argue that it is hostile to feminism precisely because it reproduces rather than transcends an essentialist conception of gender difference? Both approaches may equally claim to be emancipatory in bringing a gender critique to bear, yet what one critic's reading may reveal to be the progressive aspects of a text, another may argue are witness to its collusion in oppressive modes of thinking.

Now I am not suggesting that there has to be one right answer here, or that debates of this kind are not important and interesting. All I am suggesting is that once you have adopted a theoretical position which has ruled out the possibility of any objective criteria of female emancipation you will have to accept that all decisions at this level will be entirely subjective, and you are free to bring whatever normative frame you choose to the assessment of cultural history. It then becomes rather unclear in what sense we can treat literary texts as forms of cultural evidence – as in any sense objective documents of their times. The idea that traditional critical approaches have ignored or abstracted from the political dimensions of cultural production begins to subvert itself once we disavow that there are grounds for discriminating between more or less progressive developments.

Moreover, I think we should recognize that there is a certain paradox about postmodernist challenges to the autonomy of art, and the possibility of aesthetic discrimination, given the extent to which this is a contestation about the preserve of art itself. Why, after all, should we enter into a contest about art, deconstruct its canon, question its claimed forms of autonomy, and so on, unless we think there is something distinctive to it, and distinctively valuable, as a domain of cultural practice: unless we think that what it offers by way of insight or pleasure cannot be provided either through more explicitly theoretical modes of understanding or through other forms of consumption. Let us add, too, in this connection, that one effect of this is a narrowing of the canon, since works tend to get selected for critical scrutiny in the light of their susceptibility to certain types of reading. As Martin Ryle has noted:

> Some texts which have survived within Englit may ... flourish anew within the perspectives of cultural studies, but other texts will cease to be of interest. Donne's 'Anniversarie' does not really yield all that much if we are looking for evidence about early modern constructions of gender. Seamus Heaney's engagement with questions of history and identity make 'Station Island' an immediately interesting text for the cultural historian, but many of his poems in *Seeing Things* – those about perception, about the special visual quality of sea horizons – fit into no such cultural-historical basket. (Ryle 1994: 23)

One implication of my question here is that cultural critics who are disposed to endorse the populist and anti-élitist impulse of postmodernism and incorporate that radicalism into their academic teaching, should be ready to admit the tensions of a critical position which both congratulates mass taste, while seeking pedagogically always to further sensibility regarding the ways in which the commodity society 'constructs' its subjects and positions its consumers in terms of the representations offered in the soap opera, advertising imagery, romance fiction and so on. This is not necessarily a negative tension but it seems to me we ought at least to acknowledge it, to accept that it speaks to a prevarication about the analysis of contemporary popular culture: is this the site of a positive demotic resistance to hierarchical and élitist power structures, or their manipulated and self-serving product? – and thus to accept that in the very deployment of critical strategies which are designed to alert the reader or viewer to the semiotics of cultural production, we do not transcend but continue to reflect a long-standing dilemma for left critique – how to combine a democratic respect for mass taste with a socialist analysis of its ideological exploitation? Clearly, from the democratic point of view, there were good reasons to challenge the Frankfurt School emphasis on the manipulations of the Culture Industry, and to seek to rescue popular culture from that form of left-wing élitism and negative appraisal. But this is a critical perspective which necessarily erodes those distinctions between art and entertainment, 'high' and 'low' which earlier sustained the critical edge of radical cultural theory. What gets sacrificed in this reappraisal, as Frederic Jameson reminds us, is the standpoint of any 'genuinely aesthetic experience' of the kind formerly used to unmask the structures of a commodified and commercialized art (Jameson 1990: 41–3). Or at least any explicit standpoint, since what I am suggesting here is that there remains an implicit gesture towards that standpoint in the very inclination to defend a postmodernist critical approach as more alert than any other to the manipulations of subjectivity. Something of this same paradox is discernible in a postmodernist artistic practice which employs ever more ingenious strategies to debunk the pretensions of 'high' art and to transgress its conventions while seeking none the less to be received as art itself; to offer itself as a continuous 'artistic' statement about the delusions of the 'autonomy' of art.

At any rate, it seems to me that if we are to build on the insights shed by postmodernist critiques we need both to defend the political and ethical values underpinning these and to relate these to value commitments of a more purely aesthetic character. For in the end what we are talking about here are practical and critical strategies which are still, it would seem, implicitly aimed at the development of a more acute and educated aesthetic sensibility within a political programme where this is conceived as an integral component of self-realization and cultural emancipation.

NOTE

1   It was with a view to acknowledging this that I have sketched elsewhere a kind of dogs versus cats caricature of the divide: on the one hand we have 'the dogged metaphysicians, a fierce and burly crew stalwartly defending various bedrocks and foundations by means of an assortment of trusty but clankingly mechanical concepts such as "class", "materialism", "humanism" "literary merit", "transcendence" and so forth: obsolete weapons, maybe, but possessed of the distinct advantage that in all the dust thrown up by the flailing around with them, their wielders do not realize how seldom they connect with the opposition. On the other side stand the "feline ironists" and revellers in relativism, dancing light-heartedly upon the water of *différance*, deflecting all foundationalist blows with an adroitly directed ludic laser beam. Masters of situationist strategy, they side-step the heavy military engagement by refusing to do anything but play.' And I went on to suggest that if I were allowed only the mirror of this caricature in which to find a reflection of my own position, I would be feeling pretty schizoid, but would in the end have to recognize that there is something minimally less distorting of my own features in the grotesque metaphysical Cerberus than in the virtual reality of the ironical Cheshire grin. (See *Principled Positions: Postmodernism and the Rediscovery of Value*. Judith Squires (ed.), Lawrence and Wishart, 1993, p. 19, first published in *New Left Review* No. 186, March–April 1991.)

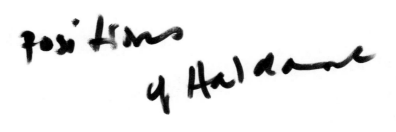

FIVE

Higher Education after Ideology: Whose Crisis? What Knowledge?

John Haldane

INTRODUCTION

This is a short chapter about a large subject. Brevity is made possible by the fact that I shall only be concerned with framework issues and not with the multiplicity of topics locatable within this framework. Additionally, however, I find it difficult to take seriously some of the 'radical critiques' of knowledge. To put the point very directly and provocatively, my enduring impression is that those who speak longest and loudest about crises of knowledge are those least possessed of it.[1]

Divisive as it may be to say this, there are hierarchies of academic study and of institutions in which such study is conducted. No one who cares about intellectual discipline and who has undergone a rigorous training in a difficult field can doubt that deep knowledge is hard won, and that what comes easier lies nearer the intellectual surface. Classical culture is a less profound subject than classics; comparative religion is less demanding and less fruitful than the scholarly study of a sacred text; the metaphysics of cognition is hard in the way that applied ethics is not. Similarly, the study of ancient disciplines in ancient universities is, in general, intellectually more serious than the practice of cultural studies in the new universities. Again in my experience, those who deny this are generally not in a position to make informed judgements or have a vested interest in seeing intellectual hierarchies undermined.

From the point of view of one engaged in professional philosophy of a sort that is very demanding and which offers daily reminders of one's inability to think effectively, talk of a 'crisis for knowledge in higher education' seems idle and quite misplaced. The more one learns the more one wishes to know and the less one is apt to think that there is no such thing as objective knowledge. Good students are aware of this; poor academics may not be. To coin a phrase: those who can do; those who cannot say, it can't be done.

POSTMODERNIST CRITIQUE

So much by way of preliminary assessment. My main title is an ambiguous one: the 'after' may be read chronologically, as higher education post ideology, or directionally, as higher education *in pursuit of* ideology. I wish to discuss both of these themes: the now oft-expressed idea that we live in a post-ideological age, but also the concern that some people still have to try and find a grounding for our intellectual and social practices in something like an ideology. What I shall do first is to observe some of the ways in which commentators try to characterize the contemporary condition and then to consider various responses to the challenges these are held to present.

Currently, concerns are expressed about the history of Western civilization. We are supposed to have passed beyond a condition of certainty, or at any rate confidence, about the values that we share and about the ways we might inculcate those values in successive generations; confidence about the basic institutions of society and about notions of intellectual, moral and spiritual authority – in short the familiar package of elements that constitute a fairly stable social and cultural order. The challenging and unsettling thought is that somehow we have left all that behind us and are now in circumstances of profound uncertainty. The problem this presents is that of how (if at all) one may construct a normative basis for social life in circumstances of diversity, plurality, scepticism and disagreement.

Sometimes these issues are put in terms of the imagery of fracture and disintegration: fragmentation of reason, fragmentation of public culture and a resulting plurality of perspectives marked by mutual incommensurability. In all of this the point is not to observe mere social diversity, rather it is intended to express the view that we lack the conditions necessary for working towards objectively warranted agreement. We find ourselves in what some people like to describe as a 'postmodern condition',[2] one in which the possibility of public discussion of matters of prime importance is undermined by apparently ineliminable features of contemporary thought: the absence of values, or extensive and irresolvable disagreement about them.

POST-IDEOLOGY

In speaking in this circumstance of the lack of 'ideology' I am using the term in a rather general way such that we might even want to speak of 'liberal ideology', though liberals themselves have often felt uncomfortable about the suggestion that they are ideologically committed. Ideology, as I am concerned with it here, involves a set of ideas concerning human nature that have extensive implications for the conduct of individual and social life; a way of thinking about what we are which is directly relevant to how we ought to live. There are narrowly drawn, rich and powerful ideologies, and there are somewhat looser, broader more encompassing ideologies. One kind of ideology is the religious world-view offered by certain strands of Christianity; Marxism is another obvious instance. However, as I said, liberalism also counts in this reckoning as a type of ideology; at any rate those versions of it which involve a conception of human beings as, for example, essentially political animals, and an interpretation of political identity in terms of democratic citizenship. Certainly, its postmodern critics such as Richard Rorty regard traditional liberalism as part of the ideological history of the West, and view it as rooted in certain rationalistic (and thus untenable) ideas about how we should think of ourselves (Rorty 1989).

Let me mention four postmodernist ideas about the undoing of ideology, and in describing them I shall follow the literary style favoured by their advocates. Thus: (i) the end of meta-narratives; (ii) the rejection of transcendentalism; (iii) the abandonment of universal humanism; and (iv) the instrumentalization of rationality.

The end of meta-narratives

One claim of postmodern critics is that the ways of thinking about ourselves that have dominated Western culture for the last 2,500 years involve hermeneutic and normative conceptions of history, ways of thinking about events that do not see them in purely empirical fashion, as devoid of any kind of evaluative meaning. On the contrary, they conceive of the course of human existence as having some kind of significance or value (and often as ascending or declining). Obvious instances of this are conceptions of sacred history; for example, the 'developmental' view found in Hebrew scripture and taken up and extended by Christianity. Thus, St Augustine thinks in terms of the sequence of creation, fall, incarnation, atonement, redemption and so on. Likewise we can see a de-Christianised version of the flow of events in someone like Hegel who tries to make sense of the human condition in terms of a narrative history. Even liberalism presumes a kind of meta-narrative, as when, for example, the conception of citizenship is presented as a rational product of history. John Rawls has his own particular version of this which has featured ever more prominently in his writings about the idea of an overlapping consensus (Rawls 1993 and forthcoming). He looks back to the age of faith followed by the religious wars of Europe and sees these as giving rise to the Enlightenment, which in turn generated our modern Western notions of citizenship and of public reason. Accordingly, this meta-narrative views contemporary liberalism as in some way naturally and rationally emerging from history.

Postmodern critics contend that we simply cannot deceive ourselves into thinking that human events have any kind of significance. The contemporary substitute for legitimizing myths is critical sociology. We can describe events (though mindful of the impossibility of objectivity), and if we choose we can interpret them in various ways; but we must not think of these descriptions and interpretations as anything other than convenient modes of organization. There is nothing of significance to be found in human history itself; we cannot discover therein any clues as to what we are and how we ought to live.

The rejection of transcendentalism

This follows on inasmuch as it insists that there is nothing to look to, apart from the simple empirical factors laid bare before us by science; and once again, mindful of the rule of subjectivity, there may not even be this. At best there is just a continuing process of chemico-physical interaction between bits of matter. Any effort to find a perspective that goes beyond this is impossible, be it the transcendental viewpoint of religion or the transcendental perspective of pure reason. Even the latter is undermined by the idea that science and social criticism have taught us that there is only a valueless material universe to which human imagination has added the myths of rationality.

The abandonment of universal humanism

This refers to the rejection of attempts to discover defining features of the human condition. Such efforts have taken various forms including the Continental rationalisms of Descartes and Kant, and the Scottish socio-psychology of Adam Ferguson and David Hume. While the latter authors rejected the *a priorism* and essentialism of the former in favour of empirical observation and conjecture, they none the less proposed that human nature may be universal, and that on this basis a normative theory of value might be advanced. Unsurprisingly, postmodern critics argue that this retains the form of untenable essentialism inasmuch as it assumes something called 'the human condition' in terms of which one might understand society by discerning the relations between primary and secondary natures, the underlying universal base and its variable culturation.

The instrumentalization of reason

Whereas in earlier times people supposed that rational deliberation about questions of conduct and values could yield defensible policies, the present suggestion is that reason has been forced into full-scale retreat. People began by thinking that reasoning could determine goals and purposes. Then, as one attempt after another to demonstrate how that could be so seemed to fail, they moved to ideas of practical reason as simply the organization of desires and aversions. Thought cannot lead to conclusions about what we should aim for, instead appetite or desire directs us in certain ways. All that reason can do is co-ordinate preferences and work out means to their satisfaction. In the eighteenth century, Hume drew this conclusion when he wrote that reason is and can only be the slave of passions, and his 'instrumental' view has been adopted by most contemporary conceptions of individual and social choice which conspicuously withdraw from any ambition to try to decide what we *should* desire or what we *should* want.

AFTER IDEOLOGY?

These four ideas have been invoked by postmodern and other 'radical' critics in would-be refutations of attempts to make sense of the human condition through an account of human nature, extracting from it various norms, values and requirements. In other words, these ideas appear to put paid to any possibility of ideology.

Notwithstanding all of this, however, I think it is very significant that we still seek some unifying and ennobling vision. We live in an age that is supposed to be post-ideological, yet all around one can see attempts to re-construct old meta-narratives or to fashion new ones. In the United States especially, no quarter passes without somebody producing a book on the modern mind, or the condition of society, etc., and although these are often pessimistic in outlook they are also struggling to try and answer the questions of who we are, of what we have become, and of where we ought to be heading. The issue, therefore, is whether such efforts are in vain.

As above, I wish to mention four ideas. To introduce these it may be helpful to describe something of the situation so far as ideology is concerned in the area of creative culture. Postmodernist thinking seems to have taken a particularly secure grip among art theorists, which raises an interesting question about where art, architecture, literature and music go 'after ideology'. If one thinks of the history of painting in Western Europe, for instance, it has long been something of an ideologically rich field. At various stages European painting has been informed by changing conceptions of the human person, the natural world and so on. It is not possible to study the work of artists like Giotto, Poussin or Claude Lorrain without seeing in their paintings certain interpretations of landscape as a bearer of significance, be it a different set of meanings in each case.

This is most obviously true if you consider religious art, but even supposedly secular painting has been resonant with moral and philosophical conceptions of human beings and their place in society and nature. Interestingly, Marxist art historians have tried to provide histories of Western painting as ideologically structured and dialectically ordered. To give an example, Marxists have sometimes argued that portraiture is a product of, and a reinforcement for, certain power relations within society. In such ideological accounts the rise of the portrait is related to the rise of a mercantile class who reassured themselves of their superior condition by having their images depicted either as beneficent characters or as figures of power.

Although I think that Marxist art history is ultimately implausible, it is right to claim the influence of ideology (in my broad sense) throughout the history of art.[3] Furthermore the relation is not a merely historical one. People regularly ask such questions as whether we can still make inspiring paintings, and the worry lying behind this is the thought that somehow we have nothing 'meaningful' to say. Without an animating conception of humanity, portraiture is just a decorative form of documentation. If there is no *idea* imbuing the human image with meaning then all we have is just a likeness, a *mere* resemblance.

These worries are legitimate and they call forth at least four responses to the purported loss of ideology: (i) romantic affirmation; (ii) endless irony; (iii) pragmatism; and (iv) reform and renewal.

Romantic affirmation

This involves going on doing the same things as in the ideological past but in a romantic spirit, doubting that one can really ground practice in some meta-narrative, or philosophical anthropology. For example, one may continue with the tradition of producing royal portraits. Without ideological conviction, however, this is apt to fail as serious art. If one looks at contemporary portraits of the Queen they are generally lacking in symbolic significance and they have little, if any, cultural resonance. There is no sense of awe or mystery; and there is little indication of the artists comprehending the distinction between the office and the occupant of it. When people made portraits in the past they were sometimes primarily recording an individual; but more often they were celebrating (or challenging) a role. Pictures of the papacy following the First Vatican Council (at which the infallibility of the Pope was defined) are avowedly portraits of the Bishop of the Church of Rome, Vicar of Christ and pastor of the universal Church, not pictorial studies of this or that middle-aged or elderly Italian. The individuals in question were thought to be elevated by the office, and official portraiture aimed to depict its authority.

Nowadays, however, artists and others find it near-to-impossible to think in such terms. It is no surprise, therefore, that portraits of the Queen are reduced to the status of pictures of an affluent woman of a certain age. The response of romantic affirmation is to play with ideas of monarchy, bringing in various icons of royalty, but this activity is ideologically unserious. It is a form of nostalgia-driven entertainment. The counterpart in architecture is perhaps more familiar: picking up features of Classical, Gothic and other historical styles, for example using the portico in various romantic ways but without really believing in the metaphysics of the classical façade.

Endless irony

The previous response involves a degree of tension as one tries to enter into the spirit of the older order, even though one cannot believe its ideological presuppositions, or even credit them with much if any coherence. By contrast, the way of endless irony imposes no demands upon the intellect or the imagination. It is simply a form of play. Without believing in its philosophical or theological foundations, or even aspiring to believe in them, one keeps quoting the forms of past culture. This attitude is prominent in contemporary literature where authors deploy – with self-announcing irony – the devices of certain genre.Thus, while having no faith in the institution of the family, and certainly without endorsing its celebration in grand narrative tales, a writer may nevertheless adopt elements of that literary form to produce an 'intergenerational saga'.

The main point against romantic affirmation is that it is unconvincing. If you do not believe in the supporting ideology, the attempt to identify romantically with it is doomed to failure. Additionally the practice of cultural quotation is subject to diminishing returns. If one simply draws from the stock of cultural forms without adding to it, and is in turn drawn upon, a process of continuing impoverishment is established. Consider once again the case of architecture. It is striking how in a city like Los Angeles, for example, the practice of making ironic reference to the styles of the eighteenth century has led very quickly to architects quoting recent postmodern buildings. Thereby the resources are diminished and the meaning of the original inspiration is lost.

Pragmatism

The third response, though un-ironic, also eschews the aspiration to achieve anything significant and instead offers effective design and decoration. Remaining for the present with the built environment, an example from my own experience may be apt to illustrate this. The arts faculty departments in St Andrews are generally housed in older buildings that have been in academic service for some years.The departments of Logic and Metaphysics and of Moral Philosophy are in a Victorian baronial mansion on a clifftop overlooking the sea. This is redolent of nineteenth-century ideas about Scotland's cultural past, including its relations with the continent and its Gothic grandeur. Also the historical orientation of the building is well-suited to philosophy which has been taught at St Andrews during the course of six centuries.

As part of a university wide policy of continuous improvement it was decided that the building needed extensive refurbishment and that process has been started. Curious to see what might lie in store for us I went to look at another department whose historical building had recently had the same treatment. I am not quite sure what I expected but it was not what I found. The interior has been refashioned in what might be termed 'accountancy service style'. You enter a building of muted colours and grey carpets and find a foyer with chairs and plants. It is certainly airy and pleasant but what it entirely fails to offer is any sense of either the history of the building or of its being a place of higher learning. It is devoid of any sense or purpose other than general utility. There are no portraits of former professors or any other historical or academic points of reference.

Overall this constitutes a largely unwitting retreat from the aspiration to do something culturally or ideologically significant with one's environment. Instead there is formal design and decoration achieving a pleasing but unassertive form. This explains the anonymous quality, for it could be any kind of upgraded office. The design is shaken free from any of the particular resonances associated with the nature of the subject practised there, the history of the building itself and the ancient traditions of the University. I leave it as an exercise for the reader to consider how post-ideological pragmatism expresses itself in other aspects of university life.

Reform and renewal

The final response I wish to consider is one of reform and renewal. This involves asking what was wrong with ideology. Standing firm in the face of postmodern criticism, one questions whether the things that have been held to be problematic really are so, asking why exactly meta-narratives are impossible, what precisely the problem is about transcendentalism, why universal humanism is untenable, and so on. And having been bold enough to challenge the various postmodern orthodoxies one may then consider the possibility of re-establishing confidence in some of the central philosophical and moral ideas of Western culture.

My own view is that what is called for is a re-articulation of pre-modern conceptions of human nature, human values and public culture. Certainly one cannot operate as if 'modernity' had not been, and nor should one simply ignore the points made by postmodern critics. Reform and renewal are recurrent necessities in any living tradition: naive pre-modernism is not an option; and the idea of a Golden Age of learning untroubled by scepticism is a fantasy of the ignorant. But before we try to finesse older ways of thinking we need first to show that they are not bankrupt and that they can resource current research and study.

NORMATIVE NATURALISM[4]

Consider then the idea that no full and adequate account of human beings could fail to be, at least in part, a normative understanding, one in which the facts of human nature are seen to establish a system of objective purposes and values; add to this the claim that one cannot wholly separate individual and communal life, or moral and social reasoning, and what begins to emerge is the recognition that any attempt to understand human nature in the round must lead us to a certain ideological conception in which practice is answerable to requirements of reason and nature.

Some questions about values are psychological and sociological. Biographers and historians are often interested in the ideals that motivated people; and periodically there are surveys of social attitudes designed to keep track of changes in morality, that is in people's thoughts about certain kinds of behaviour and in the behaviour itself. These are empirical questions to be investigated and answered by various means including very sophisticated social science methods. But however successful these means may be, all they can tell us about are people's attitudes and behaviour. They cannot settle the many particular questions that people ask about what is good and bad, right and wrong; and nor can they settle the more abstract question of what it is for something to be good or bad.

This said, there is a well-established empiricist orthodoxy that continues to exert its influence even on those who regard themselves as 'post-empiricists'. To understand its power it is helpful to appreciate something of the philosophical history out of which it developed and to much of which it was a deliberate reaction. The principle concern of thinkers prior to Socrates was with the question of how the world can be thought about in a systematic way. Their interest was as much with the possible structure of the world as with the powers of human understanding. For in order that there might be general truths about the nature and behaviour of the cosmos it must have some order. This thought led in due course to an idea about the natures of things that is expressed in a Pythagorean formula: limit (*peras*) imposed upon the unlimited (*apeiron*) producing the limited (*peperasmenon*). Further refined this became the doctrine of 'hylomorphism' (*hyle* = matter, *morphe* = shape), the principle that everything can be analysed in terms of a medium and an organizational form. So a wooden ball is so much matter having spherical form; a horse, so much flesh and bones arranged in a certain living form; a galaxy, stars and planets in a certain configuration.

Clearly this ancient philosophical analysis is a powerful one, and it remained the central doctrine of philosophical thought through the middle ages only beginning to weaken in the fifteenth century. The reasons for its demise, which accelerated in the sixteenth century and seemed complete by the end of the seventeenth, are complex but the central force in its displacement was the rise of new analytical schemes associated with a particular method of enquiry: metaphysically unburdened empirical investigation conducted through controlled experiment. In short, the rise of modern natural science.

One important aspect of the difference between Aristotelian and modern science consequent upon the substitution of mechanics for organic activity is the way in which explanation and understanding no longer invoked purposes and functions. In the older view one understands the behaviour of organisms and of their parts in terms of teleologies or directed activities. These link together various sub-organic processes and the different stages in the history of an organism. A fruit is a seed carrier; a seed is in process of developing into a sapling which is on the way to becoming a tree; the tree puts out blossoms and in due course fruits which are for the sake of propagating the species. On it goes: the parts and functions of living things contributing to larger processes themselves regulated by governing forms or natures. Now notice two features of this view of the natural order: first, it is *non-reductive*; and second, it is *normative*. It is non-reductive because it does not think that the structure and behaviour of whole entities is a function or 'upward-generated' consequence of its basic material elements. It is normative because it implies that certain states and processes are good or bad inasmuch as they contribute to or inhibit natural processes of development. Given, for example, that the heart has the function of pumping blood, and that the circulation of the blood is necessary for the distribution of minerals and other nutrients throughout the body, and for the clearing of other substances out of it, it follows that damage to the heart is *ipso facto* bad. This feature, which I shall call the 'normativity of nature', is quite general. If it makes sense to describe objects in terms of functions, and events in terms of processes then questions of efficiency, harm and benefit arise.

In rejecting the teleological view of nature and replacing it with the idea that the ultimate reality is one of mechanically interacting particles and that all the rest is just a complication of this, a matter of quantitative not qualitative differences, the modern view created a problem of the relationship between *facts*, the domain of science, and *values*, the domain of who knows what? In an age of religious belief it seemed that theology might take care of the issue: the world provides the facts and God dictates the values. But there were two problems with this. First, the science that dispensed with purposes also seemed to remove one basis for belief in God, that is that He was the designer of nature and the inventor of purposes. Second, even if one believes in God there are problems with the idea that His commands are the sole basis of values.

The most familiar of these problems is usually presented in terms of the 'Euthyphro Dilemma' (a title deriving from Plato's dialogue *Euthyphro* in which a version of it features). Consider the question: is something valuable because God commands it? or does God command it because it is valuable? To favour the first seems to make value inexplicable and arbitrary. If God were to have commanded the ritual torture of infants it would on this account thereby be valuable, but that strikes most people as absurd. However, if one favours the second option the implication is that things are valuable independently of God's commanding them.

Nature having been reconceived in atomistic-cum-mechanical-cum-mathematical terms and thereby no longer being seen as a repository of teleological norms, and the effort to provide a theological basis for values seeming to be ineffective, some writers tried to work out accounts of objective value based on reason and/or conscience. Although these are of interest, however, they were confronted with a series of objections from David Hume which, in the following two centuries, came to be widely regarded as destructive of the possibility of any kind of value objectivism.

Hume's theory of knowledge is in the tradition associated with the modern scientific world-view. As in the rest of nature, changes in us, such as the acquisition of new beliefs, are to be explained by reference to interactions within and between objects. So far as our knowledge of the world is concerned these originate in the impact of the environment on the sense organs. Generalizing, therefore, the empiricist maintains that knowledge of how things are is a function of (and probably reduces to) the content of sensory experience. Combining this with atomistic metaphysics the conclusion is arrived at that all we can be aware of are the motions of material objects and study of these fails to show us any values: good, bad, right and wrong.

Nothing in the world or in our experience of it provides grounds for belief in objective values.

This, in brief, is the basis of the proclaimed 'fact–value gap'. No observed facts reveal or entail any values. Additional to this claim is another one, equally important in the empiricist argument against moral objectivity, and suggestive of a subjectivist account of moral thinking. Hume observes that in his reading of theologians and moralists he found that they move from propositions about what *is* the case to claims about what *ought* or *ought not* to be done; but this he professes (ironically) to find surprising. On the basis of these remarks Hume is generally credited with having established a further logical gap: that between *is* and *ought*. Of course, we may argue from observed facts, such as that a man is starving, to a prescriptive conclusion, for example that he ought to be fed. But of itself this is no refutation of the Humean thesis since the response is that the conclusion only follows when a further premise is added, viz. that starving men ought to be fed. Once more, generalizing, the empiricist claim is that no ought proposition follows from a set of premises unless this includes an ought statement.

Part of the interest and power of Hume's view is that it suggests an alternative basis for values and requirements, a naturalistic and empirical account of the source of our thoughts that some things are good and others bad, some actions right and others wrong. Instead of looking to facts in the world around us we should attend to attitudes and sentiments within ourselves. In short, judgements of value and requirements are expressions or projections of our subjective desires and preferences. The approach has received a variety of refining treatments producing a range of 'expressivist' 'emotivist' and 'projectivist' theories. But the differences between these are less significant than the unifying thesis that values are subjective.

Before responding to this empiricist orthodoxy it is necessary to observe two points about the subjectivist theory of values. First it need not hold, and Hume himself did not maintain, that all values are simply expressions of individual preference. Rather it can allow that many values are socially constituted out of commonly held attitudes and preferences. The importance of this is that it provides a reply to one kind of objection to crude subjectivism, namely that we think that individuals can be in error in their evaluations. For example, we simply do not suppose that it is a matter of personal attitude whether torturing animals is wrong, and we would regard anyone who approved such conduct as morally wicked. This might seem to constitute strong evidence against a subjectivist theory until one appreciates that it is open to such a theory to identify wrongness with general disapprobation. Thus while it may not be a matter of fact but of feeling that torture is wrong, someone who did not share this feeling, or possessed contrary ones, might still be held to be 'mistaken' inasmuch as his response is at variance with the social norm in such matters.

The second point to note is that subjectivism is a *meta-theory*. Unlike consequentialist and deontological theories of value it is not concerned with the content or justification of moral and other valuations but with their 'metaphysical standing' that is as factual or non-factual, truth-bearing or non truth-bearing. That being so a question remains open for the subjectivist, namely which if any sort of first-order moral theory should he or she adopt? Largely for reasons that are easy to work out, the empiricist tradition has strongly favoured consequentialism. If values are just preferences then it is natural to think of moral theory, say, almost as a branch of social psychology. And asking the question 'What do we approve of?' writers in the empiricist tradition, most famously Jeremy Bentham and John Stuart Mill, have responded in terms of such notions as utility and happiness. Happiness is what we want and approve of, unhappiness what we shun; and ultimately we approve and disapprove of other things to the extent that we judge them to be conducive to or to constitute such states.

Thus we see the passage from a pre-modern view of nature as a system of formally structured living substances and of values as objective features pertaining to proper functioning and natural well-being, to a modern conception of reality as constituted of basic physical units and forces, and of values as projections of the states of some objects (human beings) on to other objects and situations. Postmodern ideas on these matters are more or less radical extensions of value-subjectivism but often combine this with similar views about every other domain of human thought and practice – including science itself.

BACK TO THE FUTURE

Where then does this leave us? Ironically one consequence of the intellectual development that led to Hume's fact–value gap might be the adoption of forms of postmodern thought in which that gap is itself transcended. If everything is subjective then there are no 'hard facts' to be contrasted with 'soft' attitudes. At most one might find reasons (that is attitudes) to distinguish between 'harder' and 'softer' attitudes; less and more locally subjective phenomena. This way of responding to the problem of values certainly finds support among contemporary philosophers both in the English-speaking world and in continental Europe. However it rests on claims hardly less controversial than theological ones and is not likely to be found attractive by those whose concern is with whether a place for values can be found in an objectivist world-view.

Clearly the question 'Are there objective values?' will continue to stimulate controversy, and it would be absurd to try and resolve it conclusively here. This said, however, those inclined to old or new style subjectivism need to consider very seriously whether it is consistent to hold this as the truth about values whilst continuing to treat issues of personal behaviour and social policy as if they concerned objective matters of fact. Indeed this raises the question of whether a general subjectivism about all values is not self-undermining. In arguing about these issues, parties on both sides of the dispute tend to assume the objective validity of cognitive and rational values. That is to say, even 'subjectivists' tend to be objectivists about the values of evidential weight, rational cogency, argumentative rigour, coherence, intelligibility and truth. They do not suppose that the determination to be guided in one's thought by such values is no more than a matter of preferences. On the contrary they share the objectivist assumption that we seek cogency, coherence and intelligibility because they are rational goods, and not that they are goods because we seek them.

If this proves unsettling for the subjectivist it also prompts the question how can one be an objectivist given the modern empiricist world-view? The challenge is appropriate; but I suggest that rather than try to reconcile moral and other axiological objectivisms with orthodox empiricism one reconsiders the opposition between the latter and the Aristotelian world-view. A very considerable merit of that view is that it permits the objectivity of values without forcing them into an occult immaterial realm. Otherwise expressed, it offers the prospect of combining an objectivist meta-theory of values with a naturalistic metaphysics. In saying this, however, it is important to recall that the older naturalism insists upon the non-reducibility of the forms and teleologies of living things. Indeed it is precisely because it discerns holistic patterns of growth, development and flourishing that it sees norms in nature.

The challenge of the new science was that these hylomorphic and teleological ways of thinking are misconceived and fail to grasp the fundamental structure of reality which strides below the level of living things, and has no place for organic functions and goal-related processes. Undoubtedly post-Aristotelian science has vastly extended our knowledge of the world and no-one could seriously doubt the physical basis of organic entities. But in urging the truth of the earlier view one need not deny these facts. Organic forms and natural teleologies are compatible with microphysical particles and electromagnetic radiation. The empiricist mistake has been to insist upon the exclusivity of the reality of entities of the latter sort and to require that all other descriptions be reduced or rejected. The truth of the matter is that not every truth is a truth about matter. There are forms, principles of organization and activity, by which things live and, in favourable circumstances, flourish.

So much for the general objectivity of natural norms. This leaves a great deal to be done in developing an account of human values. But the aim of the foregoing has been to argue that philosophy does not exclude the possibility of an objectivist account of these and to suggest the general character of such an approach. As in the case of other natural beings we have natures by which our lives are structured and directed. But, of course, human natures are not only very complex: they also include aspects which are certainly rare in nature and may be unique – such as rational psychologies. Furthermore, whilst our natures may prescribe the general course of our lives they do not exhaustively determine it. It is part of the human form of life to deliberate and to act in accord with reasons. In other words, our rationality extends the possible range of directions in which we might develop.

The task of education is to contribute to this development and is to show how reflection can provide reasons for choosing some routes and not others. Knowledge is possible; any sense of a general crisis of scepticism is therefore misplaced. Perhaps certain subjects are in trouble, but as I observed at the outset some areas lie nearer the intellectual surface and it may be that exposure has dried them up. If that should be so then those who wish to have rewarding careers as scholars should go deeper in the pursuit of truth. Those who can do; those who cannot, say it can't be done.

NOTES

1 In connection with this see John Haldane, 'Cultural Theory, Philosophy and the Study of Human Affairs: Hot Heads and Cold Feet', in J. Doherty. E. Graham and M. Malek (eds.) *Postmodernism and the Social Sciences* (London: Macmillan, 1992).

2 For specimen writings on this issue see the selections gathered in Part III of Lawrence Cahoone (ed.) *From Modernism to Postmodernism: An Anthology* (Oxford: Blackwell, 1995).

3 Here I would take issue with Scruton's account of matters. See Scruton 1979.

4 The following sections are drawn from John Haldane, 'The Nature of Values' in David Carr and John Haldane, *Values and Values Education* (St Andrews: Centre for Philosophy and Public Affairs, 1993).

PART III
Critical Voices

usef) frictions

SIX

Visions of Embattled Science

Mary Midgley

ABSTRACT WARS

It is interesting to ask why there is so much quarrelling about science. If one came fresh to the question, one might surely think that it was scarcely possible to campaign for or against science, any more than for or against language, or history, or work, or human relations, or any of the other very large things that set the scene for our existence. It might seem that facts are things you can't fight about.

But of course the role that these large things play in our lives can vary immensely and this variation can indeed cause quarrels in which the names of these abstractions serve as slogans for the most surprising causes. Poetry, for instance, has often needed to be explicitly defended against onslaughts rather similar to those that are often made on Pure Science. The Defences of Poetry that were written by people like Shelley and Philip Sidney have not just served as weapons of war. They have also helped to shape and clarify the role that imagination plays in our lives. They have altered the idea of poetry itself, and in that way have made possible new ways of writing it. This process has not just been an isolated, internal matter for poets and their readers. It has been an aspect – sometimes quite an important one – of much larger changes in the world. Sidney launched his arguments about the role of poetry within the Renaissance. Shelley launched his within the Romantic Revival, and these were movements that affected all sorts of aspects of European life.

On such occasions we surely need to be aware of these wider involvements as well as of the local battle among critics. What misleads us, what gives rise to endless wasteful friction, is confusion between the local, internal issues that can be seen from inside a particular profession and the wider ones, which are often hard to grasp at all.

Today, this is surely happening about science. During the twentieth century, that large abstraction which is called Science has acquired tremendous symbolic importance by being linked with a great range of practical movements which have profoundly altered our everyday life – movements which have been hailed as essentially and typically 'scientific'. And that claim has, during a great part of the century, gained them huge prestige.

EXAMPLES

The most obvious of these movements is the general expansion of technology, something which has always produced ambivalent responses and which now causes increasing alarm. But our lives have also been deeply influenced by many other, more detailed ideas and policies which have carried the same 'scientific' label and been seen as having the same kind of significance. There has been, for a start, industrial Taylorism, the practice of shaping industry so as to treat all workers, systematically and on principle, simply as physical components in the manufacturing process without any reference to their own points of view on the matter. As Henry Ford himself put it, workers must be regarded solely from a functional angle because they were in fact tools:

> The principal part of a chisel is the cutting edge. ... If there is a single principle on which our business rests, it is that it makes no difference how finely made a chisel is or what splendid steel it has in it or how well it is forged – if it has no cutting edge it is not a chisel. ... The cutting edge of a factory is the man and the machine on the job. (Ford 1923: 18–19)

This project, which was worked out in theoretical terms by F. W. Taylor and his colleagues in the early years of the twentieth century and first adopted on a large scale by Ford, has obviously had an enormous effect, not only on the lives of industrial workers, but, more indirectly, on the ways in which people now regard work.[1]

What is interesting about this idea is that its inventors did not just recommend it as an effective way of making money. They also justified it on much grander intellectual grounds. They called it pre-eminently *scientific*, and indeed it was widely known quite simply as 'scientific management'. This claim was meant to carry substantial weight. Scientific status was seen as an adequate defence of Taylorism against any moral objections which might be brought to it.

Taylorist theory thus served to exempt the treatment of workers from the principles which normally limit the ways in which human beings can treat one another, principles from which workers had not previously been formally excluded, badly though they might be treated in practice. It served to sideline principles such as the Golden Rule, which tells us to treat others as we would want to be treated ourselves. Equally it served to neutralize Kant's notion that the good life centres on treating people *as people* rather than things – as ends in themselves, not just as means to our own ends that we can manipulate at our pleasure. Science, according to Taylor and his colleagues, has simply disproved this sort of contention by demonstrating that workers were in fact just things and could only be treated as such. This is evidently an extremely strange way of deciding which of these attitudes to people we really ought to prefer. The fact that Taylorists could rely on using the name of science as a moral blunderbuss in this way was a striking sign of the prestige that it carried.

Another example is the effort to depersonalize medicine – especially psychiatry – by similarly reducing it to a physical operation on bodies, to be carried out without reference to the uneducated viewpoints of patients or their relatives. Another, again, is behaviourist psychology, which argued explicitly that the subjective angle on human experience could be wholly ignored because it had no effect on conduct. Though this strange view proved in the end unsuitable for psychology, its ghost still haunts many areas of the social sciences and as long as it prevailed it produced some extraordinary practical advice, especially about such things as child-rearing, advice which did a good deal of harm to many people's lives.

Yet one more example is Marxism, a thought-system which also claimed to be scientific and used that claim as a defence against moral objections. Though this claim may have been less central for Marx himself than it was for his followers, Engels took pains to build it into his version of Marx's ideas. And during the mid-twentieth century a remarkable group of polymathic British scientists – J. B. S. Haldane, J. D. Bernal, Joseph Needham and others – developed this notion in many influential popular writings[2] as being tremendously modern and scientific.

THE NEGLECT OF KICKS AND SCREAMS

These are not isolated examples. Throughout the twentieth century the claim to be scientific has repeatedly been brought forward as an all-purpose justification for policies to which there were obvious moral objections. The notion of advancing science was closely linked here to a more general euphoria about progress in a way which made it seem that those developments were predestined and must not be opposed. Thus the word 'modern' began to be used almost as a synonym for 'scientific' to label changes which were supposed to be both inevitable and finally satisfactory. When these proposals were distasteful, calling them 'scientific' and 'modern' served to protect them against criticism. It conveyed the notion that no reply was needed because (in an extraordinary but much-used phrase) people ought always to be dragged kicking and screaming into the twentieth century.

This propaganda was often successful. That is why both terms are now becoming discredited. The reaction against them produces, on the one hand, a good deal of hostility to science and on the other the somewhat jumbled range of ideas that are now lumped together as postmodern. Nobody, therefore, should be surprised if the public does now tend to see 'science' as supporting ideologies like those just mentioned, nor if it doesn't much like what it sees. As for the term *postmodern*, it makes the sound point that the word 'modern' ought never to have been used as a potent, all-justifying term of praise in the way that it then was. But it is surely a most awkward way of making that point.

The particular things that were then praised varied greatly. The word 'modern' is far too vague to be used as a label for all of them. Still more obviously, we cannot go on using the word modern – as people now do – to mean 'old-fashioned, objectionable because belonging to the early twentieth century or possibly to the Enlightenment'. That word will have to go back to its literal meaning of 'recent' and the particular movements which were once called 'modern' will have to be called by more informative names – names that really classify what they are and what is wrong with them. An important part of those movements was indeed a certain kind of dogmatic fundamentalism about morals – a simple-minded claim to finality – which has often characterized the supposedly 'scientific' outlook of that epoch, and which is challenged today by various forms of pluralism and relativism. (B. F. Skinner's bizarre views about justice and freedom are a typical example of this pseudo-scientific moral dogmatism.) We will come back later to this aspect of 'postmodern' thinking.

IS SCIENCE NEUTRAL?

In the backwash from these disturbances, those who currently fear science often bring charges against it which strike its defenders as unfair.[3] But they can give two quite different reasons for rejecting those charges. On the one hand they can say that science is not ideological at all but neutral, purely factual, a mere tool that can be turned equally to any use. Or, quite differently, they can say that science does have its own moral program, and that program is an admirable one, free from the blemishes of Marxism and Taylorism. In that case, science is not just a fact-store but an active enterprise devoted to forwarding its own characteristic ideals. Perhaps it may then even be an enterprise so important that it can dominate and guide our whole lives, as its champions have sometime claimed. We could then accept the words that Pandit Nehru addressed to the Indian National Institute of Science in 1960 – words much quoted, but a perfectly fair example of a widespread faith;

> It is science alone that can solve the problems of hunger and poverty, of insanitation and illiteracy, of superstition and deadening custom and tradition, of vast resources running to waste, of a rich country inhabited by starving people. (*Proceedings of the National Institute of Science of India* 1960: 564)

By 'science alone' Nehru cannot just have meant 'facts alone'. Pure knowledge of facts would obviously do nothing to solve those problems without good will, clear, well-chosen aims and wise policies. He expected guidance. He expected wisdom. He looked not just to scientific know-how but to scientific ideals. In some sense, he was calling for a factor that could take the place of religion.

But if this is the hope, it is surely urgent to ask just what the special ideals of science are and how ideological prophets such as Taylor and Marx got them so wrong.

It is not possible to claim that scientific values and ideals – whatever they may be – have a right to override all other ideals without specifying those other ideals and arbitrating between them. If, for instance, scientific progress seems to conflict on a certain issue with justice and compassion or with inner fulfilment and the quest for happiness, has it an automatic right to prevail?

'Science' cannot be treated as a conquering invader, an ideology that can simply override existing standards without explanation. Scientific ideals need to be placed in the context of other human ideals, just as scientists themselves have to place their work in the context of their whole lives. The importance of those ideals in that whole spectrum has then to be soberly assessed. It becomes necessary, in fact, to do some serious ethical thinking.

These two defensive strategies cannot really be combined. It is not possible both to treat science as a harmless neutral tool and to hail it as an infallible guiding star or a cause to be fought for. Its more vocal champions tend, however, to oscillate between these claims and end up by making both. Officially, most of them at present back the modest view that science is inert, purely factual and neutral. That stance represents a strong and natural reaction, led largely by Karl Popper, against the ideological excesses of Marxism. But one cannot maintain this position consistently if one still also wants to claim for science any high spiritual status or, indeed, any influence at all on practical affairs.

Historically, too, the main tradition of the profession is against such modesty. The movement which we call modern science was never an inert, unworldly phenomenon of this kind. Its founders and champions in the Renaissance did not present it only as a means of informing people about the physical world but also, boldly and primarily, as a way of changing their attitudes and improving their life. Led by Francis Bacon, they pointed out that knowledge is power. They called for a more confident, interventive or even violent approach to nature. They wanted their new discoveries to lead to active control, replacing the resigned and awe-struck submission that had previously inhibited curiosity.

BATTLE LINES ARE DRAWN

At first, there was room for both the attitude of active control and that of submission within the vast, rambling Christian tradition. The Bible had, after all, both endorsed human domination over nature and also called on people to respect the world as God's creation. As time went on, however, conflicts developed on many detailed points of fact such as the details of the Creation and the Flood. Although scientists themselves were still usually Christian until the late nineteenth century, public opinion came gradually to amalgamate these conflicts into a supposed general clash between the two abstractions, science and religion. This produces some fairly absurd results.

Thus, when the heroine of Trollope's novel *Barchester Towers* – who is not supposed to be silly at all – is asked what she thinks of recent scientific theories which suggest that the moon is uninhabited, she replies, 'I really think it's almost wicked to talk in such a manner. How can we argue about God's power in the other stars from the laws which he has given us for our rule in this one?' (Trollope: ch.XIX). Similarly, from the other side, Peter Atkins, declaring the 'omnicompetence of science', feels that his work will have been done if he can only get rid of religion and soars to remarkable metaphoric heights to do so:

> Science's cautious, publicly monitored gnawing at the cosmic bun is a far more honest approach to universal competence than religion's universal but empty gulping and the verbal flatulence that passes for theistic exposition. ... The stern and stony eye of science seeks answers that are not grounded in the fundamentality of purpose. (Atkins 1992: 32)

This way of thinking treats those two concerns as quite separate items, indeed as separate people, in a way that tends to make clashes between then look final and non-negotiable. It then seems that such issues can be settled only by war. It was doubly unfortunate that, although many of the early Christian fathers had endorsed symbolic rather than literal readings of the Bible, their descendants during the Reformation (both Protestant and Catholic) largely came to insist on a literal reading which did indeed bring them into conflict with the science of their day, thus generating an unprofitable warfare of abstraction in a way that would have shocked St Augustine.

Once this has happened, it becomes extremely hard to deal with these clashes one by one in a rational fashion, on their merits, and extremely easy to class them all wholesale as triumphs or disasters of war. It is very interesting to see the workings of this process in the row which arose out of Brian Appleyard's lively and attractive book *Understanding the Present: Science and the Soul of Modern Man* (Appleyard 1992). Appleyard's chief aim was to examine the role that the idea of science played in present-day thought and to see what might be wrong with it. His discussion was undoubtedly thoughtful and serious. The book produced vigorous discussion from all sides and many people agreed with the author's expressed alarms about the current influence of science. However, in the preface which he has added to his second edition, Appleyard writes that he was astonished to get a violently hostile reaction from many scientists, who accused him of launching 'a New Ignorance Movement'. Until then he had not realized (he says) that he was attacking an institution.

WHO OR WHAT THEN IS SCIENCE? TROUBLE WITH DEMONS

It is interesting to ask, however, what kind of entity Appleyard supposed that he *was* attacking. Throughout his book – which contains a great deal of fascinating discussion – readers are constantly confronted with this puzzle. Appleyard often uses language about science which is just as anthropomorphic as that of Peter Atkins. In his prose, science keeps doing things which one would think could only be done by a person. For instance it 'possesses an intrinsically domineering quality' (p. 2). It is 'incapable, whatever it may pretend, of co-existence' (p. 238). More alarmingly, 'it has made exiles of us all. It took our souls out of our bodies' (p. 203).

Passages like these are written in the mythic mode. They accept the convention used by scientistic writers like Atkins of treating science as a potent figure, a kind of demon. Anything written in this style has an extraordinarily strong and primitive appeal. In such sentences, deep speaks unto deep without the inconvenient interruption of serious thought. These passages sell books all right, but there is always a price to be paid. An author who uses this kind of language, even for two or three sentences in the course of a book, can be sure that those are the sentences which will be remembered and that his critics are likely to respond to them at the same gut level – as they have done in this case.

Most of Appleyard's book is far more subtle and reflective than this. It contains some really valuable discussions of the nature of science and the many ways in which it has affected us. But he seems to have swallowed his own rhetoric to the extent of regularly treating the various abstractions he deals with – Science, Liberalism, Environmentalism, Religion – as though they were monolithic, given immutable wholes or even separate people rather than loose, jumbled ways of thinking which are constantly changing and developing along with the society that uses them.

By personifying and over-simplifying this cast of characters, by separating them so drastically from one another, he ends up with a tragedy that looks as foredoomed and unavoidable as a play by Racine. In theory Appleyard is trying to find a new way of thought that can replace the demonic and discredited scientific outlook. But this project is constantly hindered by an excess of drama:

> Science made us; science broke us; it is time to start making repairs. ... Science inspired a version of the universe, of the world and of man that was utterly opposed to all preceding versions. (Appleyard 1992: 227)

This, for a start, is an extraordinary claim. It quite ignores the continuity of Renaissance science, not only with Greek thought but with the rationalistic element in Christianity. The idea of an ordered universe organized by a single creative mind has always pervaded Christian thought about the world, as it does that of Judaism and Islam. It was as crucial a part of Newton's and Galileo's world-view as it was of St Thomas's. And the fact that Christianity was a religion of the book, a world-view centred on the truth of a single sacred story, prepared the niche into which science subsequently stepped.

Indeed, this same unlucky notion of one given monolithic truth, rather than the patchy, piecemeal struggle towards truth which we actually deal with, lies at the root of the science-versus-religion rivalry today. Narrow-minded fundamentalism – the claim to a monopoly of truth, the inability to see how much room is left for other aspects of it – has been a blot on both sides of this debate. Though it does not dominate either of them in a way that could possibly justify Appleyard's despair, its past excesses do provide him with the quotes that lead him to think that no movement is possible. (Peter Atkins, now almost an isolated coelacanth, still does his best to maintain this tradition.)

In this way and many others, the continuity of modern science with its predecessors is strong. Renaissance science only looks like a complete innovation if you insist on treating it as a new character in the drama – a demon who has just stepped onto the stage. However, Appleyard's main charge against it is still to come. He goes on:

> Most importantly, it denied man the possibility of finding an ultimate meaning and purpose in his life within the facts of the world. If there were such things as meanings and purposes, they must exist outside the universe describable by science. (Appleyard 1992: 227)

But this separation of facts from meaning and value was not a product of science. It came from a mistaken philosophical tradition, which in turn reflected wider trends. The first step in this tradition was Descartes' drastic division of human beings into two separate and disconnected components, mind and body. This cleavage, which was indeed partly designed to protect science from outside interference, did cause it to become gradually separated from the rest of thought. But the worst effects of the split did not flow from what science then did in isolation. They came from the confusion that surrounded the status of mind and its relation to matter.

Since Descartes' idea of a world divided into radically disconnected halves seemed incomprehensible, theorists set about trying to reduce one half to terms of the other and debating about which half should prevail. At first some serious thinkers (Leibniz, Hume, Hegel) tried to dissolve matter away by showing that it was really a form of mind. Gradually, however, hopes shifted to the opposite enterprise of proving that mind was really a form of matter. This materialist contention became increasingly attractive with the growing success of physical science. Much of its strength, however, has always come from simple opposition to religion – a consideration of a quite different kind which often exercises a force irrelevant to the real issue.

Today, we are gradually managing to recognize that both kinds of reduction are unworkable. It is not realistic to draw the sharp line between mind and body in the first place which seemed to make them necessary. The proper unit is the whole person. But our whole way of thinking has been deeply shaped by this tradition of mind-body warfare, in particular by the very influential form given to it in the early nineteenth century by Auguste Comte's doctrine of Positivism.

Comte simply proclaimed that matter was all that we had to deal with. The only proper kind of thought must therefore be scientific thought which dealt in facts about material objects. Any other kind of thinking was merely a temporary product of our primitive, childish state of development. All civilizations (he said) passed through three intellectual stages – Religious, Metaphysical and Positive or Scientific – shedding at each stage some of the superstitions which had led them to look for anything other than scientific facts. All forms of thought other than science were, then, superficial and inadequate. History and ethics, for instance, must be reduced to statements of scientific fact, and anything in them which resisted that process must be abandoned.

This extraordinary fantasy – itself visibly a piece of prophetic metaphysic – caught on partly because, when it was proposed, hopes for the sciences, (especially for the new social sciences) had soared unrealistically high. More deeply, however, it succeeded because it seemed to offer an all-purpose weed-killer which would remove traditional religious ideas that obstructed the development of thought in many areas. This was the time when the word 'scientific' began to be used as a loose term of praise which was almost equivalent to 'non-religious' or 'anti-religious', without necessarily bearing any clear relation to any actual science.

Enthusiastic theorists eagerly tried to put Comte's scheme into practice, but as they did so its inherent difficulties became obvious. At first, they proceeded by colonizing large non-scientific areas of thought in the name of science. They built large, supposedly scientific systems such as those by which Marx and Spengler scientized history and Freud claimed to organize psychology. These were at first widely respected and successful. Gradually, however, scientifically-minded persons saw that these schemes bore little relation to any known science.

At this point, Positivist policy went into a rather startling reverse, abandoning colonization in favour of isolationism. Karl Popper, defining science much more narrowly, now drew in its boundaries in a way that excluded from it, not just Marx, Spengler and Freud, but a great deal of the social sciences as well, while leaving the humanities still unconquered. Modern positivism thus quietly dropped Comte's ambition to make the whole of commonly recognized thought scientific.

It did not, however, part with his flattering notion that only scientific thought is truly rational. The effect is to suggest that all thought which lies outside science also lies outside reason. While history is now rarely mentioned, this ban was expressed quite explicitly against both ethics and metaphysics. The project of reducing ethics to a set of scientific facts, which had not proved very successful, was dropped in favour of simply declaring the whole of ethics, along with metaphysics, to be meaningless nonsense. This ukase can be found expressed in handy form in that highly metaphysical and prophetic manifesto of Logical Positivism. A. J. Ayer's *Language, Truth and Logic* (Ayer 1936). And although not all positivists wished to endorse this rather emotive wording, they standardly did (and still do) accept the idea of a fact–value gap which was also a frontier between the rational and the irrational.

IS PHILOSOPHY THE VILLAIN?

In modern times, scientists have largely followed Popper in simply endorsing the split between facts and values. (Popper never questioned this aspect of positivism, though he attacked a good deal of its scientific methodology.) Scientists were undoubtedly reacting against ideologies such as Marxism which tried to bestride that split. But modern specialization, too, makes the split popular with scientists because it absolves them from dealing with matters about which they do not feel confident. Of course it is also true that Descartes had the position of science in mind when he designed the split in the first place. And Appleyard is indeed right that the immense prestige of scientists today leads to their being credited with prophetic status on such matters – even though, when they are wearing their neutralist hats, they insist that science is impartial and purely factual.

Positivism, however, is not a part of science. It is a philosophical doctrine. Ought perhaps the guns, then, have been turned against philosophy instead of science? It would certainly be possible, and no less convincing, to rewrite much of Appleyard's book in that way, making philosophy the chosen demon. No doubt it is true that philosophers such as those mentioned do carry some responsibility for today's distresses. But it would surely be bad faith to make much of this, since these positivistically-inclined philosophers, from Hobbes through Comte to Bertrand Russell, were campaigning against ecclesiastical oppression which was indeed a real and serious evil. And in this country especially it would not be a very convincing story. There would be something comic about suggesting that a people so robustly philistine as the British, so resistant to intellectual stimuli, has been the helpless victim of a philosophic conspiracy. The philosophy, in fact, has reflected the life of the age much more than the other way round and scientistic ideas have grown from many sources.

COLD WINDS FROM A WIDER WORLD: THE MEANING OF LIBERALISM

If we were indeed looking for a single source of modern moral confusion – if we were forced to consider only one candidate for the demon's role – another likely nominee would surely be the simple fact of geographical exploration, the process of world-discovery for which the Renaissance is so famous, and which set off the process of European colonization. This widening of horizons, which Appleyard scarcely notices, was surely a central cause of the main evil that he attributes to science – namely relativism. The trouble was not just that the European discovery of distant lands led to brutal exploitation and oppression of their inhabitants, corrupting the colonizers as well as hurting the colonized. The moral damage which that exploitation did could perhaps, at a pinch, be seen as accidental, an unnecessary accompaniment of exploration. But what was no accident, what could not fail to follow these voyages, was awareness in Europe of the plurality of cultures. This is the source of Appleyard's other demon, Liberalism, a force which – in the weakest arguments of his book – he desperately tries to conflate with Science.

What he is really campaigning against here, and quite rightly, is cultural relativism – the idea that nothing sensible can be said about value judgements except that they vary with the culture. They are therefore undiscussable and are all in some mysterious sense equally valid, so that 'it's all a matter of your own subjective point of view' which you favour. The distinction between facts and values is here taken to mean that only facts can be rationally considered. Values are some kind of unmanageable gas or steam which entirely evades thought. Appleyard does not seem to distinguish at all between this kind of slop and serious liberalism of Mill's kind, which centres on a strong and well-defended value judgement, namely the judgement that political freedom is itself something good, both as an end and as a means, and that this good is more important in human life than has often been supposed.[4]

From Mill's angle, value judgements are indeed bound to arise in the world and should initially be respected, both because those holding them merit personal respect and because the truth is so complex that no one has a complete monopoly of it. Elements of truth may be found on both sides of a disagreement. Rational moral discussion which will attempt to bring together these partial truths is perfectly possible and is indeed an urgent duty. Toleration is primarily intended to leave space for such discussion – not as a counsel of despair that will replace it.

This position of Mill's not only does not support a general refusal to discriminate between values but is quite incompatible with it. Appleyard, however, does not seem even to have heard of this well-known view. His idea is that goofy relativism of the kind just mentioned necessarily follows from accepting the fact–value gap, so that – since science owns all the facts – the expansion of science is bound gradually to crowd out the space left for moral thinking:

> Given the seductive effectiveness and persuasive power of science, over time it is clear that this line will tend to move further and further over to the scientific lobby. The pressure on the other side will be decreased as science continues to conquer because of its corrosive and restless refusal to co-exist. So I have two points here; all moral issues in a liberal society are intrinsically unresolvable, and all such issues will progressively tend to be decided on the basis of a scientific version of the world and of values. In other words they will cease to be moral issues and will become problems to be solved. The very idea of morality will be marginalized and, finally, destroyed. (Appleyard 1992: 23)

THE LEGACY OF NAIVE SCIENTISM

It has been a chronic misfortune of the movement now called postmodern to encourage – at lease in the public perception – exactly this confusion between goofy relativism and the kind of intelligent pluralism which is simply the recognition that the truth is so complex that none of us has the whole of it. These two very different ideas have been widely confused together and indiscriminately promoted as defences against the dogmatic claims made in the name of 'modern science'. The notion that this science is in some sense 'omnicompetent' that it contains all serious systematic thinking and will eventually oust all competitors from the intellectual world – an idea that is sometimes called 'scientism'[5] – is not, of course, an invention of Appleyard's but a legacy from crude Positivism. Its diagnosis and prediction have been eagerly pronounced by scientistic prophets throughout much of the twentieth century. A recent version may be of some interest:

Scientists, with their implicit trust in reductionism, are privileged to be at the summit of knowledge, and to see further into truth than any of their contemporaries. ... Scientists liberate truth from prejudice, and through their work lend wings to society's aspirations. While poetry titillates and theology obfuscates, science liberates. ... Reductionist science is omnicompetent. Science has never encountered a barrier that it has not surmounted or that we can at least reasonably suppose it has power to surmount and will in due course be equipped to do so. (sic) ... Science, with its currently successful pursuit of universal competence, should be acknowledged king. (Atkins 1995: 123, 129, 130)

B. F. Skinner systematically took a similar line, especially in his last book. *Beyond Freedom and Dignity.* Thus, recommending science in general and his (allegedly) scientific behaviourist psychology in particular as the only cure for the world's evils, Skinner wrote that we cannot

carry on, as we have in the past, with what we have learned from personal experience or from those collections of personal experience called history, or with the distillations of experience to be found in folk wisdom and practical rules of thumb ... [Science must be invoked instead, and that science must be behaviouristic psychology ...]

We need to make vast changes in human behaviour, and we cannot make them with the help of nothing more than physics and biology. ... *What we need is a technology of behaviour.* We could solve our problems quickly enough if we could adjust the growth of the world's population as precisely as we adjust the course of a space-ship, or improve agriculture and industry with some of the confidence with which we accelerate high-energy particles, or move towards a peaceful world with something like the steady progress with which physics has approached absolute zero. ... But *a behavioural technology comparable in power and precision to physical and biological technology is lacking,* and those who do not find the very possibility ridiculous are more likely to be frightened by it than reassured. *That is how far we are from 'understanding human issues' in the sense in which physics and biology understand their fields,* and how far we are from preventing the catastrophe toward which the world seems to be inexorably moving. (Skinner 1973: 10–11, emphases mine)

H. G. Wells in his day made similar proposals, advising that government should be handed over to a scientific élite who alone had the knowledge needed to handle it. The difference is, of course, that the prospect which these prophets confidently celebrated fills Appleyard with horror. And here too he is not alone. Whatever may have been happening to science itself, there is no doubt that this dream of a general take-over of society by scientists has become less and less attractive to thoughtful people – including many scientists themselves – as the century has worn on. Eventually, it has begun to appal a wider public. Serious science fiction, once full of euphoria, deals now chiefly in dystopias and warnings. Very few scientists today share Wells's urge to take over the government.

Does it follow that Appleyard's alarm is misplaced, that people have already seen through the whole silly project? To some extent I think they have, but by no means completely. Scientistic propaganda has been very successful and much of it will outlast its authors. Whatever else he was, Skinner was a publicist of genius. His ideas still live. Moreover, the confusions that underlie his position are so deep that it can be really hard to think one's way out of them.

For instance, the problem about arbitrating between conflicting value-judgements, especially those involving different cultures, is a real one, a problem which needs to be resolved separately, each time that it arises, by great goodwill and careful co-operative investigation. We are constantly puzzled by disagreement about crises, not only about familiar controversial topics such as marriage-laws and education but also about newer ones such as environmental pollution, transport policy and climate change. Though science can of course help us to get the facts right here, there is no obvious way in which it could be invoked to resolve the clashes of values which arise. Where (for instance) personal freedom needs to be controlled if the environment is to be protected or art competes for funds with medical care, we have to use serious moral thinking to balance the various ideals involved. Skinner's promise to solve such difficulties by behaviourist psychology was mere bad faith.

Many people, however, are indeed puzzled by the fact that these difficulties are there at all, by the constantly recurring need to face unresolved moral conflicts. They have somehow imbibed the view that, in a scientific age, such awkward problems ought not to exist. They expect science to do what Skinner promised and provide a simple way of dealing with them. This puzzlement does often lead to a kind of paralysis which is indeed expressed in the goofy relativism that Appleyard mentions. If science does not help, they tend to think that the trouble must be past cure.

Thus, the prominence of science does cause a difficulty here, not because of anything particular that scientists do, but because of the wild over-estimate of their power that has grown up, partly unavoidably and partly through deliberate propaganda, in the course of the last two centuries. But what part does Appleyard's other villain Liberalism play in this malaise? And what rescuer does he want to invoke to save us from it?

At times it almost looks as if he is simply denouncing permissiveness from the right and will call in the US Cavalry to restore law and order by censorship. But he is actually much too sharp to suppose that this would help, and anyway what bothers him is not so much public disorder as intellectual anarchy, the moral bankruptcy that paralyses judgement.

STABILITY, MYTHIC AND OTHERWISE

What Appleyard wants, then, is the kind of stable background to life and thought which he takes Christianity to have provided in the past, a solid context of agreement within which life has an obvious meaning and disagreements could be much more easily settled. The wish is reasonable enough but there is something fatally unreal about the way in which Appleyard expresses it.

In the first place, he greatly exaggerates the monolithic certainty which obtained in that past epoch. Despite the best efforts of churchmen to produce both an apparent and a real unity, Christianity was always a vast, sprawling system, full of muddle –

much of which was often fertile – and riven by all kinds of disagreements. These clashes came to a head in the Protestant Reformation a century before modern science began to be widely known. Even if that science had never developed, those disputes would surely have led to wars of religion and – along with exploration – would have produced the kind of pluralism that Appleyard deplores. Christians were involved, too, in conflict with outside religions such as Islam, and the Crusaders' swords do not seem to have provided a better way of resolving that clash than the fuddy-duddy liberal devices that are used today.

Appleyard expresses his nostalgic exaggeration of Christian solidarity in a strange and significant graphic example. He writes:

> The cathedral at Chartres was completed thirty years before the *Summa*. It is, perhaps, the most eloquent of all expressions of medieval humanism and the Gothic spirit – an *overpoweringly consistent celebration of an all-inclusive intellectual synthesis*. After many visits Chartres still renders me speechless with the certainty and unity of its vision. The building is obviously beautiful but also *brutal in its single-mindedness*. (Appleyard 1992: 22 emphases mine)

You could say the same, of course, about the Parthenon. The point of such great buildings is to convey a single-minded message. This certainly does not mean that their builders passed their lives in a state of chronic oppressive agreement. As it happens, Chartres is quite exceptional among cathedrals in having been quickly built, so that it actually does have this unified effect. (A glance at certain other cathedrals – Wells, for instance, or Ely – could lead one to assess Christianity quite differently as showing amazing flexibility in responding eclectically to unexpected challenges.) Appleyard's comment shows, however, a fatal ambivalence, an uneasiness about the idea of that very solidarity which he is officially demanding. In fact, by exaggerating the narrowness and triumphalism of serious Christian thought he makes Religion, as well as Science, seem incapable of development. Thus it becomes another foredoomed, Racinian character, a stereotype in his drama, useless for any kind of rescue.

Other possible rescuers get similar treatment, notably Environmentalism, which he says has (most reprehensibly) also frozen itself into an unusable stereotype, having:

> expanded to become an entire moral, social and political orthodoxy. As such it has joined forces with a whole range of other anti-progressive movements which advocate the abandonment of economic growth and the return to natural ways of life. Their conception of meaning and purpose is wholly negative. (Appleyard 1992: 228)

How's that for a sweeping, fatalistic dismissal of a major issue?

CONCLUSION

I have been using Appleyard's very interesting and lively book, in a way that I hope is not too unfair, to illustrate the crucial role that rhetoric and symbolism play in our current confusions about science. My chief aim is to draw attention to these powerful imaginative factors, so that we can be on our guard next time they start to carry us away, and can sometimes exert ourselves to divert them into better channels. If we can just calm down and stop ourselves using words like 'science' and 'religion' as mythic abstractions, we will probably get on a good deal better.

I have not tried to say much here about the various detailed errors which tend to make us reify 'science' into a single entity. I have concentrated rather on the dramas in which that single entity can seem to be involved once it has been formed. I think, however, that these dramas are not a secondary matter. They are already part of our culture and have a strong attraction for many of us, so they may well be among the causes that drive us to over-simplify 'science' as if it were a single thing or person in the first place. In higher education, these dramas do a great deal of damage by driving the various disciplines apart, by tribalizing both students and faculty, by blocking the growth of new ideas and impoverishing the legacy of old ones. When philosophers lose interest in history and historians in philosophy, when the science block is in a different street from the language lab, when the range of subsidiary subjects available to students continually narrows because of timetabling difficulties, then it becomes harder and harder for academic people to form a realistic idea of other disciplines which can compete with the stereotypes offered by current myths.

So these myths and visions are indeed very important. Appleyard's diagnosis of their current state, however, seems to be stuck in something of a time warp. Our imaginative life has changed a lot since the positivistic picture that he conveys was coined. That picture did indeed show 'science', as a monolithic entity which was somehow secluded from the realm of practical choice, a kind of pure scholar in an ivory tower, but a scholar who, in spite of his isolation, had somehow a monopoly on useful knowledge and could be trusted to make all important decisions. This was the vision that led eminent scientists in the 1940s to disclaim any responsibility for nuclear weapons, claiming that science dealt only in providing factual knowledge. The use that politicians might make of that knowledge was (they said) then 'the responsibility of society' – a body to which, apparently, they did not belong.

Since that time, not only nuclear weapons but environmental damage have made this stance look increasingly absurd and repulsive to many scientists, as well as to outsiders. The social responsibility of science has become far more widely accepted. Indeed, it is now something that few people would be bold enough to disown in public. Moreover 'the environment' is not, as Appleyard so quaintly suggests, just the name of an idol worshipped by some weird Californian sect. It is the name of a great range of urgent practical concerns which now occupy about half of *New Scientist* every week and fill the time of an increasing number of scientific workers. These people know that their business is a matter of life and death for all of us, and so does a large part of the general public.

Essentially, Appleyard was looking for a religion. He was also expecting that religion to resemble an unreal model of medieval Christianity. So he seems to have missed this development entirely. It is, however, the place where a usable outlook is growing up, one in which scientists from difference disciplines regularly co-operate both with each other and with the rest of the public without the slightest need for war. That growth, however, is still young, and it is true that some of the absurd forms of scientism which Appleyard describes are still very strong. Their first component – the belief that 'science' is an entity formed in isolation and not accountable to the ordinary standards of society – has taken a considerable knock. It no longer looks reputable. But the second absurdity – the excessive trust in science as compared with other forms of thought, the belief that it has answers to all questions on all aspects of life – is still powerful. It will take much longer to die away.

Books like Appleyard's can still be useful in exposing these things. But those who write them need to be quite clear that they are talking about myths that have gathered round the idea of science and not about the doings of a bizarre entity called 'science' itself. Otherwise they merely prolong a fantasy-war of which we have had far too much already.

NOTES

1. See a fascinating discussion in Bernard Doray's book *From Taylorism to Fordism, A Rational Madness* (tr. David Marcey, Free Association Books, London 1988). For Taylor's own views, see his book *The Principles of Scientific Management* (1914, Harper, New York/London).
2. See *The Visible College* by Gary Werskey (Free Association Books, London 1988) for this very interesting story.
3. See for instance *The Unnatural Nature of Science* by Lewis Wolpert (Faber and Faber, London 1992).
4. See J. S. Mill's *Essay on Liberty* (multiple editions) ch.2.
5. On this whole topic, see Tom Sorell's excellent little book *Scientism: Philosophy and the Infatuation with Science* (Routledge, London 1991).

SEVEN

Whose Knowledge? Whose Postmodernism?

Anne Seller

What follows may appear to be fragmented, to speak with different voices, and that may be thought appropriate in a postmodern age. Writing it, I kept asking: who would be reading it? Academics interested in epistemological issues will include sharp, sceptical men, with their intellectual habits firmly rooted in an over-refined version of the common sense of the good and the great, and an intense scepticism over the claim that philosophy is gendered which I want to meet. But such an academic group would also include feminist thinkers, who have developed their thinking in a context of teaching students who not only demand that the knowledge they acquire be useful, but also provide a direct route to the culture of the city lacking in our older institutions. They take cultural studies and women's studies for granted, and because they already believe that philosophy is gendered for them, the issue is how it should be taught, and how it should relate to the rest of the curriculum. The discussion is at a different stage, between people with a shared political agenda. It looks like a postmodernist set-piece: different people in different discourses speaking different languages, and of course, many of us spend our time speaking first one, and then the other, for we belong to the same universities. I want to demonstrate the need for something like a feminist postmodernism to the philosophy establishment, but while speaking to the feminist philosopher, I want to begin the discussion with the difficulties and dangers of post-modernism.

At the same time, I think of those generations of students who came to philosophy because they were excited by certain ideas, because they wanted the truth, or at least wanted to pursue certain questions with the prospect of an answer in view. They learnt some useful skills, but went to other fields, because a life-time of elegant play was insufficient. From their perspective, the discourses of academic philosophy on the one hand, and postmodernism on the other, look markedly similar: a small group, intelligible only to each other, with their own set of problems, their own language, their own rules. It may be fun it may be exciting, it may stretch you. But at the end of the day, none of them has much to contribute to all of those who come to the university not simply for skills, but for an understanding of the world and connection to it which facilitates intelligent responsible action.

Thus I am writing for at least three different people: the Oxford philosopher, the feminist philosopher, my students (perhaps the student that I was), and behind them all those who have appeared as either the victims or play things of our knowledge: the others, objects of knowledge to be studied or ignored.

I want to notice that the grander the claims we make for higher education, the more we marginalize those who, for whatever reason, do not get it. If academics were simply a minority, playing very clever and irrelevant games, it would not matter to those who do not understand. If they control access to positions of power in society, it matters somewhat. (Only somewhat, because the excluded will develop alternative routes to power.) If they arrogate to themselves the power to define the meaning and value of our lives and our culture, it matters desperately, because then the excluded become non-persons. This consideration means that if we aim for a democratic society, characterized by the respect with which its members treat each other, we must either take seriously the proposal that our universities become supermarkets offering educational products which can be chosen/consumed by any customer without change in that person, beyond the satisfaction of a desire, need or whim. Or, if we persist in the idea of education of a *person*, we must find ways of ensuring that the values implicit in that education are genuinely democratic, not simply reflective of an élite. It is this option that I am committed to.

These brief introductory remarks indicate my commitments and my agenda. I intend to tackle it by looking at a series of questions:

1. Why was there a need for women's studies?
2. Why was postmodernism so attractive to feminism? Was it a snare and delusion?
3. What are the paradoxes of being a feminist postmodernist?
4. If we reject postmodernism, and cannot go back to modernism, how do we resolve that crisis? How can we move forward? In particular:
   (i) How can we disconnect knowledge and power?
   (ii) How can we avoid the choice between either a postmodernist epistemological free-for-all, or a model of knowledge which also legitimates the domination of particular groups?
   (iii) How can we educate without dominating?

I shall conclude with a brief list of strategies for dealing with these questions. I have no answers, but my intention is to open up a discussion of for whom we intend this knowledge, about which we are so anxious.

Before I embark on that, I want to give a preliminary context to all of this. In 1993, I was at a conference on the issue of gender in higher education. The discussions were wide and varied, but one theme was strikingly repeated in them: that women had gained access to the institutions of higher education, but that the experience has dominantly been one of *dis*empowerment rather than empowerment. The second feature of the conference that impressed me was the way in which the speakers placed that claim within accounts of what they were aiming at in educating students, accounts that would probably be widely agreed upon by *all* educators: as enabling students to scrutinize their world and their response to it, to place themselves in relationship to their culture, so that they can act responsibly, both for themselves and for their society. It seemed that although their views of how to go about this might be informed by postmodernism, you could not really tell that by what they thought that education was, and I mention this because I think that although no single view is possible of what goes on in higher education, and although our views of what constitutes or legitimates knowledge might be widely divergent, I suspect that we share significant common ground in our views of what education should do.

WHY WOMEN'S STUDIES?

This section is for the sceptics. When I first arrived in university I discovered philosophy with a kind of wild joy. In the early 1960s, it seemed to me the perfect subject: all that it demanded of you was that you think clearly and carefully. So it did not matter who you were, what you were, where you came from; you were not disadvantaged, did not need any particular background to do it. For me, this contrasted starkly with most arts subjects, where, without having read any critical theory, I instinctively felt that up-bringing was all, and my perceptions and responses did not fit. (It also contrasted with the sciences because of the freedom of speculation it allowed, because you could play with ideas.) So I had twelve months of sheer liberatory pleasure, until one day my boy-friend, also a philosophy student said 'You think like a man'. I didn't know what he meant by this, his tone was neither clearly critical nor complimentary, and perhaps both, and it was a few years before the emergence of second-wave feminism, but I knew it was too dangerous to discuss: it was an invitation either to give up philosophy or to give up being a woman. So I tucked it uncomfortably away, compartmentalized a little more sharply the way I talked and thought, became less comfortable in both the seminar room and my own body.

I tell that story because it is a quick and dramatic way of showing how an apparently gender-neutral subject precisely by appearing as neutral, both liberates, and makes invisible its own biases and exclusions, even to the excluded. (Characteristically, students used to say: I'm not *clever* enough to do philosophy. Yet part of the joy I had found in it was that I had been doing it all my life, and so had they.) It is a story that is told countless times, in countless ways. Nobody says 'You can't do that because you are a woman', there are no closed doors with 'No Entry' written on them, but when you go through those doors, engage in the activity, you find that you have abandoned a part of yourself in ways that make the activity increasingly difficult, and the recovery of your self hard, if not impossible.

Women's studies was developed in response to that situation, to the recognition that women were not only invisible in the university but that also the apparently gender-neutral curriculum was masculine, so that we rarely discussed books by women. 'There aren't any', I hear the sceptics say, and then we raise the question of why not, and the dialectic that results in women's studies is under way. Or feminists asked why we did not look at women's contributions to the economy, or history. When the sceptic replies that women did not make a contribution, the masculine bias becomes a little clearer, and women's studies develops a stage further as it develops techniques of questioning and judging which reveal those contributions.

These brief remarks show that women's studies did not spring into being, ready armed as a discipline with a subject matter and method. It has been, and at its best continues to be, a process whereby (mostly) women come together to work on hunches about the way that knowledge is constructed so as to exclude most of them in that process. It became increasingly clear to me that we were opening up the discussion so that women could speak freely without having to abandon their gender.

It is very difficult to explain that to a sceptic, particularly in my own subject, philosophy. Countless male colleagues welcome us as one of the chaps, without seeing any problem because they have identified what chaps do with philosophy itself. And of course, so did we feminist philosophers. That was the subject we had learnt, we were simply in there with different bodies and a political view about the position of women. But we had a hunch that the problem was deeper than the bits of explicit misogyny in Aristotle, Rousseau, Nietzsche (and nearly all the others), and got together to explore what that more might be. That is, we made a space in which we could be *both* philosophers *and* women, and in which we could begin to experiment with the way that we would do philosophy if we were free. Some examples, to explain the problem to the sceptic, and to indicate the solution: every woman who came to those meetings 'confessed' at some point that she did not think of herself as a philosopher, that she was not doing 'proper' philosophy. But each of us thought that the others were: 'proper' philosophers were always someone else.

When Christine Battersby (1989) wrote her book she said that the only way that she could write it was by telling herself that she wasn't writing philosophy, but writing about the problems in art that interested *her*, and she could only write it because she knew that she was not doing it for an academic press. These examples show women constrained, yet philosophizing about what interests them in ways that they feel to be appropriate. It was only with the provision of a community which validated us that we began to discover what we had to say. So, for example, instead of identifying with men in Aristotle, and dismissing his views on women as local prejudice, (a practice still wide enough for students to carelessly assume that his views on women and slaves are alike enough to make no matter) we read Aristotle as women, looking at his arguments to see what is meant by the claim that in women, reason lacks authority. That leads into a consideration of what reason is, how it is being conceptualized, (for example reason as control?).

Another sort of example: philosophy has defined the problem of abortion as the issue of whether or not the foetus is a person, and hence has rights. If you can get the definition of personhood right, then you can deduce the correct answer to the question of the woman's right to choose. And there the issue is stuck. But the crucial question for most women is not the issue of rights, but how to come to the decision of whether or not to have an abortion (legally or illegally). And that, as Gilligan (1982) has shown often turns upon a consideration of a whole raft of responsibilities and dependencies, to find the 'right' answer. The question then becomes that of how to take a responsible decision so that a network of relationships is not irreparably torn. Looking at the question from the perspective of the women involved changes the issue, not to mention the way that you will explore and develop moral philosophy with a seminar of students discussing the problem. If medical ethics were written to include that perspective (rather than simply to seek criteria for taking hard decisions, which will be as close as possible to dominant moral sensibilities), it would be a different subject.

The examples can be multiplied, and this is not the place to give a potted history of the way that feminist philosophy is developing. I want to pull out some schematic points from them in the following discussions.

First, although there would seem to be no logical reason why men could not see the way in which they were privileging a male perspective, in fact it is only possible to make it visible when outsiders are looking in. It is this that leads to 'standpoint' theories: the excluded and silenced have a privileged vision, because they can tell that the silencing is working. But they need more than a feeling of unease or alienation. They can only 'tell' the silencing, both in the sense of speaking about it, and in the sense of recognizing that that is what it is, through the reaction of a community where that 'sense' of a problem can be articulated, where concepts can be developed, and where, instead of thinking that you are the problem, you begin to see that the way your subject is defined is the problem. You can only read a text against the grain, and get beyond the point of thinking that you are mis-reading it, if you have others to check that reading with. 'Does this make sense?' is a question we continually need to ask each other in all areas of intellectual life. There is no litmus test of sense, but the up-take of an idea by others is a good indicator.

As I have told the story so far, it seems to imply two possibilities: the development of a more coherent, or integrated self on the one hand, as the silenced begin to make their point of view heard, and the development of a more inclusive knowledge on the other, as that perspective is incorporated. But although many writers (perhaps most notably Afro-American women[1]) have testified to the recovery of the self through speaking out, developing a language, this has been accompanied by the developing awareness that there is no authentic self, nor a woman's voice. For just as the apparently objective, neutral rational voice of philosophy surreptitiously privileged the viewpoint of the middle/upper class European male, rendering all other perspectives, experiences, voices – in brief people – simply as 'other', the idea of a woman's voice made invisible all the differences, such as class, race, sexuality, etc.

between women. Standpoint theory collapses into a multiplicity of standpoint theories, with no way of choosing between them.

Of course, standpoint theory would not, or should not so collapse, if different voices were all simply incorporated into a more inclusive knowledge. But, on the whole, they have not been, and for good reasons. First because the way in which they are developed is not in the form of adding a piece of knowledge in the appropriate form to the heap. Like Kuhnian paradigms (Kuhn 1962), they constitute a revisioning of what is to count as a problem in knowledge, and a solution to it. So, for example, that Hobbesian man cannot have babies is not really a problem for 'mainstream' philosophers, so they do not even see the necessity of the patriarchal family and of non-voluntary obligations for women to liberalism.[2] Or, if we look at the abortion debate, we seem to find that the mainstream and feminist philosopher do not so much have an argument over abortion, as over how to argue about abortion.

Just as the differing standpoints cannot be incorporated into one, inclusive knowledge, so the differing parts of the person cannot be incorporated into one authentic self. For, if I can put it this way, it was I that thought like a man, and that was, and continues to be, one of the things I do. Like everyone else, I can play a variety of games, engage in a variety of conversations, and they do not all cohere. As Griffiths (1995) says, which one I identify with at any particular point depends upon who is trying to exclude me from what. But how can I decide on one of those as my authentic self?

In conclusion to this section, I want to summarize by saying that the experience of women in universities showed up the connection between knowledge and power: that the legitimation of knowledge-claims is intimately tied to networks of domination and exclusion. The apparently neutral enquirer seeking objective truth is in fact privileging the experience and perspective of a particular group, silencing the voices of those who understand the world differently, as he divides the world into the rational knowers and their objects, into thinking, acting subjects and the others, who are different. The way in which we have institutionalized knowledge, it seems, is to serve the interests of domination, rather than emancipation. But these revelations leave us feminists with a dilemma: our politics requires that not all views of the world are equally valid, our search for emancipatory knowledge suggests a system of values together with a critical view of the world. So here I leave my discussion with the sceptic, and move to a consideration of why postmodernism is attractive.

WHAT IS POSTMODERNISM, AND WHY IS IT ATTRACTIVE TO FEMINISTS?

I do not intend anything like a comprehensive account of postmodernism here, and I am certainly not going to engage with any of the theories which constitute it. Suffice it to say that like modernism, it is a mammoth abstraction, embracing a diversity of epistemologies and theories. I am interested in the critical moments that it shares with feminism, for it is these which make it attractive, and hence my concern is with issues, rather than with a correct characterization.

My starting point must be with postmodernism's rejection of modernism: a system of institutionalized knowledge which it perceives as: 'positivistic, technocentric and rationalistic – a belief in linear progress, absolute truths, the rational planning of ideal social orders, standardization of knowledge and production' (Harvey 1992: 9). This resonates with the perceptions I have described in the previous section: a view of knowledge and reason as exclusionary, flattening, bullying different voices into silence. And when Bernstein describes the postmodern revolt as the 'revolt of nature against oppressive, purely instrumental reason' (quoted in Harvey 1992: 13), I am reminded of Mary Daly's claim that feminist philosophy is 'a form of consciousness that is in harmony with the wild in nature and the self' (Daly 1984). Except that, of course, there is no 'self' in postmodernism. It covers a range of linked claims, from the plasticity of the human personality to pragmatism in philosophy, from the view that everything is what we make it because of the infinite malleability of appearances with nothing behind them, to a concern with the dignity and validity of the other. The reason for this approach is a three-fold rejection of the Enlightenment project:

1. Epistemological: in fact, philosophers have failed to find a basis for claims to truth or objective knowledge, or any of the grand theories of social change and human nature. Neither science, nor Marxism, are epistemologically soundly based.
2. Political: in fact, these apparently neutral uses of unbiased reason have served the interests of a particular group, and led to oppression and domination. A critique encapsulated in the irony circulating in St Petersburg on the collapse of the USSR: Radio announcement 'Good morning ladies and gentlemen. The experiment is over.'
3. Sociological/psychological: that thinkers/knowers are people, constructed by their class position/personal history, etc. and the knowledge that they produce, the way they understand the world is bound to reflect this. Again, it is clear how this parallels and recapitulates the growing discomfort that feminists felt with the way knowledge is produced in the academy.

First, there is the perception that any theory (such as Marxism) which attempts to give a total account of history, of society, of the human subject, of knowledge, must mean the suppression of difference between people, the expulsion of some elements to the margins, the outside, to 'otherness'. This implies a particular way of reading texts, which I think is moral and political. You scrutinize them for who is left out, silenced or ignored. And to hear that, you need them to be read from a variety of perspectives. As Harvey expresses it: 'The idea that all groups have a right to speak for themselves and have that voice accepted as authentic and legitimate is essential to the pluralistic stand of postmodernism' (Harvey 1992: 48).

Postmodernism's rejection of 'totalizing theory' or 'meta-narratives' is part and parcel of its insistence on the validity and dignity of 'the other', so its political and epistemological critiques are inseparable. So, second, this emerges in what I shall call responsible knowledge.[3] I embrace my implication as a knowing subject in the production of knowledge. The text is what I make of it, I am not compelled to accept what it says, because the way in which I interrogate it will determine what it says. (Think of the Hobbes example again: I can turn the Leviathan into an examination of the need for the patriarchal family within liberal theory.) So the crisis of knowledge in higher education is less about *what* texts to read, as right-wing critics in the United States seem to think, more about *how* to read. And third, it means that our readings and our knowledge, are permanently critical, permanently shifting. For I am continually re-reading the texts in the light of newly noticed exclusions. This appears to distinguish postmodernism from mere relativism which, with its view that knowledge is correct, true and relative to a particular group or person, appears to be static, to leave knowledge as it is. Postmodernism is continuously unpicking knowledge claims, wherever it finds silencings.

WHAT ARE THE PARADOXES OF BEING A FEMINIST POSTMODERNIST?

As I have described this, it sounds a bit like the apogee of liberalism. Let everyone be heard. But, of course, it isn't, because in unpicking the rationalism of the Enlightenment, postmodernism must also reject the idea that language and experience are transparent, and that the subject is clear. All are shifting constructions. Not only can we not have a unified and coherent account of reality, the mirror of nature, and not have a unified and coherent account of the experience of women, but there is no unity or coherence within each individual subject. We, too, are the texts of our cultures, to be read in multiple ways even by ourselves. As Lennon and Whitford put it: 'This subject is more like a railway junction, where signifiers, discourses and messages meet or flash past, than a source, origin, or mirror' (Lennon and Whitford 1994: 4). At this point, the attractions of postmodernism for feminism wane. We seem to be denied our subjectivity just as we discover it or as bell hooks put it: it's easy to give up your identity when you've already got one. So postmodernism undermined the privileging of the white male voice and validated a variety of voices that had been excluded. It seemed to defeat the bullying by texts and reason, so that these became what we made of them, and it demanded of us a responsibility for our own knowledge, rather than a service to, or apprenticeship in, somebody else's. In short, it seemed to share the emancipatory vision of women's studies as liberatory, as permanently critical, and as responsible. But in the same critical movement, it silenced us all over again. There is no truth, no knowing subject, and hence no self to be emancipated, and no emancipatory knowledge. Or if there is, we must rethink our understanding of those terms.

At this stage, two strategies occur to me: first to look at postmodernism as offering a series of useful techniques, rather than a theory of knowledge. (Listen carefully, see who is excluded, etc.) This leaves open the question of how to legitimate knowledge, for it is clear to me that after the critiques of postmodernism and feminism, we cannot simply go back to modernism. We have to find some way of disconnecting knowledge and domination, of developing a system of education which is not an apprenticeship into a hierarchy of power. Then, to turn the techniques of postmodernism on itself, and ask, who does it exclude and silence? Who does it disempower?

Both of these strategies put the focus on education rather than knowledge. (It is curious to notice how, the moment they are thinking about their students, as opposed to their research or their politics, postmodernists become didactic in ways that their theories should exclude.) Writers like Lovibond (1989) and Soper (1990) have convincingly demonstrated that postmodernism reaches the theoretical and political dead-end mentioned above. I want to question the way it works in the class-room.

Everytime that I have introduced students to postmodern texts, no matter how bright, or mature, or motivated they are, their initial response has been one of total incomprehension, not just of what the writer is saying, but even of what the writer is trying to do, in the most general terms. Often, particularly amongst mature students, the response is one of anger, and I think this may have something to do with their having finally gained access to higher education, and suddenly feeling themselves excluded again, because they cannot make sense of the words in front of them. In a word, much of this material is inaccessible, and casts out the uninitiated. There is a terrible irony in Spivak, meeting such complaints with 'Do your homework', and yet elsewhere arguing that she would like to talk so that the subaltern can hear her, and this is simply a reflection of the general paradox that the theory which draws attention to the silenced and excluded is at the same time one of the most exclusive conversation clubs in the world. As Sa'id has pointed out, there are some 7,000 of us writing books for ourselves to read. Furthermore, at the same time as validating all the other voices it is developing a political correctness which is self-censoring. Overheard at a conference on feminism and language: 'But there is a touch of the Kantian objectivist in that'.

Now there are at least two good reasons why something is difficult to understand: first because it is articulating a difficult, or new idea and so is in the process of creating the concepts and language for that. J. L. Austin (1962) was a master of 'ordinary language' philosophy, so that his papers can appear so clear that students wonder what the fuss is about. But *How to do things with words* is a hard read. And second we assume that the language we are familiar with is transparently clear, but if you are not familiar with it, it is difficult to understand. Think about the way in which people with computers sounded before you had one, to see this point. The more you multiply languages, or groups, or discourses, or communities, within a university, the harder it becomes for us to understand each other. If you want to converse with physicists about physics, do your homework. But physicists do not pretend to a commitment to the oppressed, whereas many postmodernists, and especially feminist–postmodernists do. Feminists must have a commitment to putting their theories into the languages of those constituencies that they seek to empower, at the very least their students. Both of these occasions for the difficulty of a text must ultimately be overcome as new ideas become part of the currency of increasingly familiar languages. That is part of what is involved in education.

I summarize these points with the story of Ray, a mature student. We were discussing a recondite article in a class on feminist ethics. Throughout the preliminary account he was shifting and sighing, his body language betraying anger, and finally he burst out, 'I don't see what she is going on about.' I split the seminar into small groups, the text into sections with questions for them to discuss about each section, and brought them back together to report to the entire group at the end of each section. By the end of the seminar, they were picking out phrases and sentences: 'that is what she means by ...' 'that is why she says ...' I finally summarized where we had got to, and Ray angrily said: 'Why couldn't she put it like that?' On reflection, I can think of a number of reasons, from the demand that we write in a certain way in order to be published in a certain class of journal, to the impossibility of writing with clarity when you are first formulating ideas. It is then part of the work of the community to clarify, feed in examples, and if necessary, translate, a process that does not appear to belong to any particular epistemological school. But this still leaves open the question: just whose language are you translating it into?

Is this genuinely an empowering education or simply facilitating the movement of our students into the élite? A friend of mine wants her extra-mural students to be able to answer back to those élites who so enforce a sense of inferiority: 'But Quine says ...' And that is certainly liberation of a sort: her students are no longer victims to clever chaps. Another argues that postmodernism is a back-hander for the oppressed: her students discover the liberation of reading novels from their own perspective, finding their agendas in them, only, a few months later, to discover that their voice is just one in a babble, making no more sense than anyone else's, as if, at long last one gets an appointment with the consultant only to discover that the diagnosis is done by dice throwing. And, she adds, you can deconstruct the courts all that you like, they will still send you to prison. I might add: you can deconstruct the university all you like: it is still a boy's club. Which is why, at the end of the day, postmodernism serves to exclude as much as to empower.

POSTMODERNISM AND EDUCATIONAL PRACTICE

At this point, I want to break into my own argument to suggest that we are looking at the wrong crisis for higher education, when we discuss the crisis in the legitimation of knowledge.

If we begin with a model of the university as something like Balliol College in the late nineteenth century we see a community of scholars who knew each other, engaged in what they would have seen as the same pursuit. There was contention and dispute, but within a common culture and sense of purpose that many of us today might well have found suffocating. Of course, the exclusion of people from outside that culture meant that it could believe in its own universal character and rational basis, and the question of the objectivity of its activities could be raised only as a theoretical/philosophical issue – an interesting question, but not a crisis. The difference today is that not only do we appear to have lost our faith in our ability to think our way through such questions in such a way that we can maintain confidence in the purpose and value of higher education, it is no longer clear that we can even understand each other enough to discuss this. As we open our doors to a wider section of society, we throw doubt on the value of what we have to offer. We can no longer point out the path to truth, apparently, because there is no truth. And so we can no longer empower.

But just at the point that we lose our confidence in the idea that our subject-matter will direct us in what to do, (the notion of reason leading us by the nose, as it were), just as we fragment, the whole notion of an intellectual community is assaulted by outside forces of government and economy. I personally feel that this is the real crisis: at the point that we lose our clear commitments to reason, truth and empowerment, commitments which are the basis of our defence of our autonomy, we are 'invited' to become industries, marketing products at competitive prices and giving value for money. That makes us vulnerable to the highest bidder for our services, and may bind us more tightly to structures of oppression than in the days when Balliol devoted itself to preparing young men to be decent and just colonial officers.

One example: a university admissions officer, in the Middle East touting for overseas students, can see a public execution from his hotel balcony. Meanwhile his hosts explore the possibility of their women, who are not allowed to mix with men students, and therefore cannot leave their single sex university to study in the West, acquiring Western Ph.D.s through Western lecturers travelling to the Middle East to supervise their supervisors. Let the seller beware: what the market demands may not be what the discipline demands, nor what the intellectual is interested in, nor what people need to further their understanding of their situation. But how can any of these points be made without implicit reference to ideas of knowledge and progress? I want to give a two-fold answer to that: by reference to what constitutes education on the one hand, together with our grasp of the communities or constituencies which that education serves. The market model of education is destructive of both of these.

Now, implicit in all of that is a rejection of postmodernism, primarily for political reasons. It delivers the universities, without defence, into the service of the advanced capitalist corporate state and the multinational corporation. But it is equally clear that we cannot go back to modernism. Our question has to become: how can we find guidelines to help us to decide what to teach (and how), what to study, what to think about, and hence to defend what most of us reading a book like this think are worthwhile activities.

Well, I have already suggested that we share conceptions of education as empowering and liberating. Let me try to develop those.

My friend is driving around Boulder on a Sunday, looking for somewhere to buy petrol. After driving past two open garages, I ask her why she did not stop. 'Because they are self-service, and I cannot pump my own gas', she replies. I insist that we stop, and show her how to do it. This is a Marxist sociologist from an upper class Argentinian family. She can cope with exile, with hiding her Ph.D. in a tin box in the garden from a repressive regime, but not with pumping petrol. We get back in the car, and she turns to me with a huge smile: 'Anne, I feel positively liberated.' A model of learning as not touching the self, or her understanding of the world, but simply enabling her to move around more freely, literally, to do more things (like drive up to the mountains on a Sunday). Skills-based courses might look like this (for example computing, law, medicine), and best fit the market model.

But think of what is involved in learning to be a doctor, or lawyer, or accountant. Implicit is not simply a set of skills: how to remove an appendix, diagnose diabetes, but an entire way of understanding the world (consider the categories of diseased and healthy for example), an epistemology, a set of values – one learns to *be* a doctor, not to *do* doctoring, and I think any attempt to do less would not only be irresponsible (to both student and wider community) but dishonest. It is almost an Aristotelian point: in teaching skills, you develop the virtues implicit in practising those skills. And, one might add, you induct into a whole set of social relations, impart a metaphysics. Yet it is precisely an invitation to buy itemized skills, without such induction, which the market model of higher education offers.

But being a doctor is contested territory. For example, there is what I term 'the white coat approach': 'there are bodies, inconveniently inhabited by persons, which I understand better than they do. (Somewhat on the analogy of the irresponsible pet owner.)' Or a holistic approach, or a view that makes the development of new surgical techniques the cutting edge (pun-intended) rather than the links between poverty and low-birth-weight, and so on. One way of viewing this variety of approaches is to see them as emerging from the differing demands and needs of a variety of communities, as well as the different kinds of health-care an individual needs. When I have a burst appendix, I want high-tech intrusive surgery. In dealing with the menopausal swings of mood and energy, I want useful advice which respects my responsibility for myself. Sudanese villagers struggling with starvation and with a system of belief in the physical effects of malevolence demand a different kind of health-care to that of British villagers struggling with pollution – and so on. The education of a doctor, then becomes a matter of learning how to solve problems: but these problems will be posed differently in different contexts, and what constitutes a solution in one context will be inadequate, if not wholly unsuccessful in another.

I cannot answer the question of how such an education should be provided. But it is clear that educating all doctors as if they were ultimately to serve the clientele of Harley Street specialists would fail. Thus the notion of educating for one community, or constituency, particularly the dominant or most privileged one, would not in itself provide a value-free, objective, neutral education. It is clear that doctors, solving different problems in different ways, would be able to talk to each other, disagree and argue, that is in some sense, they share a community or language. It is also clear that they could be falsely educated, that they could be taught solutions which are not solutions at all, either in terms of physical harm (prolonged bed-rest after major surgery) or in terms of failing to respect the needs of the patient (rather than some other group): for example clitoridectomies for nervous excitation, or enforced inactivity for depression. Fundamental to such an education would be the notion of respect, in the sense of listening or paying attention to, another virtue that both post-modernists and modernists would agree upon, but one which the market is indifferent to, relying instead on the mechanical adjustments of supply and demand and price.

Meanwhile, our newly trained doctor is like my friend in some respects: able to do things she could not previously do, and also should have a more confident understanding, and ability to move around not only her own culture, but wider ones as well. But, unlike my friend, her self has changed and developed. She will have a more critical understanding of her world, she will, hopefully be more respectful in the sense explained above, she will have a view of what can be improved, and how, in at least some areas in her people's and her own life.

In an ideal world, I would relate this analogy in detail back to the student. But space does not permit. So I will summarize my view by saying that an emancipatory education is one which begins with the student's perspective, and behind that, a particular community which poses its own problems, background, beliefs, etc. Part of our aim must be to enable the student to help solve her community's problems, or to help solve our own community's problems, and that means developing a critical understanding of our culture and the way our particular positions are constituted by it. It means recognizing that explanations are social achievements, realized in people's abilities to use them. It means cultivating habits of scrutiny, of listening, of understanding, and of respect. And it means a model of education which is based on communication and dialogue.

To date, this view of education has been ill-served by postmodern *theories*, which have excluded, disempowered and led into blind alleys. But we should aim for a postmodern sensibility or practice: a recognition of the variety of constituencies or communities that the university should serve, the variety of languages it must be able to speak. At the same time, we should keep the dream of a common language, or of a common multi-lingual community: a further point where we would all understand each other without any particular language dominating. There is no such thing as a value-free education, we cannot produce and disseminate value-free knowledge. But there is such a thing as objectively failed solutions to problems, and implicit in my model of an emancipatory education is a rejection of the contemporary managerial practices and market place model currently being imposed on universities.

NOTES

1. For example Audre Lorde as described by Barbara Christian:

   Here insistence on speaking as her entire self whatever the consequences became the model for many women who had begun to realize that when the words 'Black liberation' were spoken, they were not referring to us, precisely because we *were* women. (Christian 1993)

2. Hirschmann (1992) gives a good example of such analysis in chapter 1.
3. Code (1988) uses this phrase in a different but related way to develop a theory of knowledge.

This paper first appeared in *Women's Philosophy Review*, Issue No. 11, June 1994 (unpublished).

EIGHT

Seductive Texts: Competence, Power and Knowledge in Postmodernity

Robin Usher

INTRODUCTION

Within contemporary education, competency-based education and training (CBET), or the 'new vocationalism', is now very much upon us. In the UK, the National Vocational Qualifications (NVQ) structure based on the notion of competences, or 'the ability to perform to pre-defined standards', is close to providing a common framework for vocational education and training and is spreading even into other areas of education.

There is a flourishing literature already in existence (for example Ashworth 1992; Hyland 1993; Norris 1991) which clearly points to serious deficiencies, both in terms of practice and rationale, with current CBET. Yet there is an acceptance at policy-making levels that it has a crucial role to play in economic regeneration and competitiveness within the contemporary globalized economy. This is coupled to a widespread belief that the education system has failed at all levels to produce a flexible, adaptable workforce motivated to learn throughout life.

UNDERSTANDING TEXTS IN A POSTMODERNIST WAY

Kenway *et al.* (1993) point out that we are witnessing a powerful tendency that de-fines 'worthwhile' knowledge in terms of a vocationalism designed to prepare people for the market-place. They point to the marketizing of education and the centralizing of curricula, resulting in vocational education being constituted in terms of behav-iourist, reductionist and instrumentalist competences. They argue that contemporary vocational practices are located in a condition of postmodernity and are best under-stood from a postmodernist standpoint.

In this chapter, 'postmodernity' refers to a number of different but related themes and tendencies. First, and most obviously, it refers to a contemporary social condi-tion encompassing economic changes such as the globalization of capital, the spread of new information and communication technologies, the growth of markets and the development of post-Fordist organizations of work. Linked with these economic changes are cultural changes such as the growth of a consumer society with its asso-ciated lifestyle practices, the undermining of hierarchies of knowledge, taste and opinion, the celebration of difference and a privileging of the local and the specific as against the universal and the abstract.

Second, postmodernity in the form of postmodernism is constituted by a set of ideas and theorizations which encompass a problematizing of imposed and singular definitions of reality, an abandoning of foundationalism and a challenge to the hier-archical dichotomies of Enlightenment thinking. Whilst postmodernity as a condition and postmodernism as an intellectual/cultural movement can be separated, they are also dynamically inter-related and interactive. Postmodernism can be seen as both evidence of and a contribution to the linked socio-economic shifts that constitute the condition of postmodernity (Lyon 1994).

In this chapter therefore, I want to examine the new vocationalism as embedded in contemporary vocational practices which can be best understood both from a post-modernist theoretical standpoint and as practices that are characteristic of the condi-tion of postmodernity. I shall begin with the former and here I will work particularly with two postmodern themes – that of 'text/textuality' and 'seduction'.

Foucault's work (1980) on the co-implication of power and knowledge (power/knowledge) provides us with the means of recognizing that 'knowledgeable' discourses embody regulatory power. Utilizing this notion, CBET could then be seen not simply as a mechanism for creating a more skilled population but as a discursive practice that reconfigures skills as a means of social regulation (Edwards and Usher 1994). However, put in this stark way there is a consequent danger of seeing CBET as working solely through a 'hidden' and impositionary power. What I want to do however is to refocus the spotlight and, without ignoring power and imposition, foreground the work of seduction and in particular, the seductions of the texts of the new vocationalism.

First, a word about 'text(s)'. In a wide sense, a text is anything in need of interpre-tation. New vocationalism is a text since it is an educational practice which projects certain interpretations or meanings and which can itself be interpreted or read for example as working through seduction rather than imposition. In a narrow sense, 'text' refers to written texts which share the characteristics of texts in the wider sense. 'Text' can therefore refer both to a signifying social practice and to a piece of writing that signifies – and indeed the two senses of 'text' are connected for very often a text in the wide sense speaks through texts in the narrow sense. The new vocationalism is itself a case in point – a social practice interlinked with a set of written texts.

My argument is that texts can be seductive as well as informative, that indeed their signifying power often lies in their seductiveness. This argument hinges on how the relationship between texts and worlds is understood. Derrida (1976) argues that there is a strong tendency to see the significance of texts as residing purely in what they are about; a something, a reality or a world which they more or less faithfully describe and explain. By emphasizing their representational nature, what is outside the text is privileged over the text itself. The text simply becomes the means of gaining access to the world outside, a vehicle for conveying its meanings. However, the something which a text is about is not independent of the text but is very much inside, something created through the text.

Following Derrida, the distinction between text and world is therefore not quite so clear-cut and straightforward. I would argue that it is through discursive practices such as education, that worlds, texts in the wide sense, come to be created. Discursive practices such as the new vocationalism combine rationalities, or ways of representing, that render aspects of the world thinkable, and technologies, or ways of intervening, that enable the thinkable to be translated into programmatic action (Rose 1991).

According to Foucault, discourses combine thinking and doing, theory and practice, meaning and action, knowledge and power. Texts therefore in the narrow sense are the means by which the power–knowledge formations in texts in the wide sense are relayed and disseminated. It is only by paying close attention to the discursive and its effects that the existence and mode of operation of power within a practice can be revealed. Texts are the means by which the operations of power are accepted and made part of the everyday.

Discourses work through texts by presenting powerful meanings with effects on readers (as participants in the practice). How they are interpreted and with what effect is open to variation. Some meanings are more powerful than others and the situatedness of readers in contexts of pre-understandings predispose certain readings over others. Readers may themselves have powerful investments in readings which hook into desires, emotions and perceived identities.

In sum, therefore, a text is read *from within itself* rather than from a point outside it. Furthermore, its meaning lies, partly but importantly, in its *effects*. It is in these features that I shall locate my discussion of the seductions of the text.

I shall start by saying something about the texts, in a narrow sense, of CBET and their seductive effects by examining a text that I have taken as representative of CBET discourse viz. Jessup (1991). I hope to show then how the text (in a wide sense) of CBET is also seductive. What I shall not be doing, is to expose errors or faulty argumentation in his text, nor to claim that Jessup has got it wrong about

CBET in the sense that it does not accurately depict its reality. My interest is in Jessup as a useful text and my argument is how its very usefulness renders it a powerful text, how its usefulness functions to seduce and how meaning is subtly imposed through this seduction. In this, I want to argue further that it exemplifies and indeed embodies the seductiveness of the text of CBET.

TEXT, STYLE, DESIRE

> The thesis put forward in this book is that if education or training is defined by its outcomes it opens access to learning and assessment in ways which are not possible in traditional syllabus or programme-based systems (Jessup 1991: 89).

Jessup's text appears at one and the same time to be simply describing in a straightforward way what is currently happening on the ground in CBET, and also presenting a new and challenging system of education and training based on outcomes.

Overall, the style is practical, down-to-earth, common-sensical, with no obvious demonstration of partiality or partisanship and no attempt to demonstrate superior academic knowledge. Yet, at the same time, an impression of expertise is conveyed – Jessup seems to know what he is talking about. As readers, then, we are drawn into the text – chapters are short and punchy (75 per cent are seven pages or less) and abundantly sub-headed (an average of seven sub-headings per chapter).

This clear, straightforward, and common-sense style subtly suggests that a competency-based system also shares these qualities. The style of the text therefore constructs and justifies a world of work-related and practical competences. It conveys a certain reality of CBET with characteristics which no reasonable person would want to question.

Many critics of CBET have highlighted its 'positive' features. Ecclestone for example points out that the NCVQ (the UK National Council for Vocational Qualifications), whose texts Jessups interweaves with his own, in highlighting relevance, increased access to educational opportunity and learner-centredness, 'speaks implicitly to us of familiar and acceptable themes' (Ecclestone 1994: 155). Norris (1991) comments on how the language of CBET has a compelling force precisely because it appears to be simply re-iterating commonsense. What reasonable person could possibly favour 'incompetence'? Competences are projected as easy to understand, precise, transparent, straightforward and flexible. As achievable ends, the means to achieve them seem correspondingly clear. This simplicity and clarity, offers the prospect of improving practice to the benefit of both learner and employer.

What all this draws attention to is that the texts of CBET are a *rhetorical achievement*. Conventionally, a text is condemned as rhetorical if it is mere words with no substance or if the way words are put together serves to obscure or mystify. But there is another way of understanding the term 'rhetorical', one which draws attention to the fact that texts communicate, that they seek to convey meanings which have effects. That texts can be rhetorical points to the fact that language is performative as well as referential. Furthermore, the classical origins of rhetoric remind us that texts are persuasive in arguing *for* something by arguing *against* something else (Billig 1990).

In a text such as Jessup's the rhetorical process works by establishing the desirability and necessity of a world of competences and CBET – for example, that they will make 'learning more relevant and available', and provide 'a more coherent system ... to ensure we get value for money' (Jessup 1991: xi). At the same time, the text's persuasive force lies not in any special pleading or obvious partiality nor even simply in the 'neutral' description of the workings of the NVQ system. Rather it lies in what is being argued against.

Running throughout the text is a critique which sometimes emerges on the surface but most of the time is implicit. It can be glimpsed from time to time – for example, in claims that 'educators and trainers exert a proprietary control over the process of learning' (Jessup 1991: 4); that the focus needs to be switched from providers to learners with teachers no longer controlling the process of learning (Jessup 1991: 99); that 'education is a pretty hit-and-miss affair and often remarkably inefficient' (Jessup 1991: 132); that 'alienation from the education system, combined with consequent poor employment opportunities, contributes to the rise of crime and hooliganism among young people today' (Jessup 1991: 132). Thus although largely implicit, it forms a quiet yet powerful centre around which the text is rhetorically organized.

In effect, the text is arguing against those who are *not* reasonable and practical, and they are constructed implicitly as politically motivated, fearful of change and with a contempt for the practical and the common-sensical of the 'real world'. For example, Jessup talks of the need to make assessment independent of programmes of learning (Jessup 1991: 18) and he argues that in the NVQ system 'assessment is brought into the real world and demystified' (Jessup 1991: 135). He claims that debates on education 'tend to be so value-laden and politicized that it is difficult to conduct a rational analysis' (Jessup 1991: 132).

What these examples show is that the text's persuasive force depends on its being organized as a critique against the critics of CBET but without it appearing to be a critique, that is without engaging directly with these critics. It is through the text's very clarity, coherence, transparency, and common-sensicality that an unreasonable, mystifying and mystified 'other' is constructed. At one level, this 'other' is provider-led education but at a deeper level it is those who argue for knowledge and understanding as against outcome-defined competence, who in effect are theorists and academic educators, cast in the role of confused and confusing mystifiers. CBET is presented as offering learning that is not only untheoretical and unacademic but *anti*-theoretical and *anti*-academic, appealing in the process to widespread popular beliefs about the irrelevance and mystification of learning provided through educational institutions. It is this 'other', absent yet at the same time present, that the text is implicitly arguing against. It is precisely through this 'other' that the text is able to present a desirable world and in this way achieve its seductive effects.

Texts with a significatory force and rhetorical power hook into readers' desires that cannot be spoken but are manifested through their concerns. For example, Jessup's text hooks into the educator's concern to be efficacious, to act effectively in ways which have useful outcomes for learners. It does this by presenting itself as relevant and 'concerned'. The NVQ system is presented as a structure where learners can achieve outcome-defined competences and move through progressive NVQ levels. Its concern, finding a ready response in educators, is with the best means for hitherto wasted potential to be tapped and realized (Jessup 1991: 5). The NVQ system is presented as a clear-cut scheme eliminating the waste, confusion and mystification of the existing educational system (Jessup 1991: 7–10). Instead, order, progression and clear understandable paths are offered to learners. Educational practitioners, to whom the text is mainly directed, are implicitly invited to connect the NVQ mechanism of progression with *progress*, and given the kind of moral pre-understandings within which educational practitioners are located, this is an invitation which is hard to refuse.

The concern for efficacy, for the 'power' to help others progress can also be seen as a desire on the educator's part for understanding and control. The text offers a way of understanding what education *ought to be* but a way which is not utopian (that is idealistic, impractical and unrealizable). A picture of CBET is presented as both concrete and understandable and therefore capable of being *mastered*. It is significant for example, that competences are mastered. With competences it is a matter of doing the 'right' thing, performing right – through mastering competences one becomes masterful. This macho metaphor of performance suggests that through being able to perform one becomes a *powerful* subject, whether as a learner or as an educator.

The text therefore hooks into the desire for understanding, and implicitly for mastery and control, by being a text that itself is understandable, masterable and controllable. The precise, straightforward and controllable reality of CBET created mirrors its own textual reality. The text therefore provides the reader/educator with the resources to tell a comforting story, to feel in control, efficacious, and 'in tune' with educational progress. It exemplifies a general characteristic of texts – that they create a world where the reader is reflected, where subjectivity is forged through the positioning afforded by the text and the way it is constructed.

The reader/educator is positioned simultaneously as a 'powerful' and 'powerless' subject. The former happens through the text hooking into a desire to be efficacious, the latter by hooking into a sense of guilt. Educational practitioners are located in a powerful discourse of modernity where the historical and cultural importance of the educational task in realizing the grand narratives of the Enlightenment is only partially achievable in contemporary postmodernity (Lyotard 1984). Yet the sense of failure in discharging it leaves educators with a strong and permanent feeling of guilt manifested in a readiness to accept an imputed role as agents of mystification and of practices wasteful of learners' potential.

The text hooks into this sense of guilt by being organized as an implied critique of schooling, of institutionalized provider-led education that has neglected learners (Jessup 1991: 3), failed to realize their potential and consequently undermined national economic competitiveness (Jessup 1991: 5, 6). The reader/educator cannot help but feel part of, and to some extent responsible for, this mess. NVQs are then presented as the way forward, as the radical yet practical answer, where everyone can realize their potential and the country can assume its rightful place in the premier economic league.

Thus the text makes a subtle appeal to the reader's desires, emotional investments and self-identifications. By simultaneously positioning the reader as powerless through exploiting concern and guilt and powerful through providing understanding, mastery and a new way forward, the reader (the educational practitioner) is seduced. Seduction, after all, works through the seduced understanding themselves as both powerful and powerless. By this process of seduction, the reader more readily accepts the message of the new vocationalism.

BEHAVIOURISM WITH A HUMANISTIC FACE

The clear behaviouristic discourse running through Jessup's text is not unknown in education. The proponents of the new vocationalism are well aware of this but they argue that CBET is different. Jessup for example, argues that the NVQ system is different because it does not require an educational model of learning and behavioural change (Jessup 1991: 39).

Conventionally, the 'knowledge' component of this discourse is that of behaviouristic psychology. Its weakness has been its failure to incorporate any notion of human agency and responsibility. Contemporary CBET is based on behavioural learning outcomes without any deterministic behaviourist underpinning. However, for critics such as Jones and Moore (1993) the behaviourist influence cannot be shaken off so easily. They argue that the effectiveness of CBET resides in the manner in which behaviour is regulated through both a particular representation of 'skills', and a technical control made possible through a particular technology (NVQ inscriptions of competence and procedures for assessment). Critics argue that the NVQ system is in effect a hierarchical system of classification and regulation and that the very structure of pre-defined (by employer-led 'lead bodies') outcomes, the reduction of human action to measurable *performance*, provides a ready means for hierarchical regulation and control.

Yet in the text, the NVQ system is presented as unproblematic, a neutral, enabling and efficient structure (Jessup 1991: 5) to bring coherence into an underperforming system of education and training (Jessup 1991: 137). Readers therefore are inclined to dismiss questions of power and regulation. Contentious issues such as for example whether employers know best what constitutes competent workplace performance are instead presented as *natural* and *necessary*, facts rather than conventional and contingent arrangements imbued with power and open to contestation.

The text therefore constructs a technicist world where questions of power seem unimportant and where knowledge is neutral in its generation and application. People, like NVQs, become flexible, transferable and adaptable, a bundle of functional competences attained and exercised according to the demands of the market. They are commodified in the very process that commodifies learning.

Yet this is no crude commodification, but on the contrary is subtle and seductive. It is because of this that I would argue against those critics who see CBET purely as a lightly disguised behaviourism. What we have rather is an interweaving of behaviourist and humanistic elements. There is, for example, an emphasis on the 'neglected' learner (Jessup 1991: 3), of the need for a system 'tailored to meet the needs of individuals' (Jessup 1991: xi), of individualized learning programmes (Jessup 1991: 99), and claims that the new model 'places the learner at the centre of the system' giving learners 'control over their own learning' (Jessup 1991: 115, 116).

This humanistic discourse provides the 'human face' for what might otherwise be an obviously and contentiously hierarchical, regulatory and unattractively inhuman system. In Jessup's text, CBET is centred on the self-directing individual and the need for learner-centredness. However, Foucault (1980) reminds us that powerful discourses are always about *something other* than power; they do not, as it were, talk directly of power. Thus the discourse of CBET talks of pre-defined outcomes which are 'more relevant and relate more to the needs of individuals' (Jessup 1991: 136). The dual but interweaving emphasis, the behaviouristic and the humanistic, the seemingly opposing elements in one discourse, is necessary if the text is to effectively do its work.

The text constructs an autonomous and self-directing subject (Jessup's chapter 17 is headed 'Implications for Individuals: The Autonomous Learner') – a subject necessary for the sustaining of agentic notions of opportunity, choice, willing commitment to flexibility and adaptability. Humanistic subjects are posited as knowing what they want to learn and as having a *natural* tendency to self-directedness, inhibited only by institutional, teacher-controlled education. Learning will no longer 'be equated in the minds of people with "academic", "classrooms", "boredom" and "failure"' (Jessup 1991: 136). The humanistic subject therefore provides yet another means for constructing and demonizing institutionalized, provider-led education as the 'other'. CBET can then be constructed, in contrast, as the only means of providing the right conditions for releasing the natural tendency to learn.

Of course, humanistic discourse is opposed to behaviouristic discourse in many important ways. Yet it can also be seen as *complementary* and indeed a necessary part of the discourse of new vocationalism. Humanistic discourse of 'access', 'lifelong learning', 'personal development', and 'negotiated curricula' becomes reconfigured and incorporated within a managerial/behaviouristic discourse of 'delivery systems' and 'units of learning'. CBET thus gains a progressive, learner-centred image where any questioning of its underlying effects seem élitist, reactionary and unprogressive (Ecclestone 1994).

The interweaving of the humanistic and behaviouristic works to block an understanding of the operation and effects of power but without itself appearing to be oppressive and constraining. The critique of the disabling structures of provider-led education projects a picture of a world where everyone can realize their full potential

and can be fully autonomous and self-directing, entrepreneurs of the self. Consequently, CBET's seductive appeal is heightened by being removed from any implication with power.

LOCATING CBET IN POSTMODERNITY

I have tried to show that the construction of the text, its language and textual devices,
in general the way meanings are organized, is effective in positioning readers. The
text as a rhetorical achievement creates a 'credible' and 'useful' world, a world that
can be read as both desirable and necessary. Through this construction, the text itself
becomes powerful as a means of effectively transmitting a powerful discourse. Yet
because the text can be read as a neutral vehicle for describing a pre-existing world
outside the text, its power is masked. It both conveys the discourse of the new vocationalism and conceals its regulatory force. As Foucault reminds us, power operates
not simply through imposing limitations but through presenting new possibilities for
constructing new capacities and modes of activity, in this case becoming competent
and efficacious.

My argument has been that texts have effects on readers, effects which are not
limited to having learnt more as a consequence of assimilating, and being enlightened by, their informative content. Jessup's text could be seen as precisely having
this effect and no other. However, it does more than this, its effect is not solely that
of informing. Here, I think this particular text exemplifies a general feature of texts,
that is that they always say more than they appear to be saying. Texts interact with
and help to create worlds and the effect they have over and above the purely infor-
mational is to draw readers into the worlds they create and by so doing seduce them
into the powerful definitive meanings embodied in those worlds. Put in this stark
way, however, it would be easy enough to understand this process simply as ideological conditioning. However, what is at stake here is much more complex than that.

First, texts as I have tried to show through my examples, are complex constructions. They may well be the vehicle for conveying and disseminating a regulatory
discourse but they do not, as it were, wear their hearts on their sleeve and they do not
work through imposition. Hence texts always say more. Jessup's text, for example,
says nothing about regulation or the possible oppressive consequences of CBET. Indeed, it appears to be saying quite the opposite; that in effect CBET is liberating.
Thus to understand the 'more' that texts are saying requires a re-focusing from the
world to the text, from what the text is about to how it is constructed and what it
constructs. It is to recognize that power is not external to signification, something
that comes before or after, but always inhabits meaning (Featherstone 1995: 138).

Second, texts work their effects in complex ways. Texts require readers; they do
their work through the effects they have on readers and through the way texts are
read. Hence the interaction between texts and readers is two-way. Readers are situated within a context, a text has effects through a context of reading and different
contexts mean different readings. From the context, readers bring with them ways in

which they interpret the text and through which the text has a particular resonance for them. I have argued that Jessup's text has a particular resonance by hooking into certain desires which those who are most likely to read his text have for understanding and control and for efficacy in the practice of teaching and learning. These desires are themselves contextually located in the crisis of the educational project that is an aspect of the contemporary condition. Ultimately, it is because of this that the texts of CBET can be seductive.

Having looked at CBET from a postmodern perspective, I want to turn now to considering its location in postmodernity – in other words, to locate the text in a narrow sense to the text in a wide sense, in this case the text of postmodernity, and try to show how seduction is foregrounded in this wider text.

Two important characteristics commonly attributed to postmodernity are the rise of markets and the cultural dominance of commodity forms. Given the former, traditionally non-market forms such as education come to be reconfigured according to the logic of the market with the new vocationalism making a significant contribution (Kenway *et al.* 1993). With reconfiguration into a market form, education assumes a consumer identity, itself becoming a commodity to be consumed. This is a particularly useful way of looking at competences since, as we have seen, they are marketized, marketable, commodified and consumable.

In postmodernity, education is reconfigured through assimilation into a new economic and cultural regime of post-Fordism; a global condition of flexible capital accumulation and specialization, characterized by dispersal and fragmentation. Post-Fordism brings more volatile labour markets, faster switches from one product to another, niche marketing and a greater consumer orientation.

As the postmodern culture of consumption becomes the hub around which the lifeworld rotates, social relations reflect and concretize its fragmentation, heterogeneity and plurality. The postmodern can therefore be characterized as a social condition where lifestyle practices and consumption become linked and where people's lives are saturated by new and ever-changing commodities and seductive images that, released from stable referents, take on their own 'reality' and become themselves consumable (Usher and Edwards 1994).

A consumer culture does not discriminate: where everything, including meaning and knowledge, can be consumed the rules of good taste and worthwhile knowledge are challenged and subverted. In the postmodern, knowledge is conceived as multiple, reflecting multiple realities and the multiplicity of experience, and generated in a multiplicity of sites. When the worthwhile can only be defined in terms of multiple and changing taste and style, knowledge cannot be either canonical or hierarchically structured. The consumer (the learner) rather than the producer (educator) is articulated as having greater significance and power. Educational practitioners become part of the culture industry, vendors alongside many others in the hypermarket of learning.

To put this another way, education is no longer concerned with transmitting Enlightenment messages and meta-narratives. Its performativity or usefulness within a market context becomes as, if not more, important. Educative processes are reconstituted as relationships where knowledge (as commodity and as image) is exchanged on the basis of its usefulness or performativity for the consumer. Learners-as-consumers seek an education that is value-adding.

Vocational practices are located in post-Fordist economic and cultural shifts within which policy is explicitly geared to producing a multi-skilled and flexible workforce (Edwards 1993). The post-Fordist organization of work, marked by informal and networked social relations and flat/lateral hierarchies, privileges individual motivation and personal change linked to reading the market and continuous adaptation to the needs of an ever-changing socio-economic environment. The learner is positioned as a subject in need of flexible competences in the flexible post-Fordist market place.

Vocationalist discourse individualizes learning and personalizes economic competitiveness by articulating individual failure as the cause of economic decline with a corresponding individual responsibility for becoming motivated and competent. Education is allotted the task of turning-out the product which the post-Fordist economy consumes, that is enterprising, consumption-oriented individuals with the appropriate attitudes and pre-dispositions, flexibility and competences. At the same time, the postmodern challenge to existing hierarchies challenges educational institutions, their control of curricula, and their monopolistic claims as sites of learning. Alternative employer-led curricula, alternative sites of learning such as the workplace, and extra-educational modes of assessment and accreditation, increasingly come to the fore. As Jones and Moore (1993) rightly point out, the new vocationalism has as much to do with the regulation of 'experts' (including the educational variety) as it does with what might be taken to be the more obvious aim of regulating their clients.

SEDUCTIVE TEXTS

Much of the criticism of CBET by educational writers fails because they do not locate their critique in the challenges of the postmodern, a failure in effect to come to terms with the postmodern text in both the wide and narrow sense. Their critique of CBET is still located within a modernist conception of the educational project and its associated significations and interpretations.

CBET is itself a good example. Obviously, vocational education can take, and historically has taken, many different culturally-shaped forms. In the contemporary conjuncture, it takes the form of a CBET shaped by the cultural matrix of postmodernity, interwoven with post-Fordism and marketization, with education 'melting into the circuits of culture' (Plant 1995) in a postmodernity where everything becomes cultural. CBET becomes not only commodified and consumable but a seductive image that is both the source of and the means of satisfying desire. In other words, CBET works through its sign-value, its effect residing not in what it *is* but in what it *signifies* and the investments which learners and educational practitioners make in the positioning provided by these significations.

Educational critics find it hard to accept the notion that an educational form can work through its seductive significations and that people may have investments based on something other than reason. Their response is to say that this is not 'really' education, or if it is, its seductiveness shows that students are being duped and that 'something else' is going on behind the scenes. Now as I have already argued there *is* something else going on behind the scenes since the text(s) of new vocationalism is implicated with regulative effects. However, this is not the whole story.

As Edwards (1996) points out, when students are positioned as consumers, demands are made on educational providers which they find difficult to cope with, and this extends not only to CBET but to all forms of educational provision. As we have seen in Jessup, notions of 'student', 'provision' and 'providers' are reconstituted. 'Students' become 'learners' and with this follows changes in both the control and content of curricula. That learners should make choices based on desire (including the desire to be optimally positioned in the market) rather than a search for enlightenment and the mastery of a canon of knowledge can no longer be considered strange and uneducational.

It is one of the features of the text of postmodernity that boundaries become blurred and break down. This is part of a process of 'de-differentiation' (Lash 1990) and its effect on the educational form is to blur distinctions between educational and non-educational discourse, sites and practices. Thus educational discourses draw upon market discourses, education is assimilated to training and vice versa, workplaces become sites of learning, the distinction between 'serious' education and 'frivolous' leisure becomes subverted.

For educators this is an ambivalent situation since boundaries have traditionally been integral to defining both the educational project and their identity. For many, de-differentiation, although troubling, also signals the breakdown of academic power-centres and pre-defined curricula based on established and excluding disciplinary knowledge. For them, its seductiveness lies in its demystifying and empowering potential both for themselves and for learners. For others, it is precisely these de-differentiating trends and their manifestations in CBET which are a troubling source of anxiety. It is the very seductiveness of CBET which for some poses a threat to education as a serious and disciplined process of development based on the stability of the canon (Edwards 1996).

Seduction has powerful metaphoric resonances of leading astray, even of corruption. Critics of CBET might well see it this way -- as something which leads education astray from what it should really be about. But this position is based on the notion that there is an ideal model defining education. I have tried to argue that there is no such model and that educational forms must be understood contextually. In the context of postmodernity, CBET is part of a new vocationalism which works through seduction.

Having said this however it is also very clear that CBET's appeal is in large measure modernist. It is structured in modernist ways, its appeal is to modernist desires for mastery, both of self and the world, and it still rests on an Enlightenment faith that education is the answer to social problems. It challenges existing classifications and hierarchies by substituting its own. Certainly, there is no postmodernist ambivalence, openness, indeterminacy and celebration of difference here. Yet this only demonstrates once again the textuality of CBET for it is the importance of significations which are foregrounded. As I have argued, it is not what CBET *is* but what it *signifies* that matters. It is not the nature of the desire it appeals to that is significant but the fact that it works through appealing to desire. That is what is meant by the textuality of CBET, why its power lies in its seduction, and why its seductive power is best understood as located in the 'text' of postmodernity.

NINE

Negotiating Truth: Some Insights from Applied Social Anthropology

Sonia Greger

Provisionality in methods and process does not necessarily imply provisionality in commitment and value. The prior commitment (to the worth of persons) is absolute and total. But everything between and in practice is provisional, negotiable and alterable. (David Jenkins 1995)

Presenting the views of an anthropology fieldworker, this paper uses her concept of *meaning negotiation* to analyse everyday social occurrences in a community fairly remote from her own English background. These analyses can lead to various forms of theoretical discussion for use outside the 'field'. Used as theoretical 'resting places' they also help her to understand, as part-insider, through a process of reasoning which must always remain open to further questioning and questing.

The process fits well into the relativist arguments of postmodernism, but it is found necessary always to have, recognize and rely upon a subjective moral stance which is, in the last resort, metaphysical; and this latter has no place in postmodernism. This subjective position clearly reaches back to many roots in the author's culture and those, too, however powerful and necessary, remain open to question. In religious terms this way of doubt can be seen as a traditional *via negativa*. Although cultural sources are recognized and, like other cultural elements, held always open to question, this particular moral aspect of subjectivity cannot be held (as in postmodern terms) as merely a matter of opinion. It is universalizable: in Kantian terms, to be recommended to and for all persons.

THE FIELD

Ethnographic work in an agricultural and pastoral group of villages in a Cretan mountain plateau shows a relatively traditional rural culture with strong patriarchal form. The public confrontational modes of behaviour among men is only one side (the outside) of meaning and value negotiations; and these can reflect some light back on similar confrontational modes of discourse in the author's experience of British academic life. More private ways of restoring community might provide useful examples for balancing such competitive modes.

Fieldwork demands a capacity to listen, and let data speak for themselves. Perhaps the best trick for avoiding over-hasty imposition of theory is to treat bodies of university knowledge with irony. The question to ask is: are these tools really adequate for the job in hand? Bracketing off academic knowledge has helped this writer to become more aware of its powers of manipulation.

The field under study here is as riddled with ambiguity and insecurity as our own; perhaps more so, and not just because it is being affected by our own. Ideals of 'simplicity', 'closeness to nature' and 'freedom' may be no more than romantic fantasies, as non-locals (for example tourists) use the region as their 'exotic other'; and a dose of postmodern irony could clear that from an outsider's perception.

It is necessary first to set out, in proper post-colonial and post-positivist style, the writer's theoretical bias. Bias, that is, within the practicalities of first the ethnographer's semi-passive activity of participant observation; and second in the much more involved, up-to-your-neck-in-it pursuit of one taking responsible part in a small development programme: what came to be described as 'action research'.

THE THEORETICAL POSITION

Three central issues: *objectivity*, *relativism* and *subjectivity*, will be approached with the following bias. Later an attempt will be made both to explain and defend those biases. It will be necessary in the process to pick a way between a hermeneutic approach as instanced in Lawrence Rosen's work:

> If language does not reflect the world but is integral to its constitution, and if that constituted world is one in which the image of a handclasp is more ... a familiarity than a proof, an understanding than a certainty, we may be called upon to forswear a quest for structural constants, however transmuted, in favour of an exploration of interpretative process, however contested. (Rosen 1984: 180)

At the same time there must be a search for some kind of socially independent objective truth as claimed, for example, by Ernest Gellner:

All knowledge must indeed be articulated in some idiom but there are idioms capable of formulating questions in a way such that answers are no longer dictated by the internal characteristics of the idiom or the culture carrying it but, on the contrary, by an independent reality. (Gellner 1992: 75)

For Gellner, 'the ability of cognition to reach beyond the bounds of any one cultural cocoon, and attain forms of knowledge valid for all' is the mode of science; which is 'an understanding of nature leading to an exceedingly powerful technology'. Should we not hesitate here to ask whether such claims to power may also be culture-relative?

A third way-marker is that moral stance instanced by David Jenkins (1995): the 'prior commitment to the worth of persons', which is absolute and total and a fundamental theme of this paper. Thus, the search for objectivity is tied, in this steering through way-markers, rather less to high level claims for scientific enquiry; rather more to a moral concern that is also tied to an ongoing truth concern.

To address *objectivity*: it is held that there are social realities (note the plural) which exist 'out there', beyond and independent of my perceiving and interpreting them. If/when I perceive and inevitably start to interpret them I become to some degree part of the complex of social realities. Thus I become a causal factor within a complicated state of affairs which is perpetually changing.

My *subjectivity* thus becomes an important focus for my attention when attempting to interpret elements within that state of affairs, and I attempt to view it impartially in relation to other elements. Finding myself involved in a state of affairs, I am concerned

1. to interpret it with growing understanding and insight (I shall call this the *truth concern*);
2. for the 'health' on ongoing affairs (which I call the *moral concern*).

Clearly use of the word 'health' in relation to social realities raises enormous and fundamental issues for further consideration. Some attempt will be made to cope with them in this chapter; for they are always there.

It would be fallacious to read either the truth concern or the moral concern globally: as an ultimate single objective. That would be to submit to dogma and would be both truth denying and morally wrong. *Relativism* is thus an essential concept in remembering that no dogma can, in itself, be claimed to take truth priority over any other biased view. Since it makes no sense, in this context, to argue for a single, global 'reality' and since the focus on subjectivity demands honesty regarding theoretical bias, it must follow that there are many points of view which may at times appear complementary to one another; but at times in competition. Nevertheless, the subjective *moral* commitment is, as already claimed, one to recommend to and for all persons. This element of subjectivity is not merely a matter of opinion.

That is my theoretical bias to date. This maps out a personal practical working procedure as anthropologist. If it were possible to understand in a different way –

whether from a different cultural background, or as a different kind of creature with different perceptual and cognitive equipment – many conceptual distinctions might dissolve. For purposes of analytical reasoning (a dominating approach in the Western culture) concepts have to be clearly distinguished. Yet *ambiguities of meaning and fluid boundaries are of the essence of creativity and adaptability*. The working distinctions between self and other; between subjective consciousness and the objective data it interprets; between strict concern for realities-in-the-plural as against a global reality-in-the-singular; all these distinctions may, in a religious or moral meaning context, merge into one concern for both truth and justice. That is the metaphysical level which working procedures reflect but do not intellectually approach. As a religious person I suspect that my subjectivity is much closer to the subjectivity of others; and that particular social realities are creatively linked to a more holistic notion of 'truth', than my working theoretical rules allow. That holistic ideal must, however, be kept to the edge of working procedures, lest it take on dogmatic form and break both the truth concern and the moral concern. As an ideal, it remains for me of ultimate and continuing importance.

To relate those working and procedural rules back to practical experience, we turn now to some anecdotal material. It should be borne in mind that the writer here is the anthropologist reporting, that she is probably unaware of many relevant realities and some of her own prejudices. Further, she is using these anecdotes to bear out and illustrate her own theoretical bias.

THE BACKGROUND

After ethnographic study of the transhumant villagers of Magoulas in the Cretan Lasithi Plateau from 1982 to 1985, further participant observation in the same village led to a women's development project (known as the Workshop) which grew between 1987 and 1990. Supported by the EC COMETT programme and the Greek Ministry of Culture, the programme involved bringing graduate students from the UK and Greece to work with Lasithi women, helping them set up a co-operative for reinterpreting Greek fabric designs and producing them on hand-crafting knitting machines.

A change of government in 1990 brought attack on the project and the local village president, accusing him and the present writer of embezzling EC funds. The Workshop was closed, the women afraid. Only in 1995 were there signs that the project may be reopened under local control and with advice from the writer. It has taken several years in the law courts to clear the project of the accusations.

We turn now to smaller, more manageable anecdotal material. One has to do with a village woman's concerns; another to do with the visit of a group of Danish men seeking collaboration with the local people (as we had done in the Workshop project) for a joint development programme. The first involves 'insider' negotiation; the second with 'outsiders'. In their various ways these anecdotes will set the complex scene for the kinds of ambiguity, tension, insecurity and modes of negotiating 'truth', which I want to discuss.

Anecdote 1: Anna

The name is fictitious, the woman – a shepherd's wife – and her circumstances are real. Picked from fieldwork record cards in the category Village Dynamics, this reminds me that we have known each other for over ten years. She knows that I know much of her family history, and she has, like other villagers, come to realize that I do not repeat locally what people say to me. Thus an anthropologist often gets used as a kind of agony aunt. She will also expect me to say nice, supportive things about her in *cafeneion* discussions. Field notes run thus:

Winter 1991 AA came to my kitchen for a coffee. Discussed her worries. She was snubbed yesterday by EE and village clerk's wife. AA interpreted this as political: they are right-wing voters; AA's family vote left. She is also worried about her second cousin's plot of land which she and her husband work because cousin and husband live outside the plateau. AA has always worked the plot, growing potatoes for her own and cousin's family with never a quarrel between them, Strong south wind last June blew down old tree on cousin's plot, and cousin's husband said AA could have the wood for her stove. Cousin's husband is godfather to AA's youngest son who is invalid after a bad road accident.

AA argues that she worked the land and was promised all the tree on the grounds of her son's weakness and need; but DD (a village man) asked cousin's husband for some of the wood and was told he could take some. AA says that DD has taken the lot. [N.B. DD asked my husband to take a gift next time we visit cousin and husband in their distant village. Was it meant to be a thank you gift for the wood? Good job we did not go yet. Don't get involved!]

AA went on to get my sympathy. Her son cannot gather or chop wood now (true); her husband is closer relative to cousin that is DD (true). During the scandal about Workshop project DD had said publicly that I was a liar. When I didn't react apart from laughing about much similar gossip, she reverted to the time of the big right: left quarrel (what a lawyer defending the case had called the era of *skandalologia*) [N.B. that at the time of attack of our Workshop project I had felt, not only a failure, but also *guilty*. Why? The Greek concept of a good person is tied to the idea of being successful; less tied to our idea of good intentions.[1] In the local context it is all too easy to lose touch with ideas of objective truth. Local negotiations appeared to ignore the possibility of our project accounts proving to be, as I knew, impeccable.]

Finding that I had no animosity towards DD, AA turned to her cousin, who is known to be my friend. 'The big problem here is men who are *egoistis* (egoistic, selfish). Second cousin has suffered all her life from a very egoistic husband.'

She continued with her other worries. She is discontented with her husband and both their sons. We then discussed the menopause. She is 56, and started the *kli-*

maktoro in her mid-forties. She is now 'finished'. Her husband is still sexually demanding but he does not love her; only swears at her. She has no optimism about her son's future and feels he should have died in the accident. [N.B. that AA's husband has spoken to me of his optimism. Invalid son is trying to help domestically. He gets up early to clean out and re-light the woodstove before his parents awake. But son has told me that he cannot bear his future, for he has no room of his own and sleeps on a bed in the tiny living room. His parents tell him he is the luckiest, because he sleeps near the stove.]

[Notes in square brackets indicate insertion of fieldworker's thought as relevant.]

In the above case we need to compare the parents' traditional hard shepherd life with the fact that invalid son studied at university and was doing well until his accident, which wounded his brain as well as paralysing other parts of his body. His parents are non-literate.

Amid this tangle of relationships few, if any, clear facts emerge. Most, if not all, are inextricably tied up with values: are matters of judgement. It is not the anthropologist's job to pass judgement. All she can do is listen and try to be supportive without preferring one person's view against another's. Note that each tries to get her sympathy in opposition to the current 'enemy'. Most village discussion works in that way. It is difficult to remain impartial, but very important to try.

The impartiality is not, however, a matter of focusing on value-free 'facts'. It is more a matter of moral concern for all participants and the general, reasonable 'health' of the village community. That, too, is an important skill practised by most villagers some of the time. *Trust* belongs within the community. Trust in objective truths, for example mathematical validity of financial accounts, seems not to exist. Truth has to be negotiated among those you know and have to live with.

MEANING NEGOTIATION

The daily struggle – what other writers on Greek communities have called 'pushing and pulling' – to manipulate 'truth' on a continuous basis is what is meant here by 'meaning negotiation'.

Rather softer in tone than Rosen's 'bargaining', which has to do with Muslim men's negotiations; manipulations from *inside* this community use gentle, affectionate modes as well as the more confrontational styles. The individual works hard, often – especially in the case of women – behind the scenes; but also – especially in the case of men – in the public arena of the *cafeneion*. Although there are cases of objective 'fact', as noted, 'truth' for the villagers, seems never to be only a matter of objective fact; but also of evaluative claims for moral support.

Anecdote 2: Windmills

Field records of the village include many cards on this topic. Windmills have been used in the plateau for irrigation for most of this century. They have a technico-romantic appeal for ecology-minded specialists, especially from Holland or Denmark. Because the traditional white-sailed windmills also attract tourists – the Greek Tourist Board being willing to pay farmers for maintaining their old mills whether they use them or not – the question of windmill maintenance and restoration has become a hot political issue right across the plateau. The notes quoted here are from one particular meeting between the village president and a formal group of visitors from Denmark.

Peter had visited our Workshop about a year before, met British students on placement to the project, and a few local people. Apparently he had been impressed by what seemed our 'green' approach to local human ecology. He had returned to Denmark and persuaded influential colleagues to return with him for discussion about possible collaboration with locals. Field notes run thus:

Meeting with Danish visitors 1992 at Psychro
Present: elected village president.
Peter – from an organization called Small & Green.
Ianis – local man married to British girl who had come on placement to our project.
Rachel – Ianis' wife.
Heine – from an organization funded by Danish Ministry of Energy to co-ordinate foreign contacts.
Bruno – Danish engineer and windmill manufacturer.
My husband Karl, and I.

Heine through Ianis as interpreter, set the form of negotiation on pattern similar to north European business meeting: all very 'reasonable', like inter-state COMETT meetings I had attended. He wanted to know if farmers on the plateau are interested in keeping the traditional environment and encourage good tourism. He said it was evident from his observations that water is being used excessively and unnecessarily. Over-pumping from petrol pumps is causing the water table to drop (true). Bruno's pumps are designed both for high yield (four times the old mills) *and* to prevent over-pumping. He has designed for World Bank and remote areas. Therefore long research behind the design. [N.B. a Villager's later comment: 'What can they teach us? Everyone knows that we know *all* about windmills.']
Village president at first confrontational, talking technically in aggressive tone about horsepower, pressure, etc.; but he gradually softened and agreed to discuss the proposal at next meeting of Union of Lasithi Communities. Heine undertook to get a formal letter to the president in time for the meeting, saying he must have a prompt reply in order to make application for funding. [N.B. Village president repeatedly turned to me to translate his words to visitors. Was this because (a) he is annoyed with Ianis – gossip has it that he thinks Ianis has changed his vote to opposing party; or (b) I must play the traditional female role of cooling the issue,

explaining opposing parties to each other; or (c) I am also a foreigner, and he is now treating us all as outsiders no longer open to negotiation; or (d) possibly all three at once?]
Apparently Heine's letter was received in time for the meeting; but he got no reply.

There is much more to the windmill stories. A bundle of green record cards (colour-coded for ecological issues) illustrate many negotiations, whilst the windmills remain as they are: rather decrepit. Farmers continue to use their petrol pumps. On a different set of record cards is a note recording the erection of an expensive statue honouring the *local* man who first brought windmills to the plateau.

The heroic stance of this local benefactor – he stands with sword poised in threatening manner – is a good example of 'shared narrative'. An outsider wondering what a raised sword has to do with windmill power may miss the local significance of the Cretan *palikari* image of the mountain freedom fighter. As already noted, windmills have enormous local political significance.

Any technical development appears to happen piecemeal and, although ecological issues are discussed, they are pushed aside when decisions are taken by farmers or shepherds whether to avail themselves of current opportunities.

That is a brief example of attempted negotiation with outsiders. Peter bravely continued trying to build a suitable modern windmill whilst getting to know local people. So he worked, for a time, as we did, by starting from the inside. Yet it was largely because my project started from the inside that I was accused at the time of government change of leading some kind of illegal mountain conspiracy.

There appears to be a direct opposition between concepts of centralized organization and ideas of local initiative.[2] Since there is no logical contradiction between forms of centralized order and local initiative, this projection of traditional confrontational negotiation into the politico-metaphysic of Mediterranean behaviour is interesting. I believe that it emerges from patriarchal forms which underlie most public discourse at least throughout the Western world, and wherever the potential creativity of science and technology pertain.

MEANING NEGOTIATION FROM THE INSIDE

In the ethnography of this plateau region I used the diagram (Figure 9.1) to summarize how ongoing village manipulations of 'truth' seemed to operate. It takes time for new ideas to be assimilated; not because they are difficult to understand as isolated notions, but because they do not fit meaningfully into the complex, constantly adapting, local meaning system. The attempt in Figure 9.1 to map out the three axes of meaning negotiation still proves useful. It helps me, as participant observer, to 'feel my way inside' the system, and to be patient when I cannot. The following three axes are illustrated in Figure 9.1:

- *The Given* – those features in the environment which villagers accept since they can do little to control them: terrain, weather, economy, centralized control, etc. These may be shifting and unstable, but only a limited degree of personal or collective manipulation is possible. They tend to be accepted as a remote 'fate'.
- *The Practical* – these features are tied to tradition: villagers' ideas of the right way to carry out their labours and technology.
- *The Symbolic* – activities and ritualistic behaviour take on evaluative connotations; so that the right way to plant seed, or the right way to conduct a village-centred *cafeneion* discussion cannot be completely dissociated from these evaluative ideas.

So the village president had to be confrontational in his discussion with Heine in order to be a strong man who knows all about windmills. His tone and manner had initially been harsh and aggressive. When he softened, appearing to agree, that was a probable sign that negotiation had already failed and would get nowhere.

So, also, Anna had to talk privately with another woman about her female pains and sorrows. A strong man does not listen to such dark, emotional and, for him, rather threatening discourse.

THE PRACTICAL
Work skills & organizations
Notions of technically 'right way'
Tied to tradition
May shift only with difficulty

THE SYMBOLIC
Ritual/sacred objects & spatial structures
The ethically 'right way'
Tied to tradition
May be under threat within shifting context

NEGOTIATION
Or the management of meanings
Organizes on a shifting basis as
appropriate to group or individual.

THE GIVEN
Terrain, economy, political
context. May itself be shifting:
e.g. weather, market or population fluctuation

Figure 9.1 Axes of meaning negotiation

MUTED MEANINGS

In the pushing–pulling manipulations of village truth-cum-value some dark things are seldom given expression. This does not mean that they do not exist. Anna's completion of her menopause is a fact. Her husband may speak of it with other men with macho talk of finding a younger woman. Anna speaks of being 'finished', and is in deep depression. Much of what relates to women's understanding is kept dark. It is regarded as emotional or polluting.

I have written elsewhere (Greger 1991) of what Anna Caraveli has called the 'aesthetics of pain' in Lasithi women's ritual lament singing. Their skill in grieving for the dead is 'kept dark'; muted by both men and Church. It is regarded as dangerously emotional, anti-rational and subversive.

Yet the coming of death is a fact. A rationale which tries to repress awareness of that fact is irrational: repressive of emotion or grief. Rationality should come to terms with feeling and emotion, recognizing that they have a cognitive core: not use up energy in trying to cover them up or hold them down.

What is meant in this chapter by a 'healthy' community is one which allows fears, sorrows and pains out into the open of collective awareness. Although I have instanced repressions in the village awareness, I find there *are* ways allowed in local meaning negotiation for sharing the darker side of experience. It is when I return to England that I am more aware of repressions and covert manipulations.

Having learned something of the village game of negotiating, I am more aware, for example, of academic politicizing back in the UK. This applies not only to jockeying for promotional favours. It applies to the very construction of knowledge and meaning as developed in university departments. Meaning negotiation is going on all the time.

Muted meanings, whatever the reasons for keeping them dark, do emerge from social realities. Anna's depression is a reality emerging at least in part from her social and family circumstances. Women's ritual laments emerge from social realities which men and Church try to repress. Such realities, in a healthy community, may be given expression; for the forms of folk art and ritual *can feed social discourse creatively*.[4] They are often repressed because that suits those who hold power in one form or another.

Meaning negotiations emerge from, and feed back into, what Victor Turner (1969) called *communitas* (briefly 'individuals confronting one another in the manner of Martin Buber's *I and Thou*'). Where society is viewed in solely structural terms (the system of statuses, roles, offices – what might be called the 'corporate ego') represses such realities as women's or peasants' only half-expressed experiences, then members of that society are exploiting those to whom no voice is permitted.[5]

At least in the kind of localized meaning negotiation outlined here, it is possible for the under-privileged to go on manipulating 'truth' to better suit themselves. In large scale societies the possibility of repression reaches terrifying dictatorial proportions.

So when the village president resists both outsiders who want to cash in on current opportunities, and government officials who wish to destroy local initiatives, he has the writer's sympathy. The sympathy rises not because I support his political party, nor because I make his enemies my enemies (the traditional role), but because I believe we must so respect local, grass roots attempts at adaptation.

Again we return to a moral stance of respect for all persons, which takes precedence over searches for objective truth. The religious *via negativa* tradition has upheld this priority over many hundreds of years, always in conflict with contradictory attempts to dogmatize. It, too, works through a kind of darkness, a 'cloud of unknowing'; and as a continuing tradition it may feed, through future negotiations of meaning, to new formulations of truth.

CURRICULA IN HIGHER EDUCATION

Focusing on various modes of negotiating 'truth', this chapter has been an attempt to show that truths or facts cannot be completely dissociated from the values of those who observe and interpret them. Such interpretation is, very broadly speaking, political; so it follows that some categories of people are in danger of being exploited by the very construction of knowledge which they inhabit.

Considered here were women and peasants; but similar arguments could apply to minority religious groups, for example. Truths are relative to various meaning contexts, and we should try not to judge between those contexts except insofar as rejecting any which break a fundamental moral principle of commitment to the worth of all persons.

Ernest Gellner holds an objective standard to be in the methods of scientific enquiry; but without denying their search for objective truth,
it has been argued that those, too, are subject to social construction and control. Thus it is crucial that educated citizens criticize in an open-minded fashion; becoming aware of their own prejudices as well as doubting the dogma of others.

It has also been argued that a safeguard lies in non-dogmatic moral or religious discourse. Figure 9.2 shows a distinction between what might be called the *fictional omniscient* fantasy of repressive political or religious structures (patriarchal forms are a culprit here), and the *mythical* concepts of religions, cosmologies or world-views which, whilst believing in some ultimate truth or morality, do not claim to have exclusive possession or clear formulation of that ultimate concern. In this form, the argument here is fairly close to Ernest Gellner's idea of scientific truth. If we take an agnostic stance while including a moral dimension, there is little disagreement.

The *fictional omniscience* marks a dogmatic, repressive corporate ego that is dangerously far from rationality. The *mythical* is a symbolic way, using various metaphors, of reaching towards ultimate truth and value, without ever claiming to possess it. That, however unfashionable, is a metaphysical or religious position.

Crisis, or a fundamental collapse of current sociality, occurs all round us. Elements of old principles and traditions may be clung to while setting out in radically new directions.[6] These adjustments are forms of meaning negotiation which seem to grow, like new plant species, up from the ground of groups who feel themselves oppressed.

Non-dogmatic concepts – working through a *via negativa* of ambiguities, tensions, conflicts and emerging out of a non-patriarchal authority-from-within which retains the moral sense of *communitas* – may gradually bring the possibility of cohesion and coherence to the human species. For now, *communitas* seems always fragmented. We have the pluralism of social groups always opposing each other.

FICTIONAL
OMNISCIENCE

MYTHICAL STRUCTURES
ATTEMPTING TO FORMULATE

FUNDAMENTALISM
and
DOGMATISM

THE UNKNOWABLE
(God?)
Open-ended enquiry

Repression by
corporate ego

Democratic openness
to muted meanings

ETHNIC FENCES

ETHNIC BRIDGES

(Power structures)

(open metaphors/cosmologies)

Superior knowledge is
claimed, whether in
religious or scientific
context.
e.g. as a quick fix
by technology*

World pictures, dramas and
fantasies that form the
imaginative background of
all our intellectual work.
Myth-making as a vital
human function *

Figure 9.2 Two approaches to 'knowledge' and 'truth'
* See Midgley 1992.

We also have a greater opportunity than ever before of reaching across the boundaries of meaning and value; learning to live among ambiguities and tension, whilst clarifying as logically as we can.

Patriarchal structures of authority which have developed within and from shepherding or nomadic groups such as those studied for this chapter, and which have emerged over thousands of years from a middle Eastern core, may not be natural forms of human society. They may be entirely inappropriate to different kinds of society such as our own.

In early subsistence groups, where *communitas* inside the group probably took precedence over hierarchical authority, and which still operates in the villages studied here, there may be a very different balance of cohesion–confrontation behaviour. If we could better understand the forms of *communitas* negotiation, so extending the range of 'who we can talk to, and how',[7] we might find a way out of inappropriate social structures inherited from patriarchy. These underpin scientifically informed society and threaten to so misuse that knowledge as to destroy our species.

Confrontational modes, acted out in public by male members of traditional patriarchal societies, have been projected into the negotiations and consciousness of 'civilized' mass societies. The more private modes of meaning negotiation, particularly those traditionally carried by women, have not been so projected. Victor Turner held that the forms of *communitas* might even be better expressed in modern mass society than in small and remote closed groups; but he noted[8] that they have not yet been recognized as normal public practice.

It seems very important that education, from childhood right through life, should provide for the development of critical faculties as well as what have been called here the 'truth concern' and the 'moral concern'. This is certainly not to evade evaluative issues, or to rest in value free study of[9] texts or of science. In the last resort each individual must become responsible for her/his own moral stance. Certain postmodern trends which focus on relativism or subjectivity can contribute to that; but for nerves to fail at the point of 'Anything goes' or 'It's all a mere matter of opinion', just as the old authority figures are under question seems, under the circumstances, very adolescent.

Thinking of young students seeking higher education, I am reminded of Hermann Hesse's Joseph Knecht in his novel *The Glass Bead Game*. Joseph, as a young man has been struck by postmodernist (or are they modernist?) doubts

'Oh, if only it were possible to find understanding', Joseph exclaimed. 'If only there were a dogma to believe in. Everything is contradictory, everything tangential; there are no certainties anywhere. Everything can be interpreted one way and then again in the opposite sense. The whole of world history can be explained as development and progress and can also be seen as nothing but decadence and meaninglessness. Isn't there any truth? Is there no real and valid doctrine?'

The Master had never heard him speak so fervently. He walked on in silence for a little, then said: 'There is truth, my boy. But the doctrine you desire, absolute, perfect dogma that alone provides wisdom, does not exist. Nor should you long for a perfect doctrine, my friend. Rather, you should long for the perfection of yourself. The deity is within you, not in ideas and books. Truth is lived, not taught. Be prepared for conflicts, Joseph Knecht – I can see they have already begun'. (Hesse, 1943: 79–80)

So what is understanding? I turn finally to David Pole's reading of the philosophy of the later Wittgenstein:

> 'Now I understand!' one exclaims, after struggling with some technique or calculation, and then one goes on happily from that point. But it may also happen that one gets lost again. 'I didn't really understand; I only thought I had!'. ... The experience of understanding might be roughly expressed as 'Now I can go on from here'. It brings a sudden sense of command, a relaxing of tension and a self-confidence which may or may not be well-founded. (Pole 1958: 24)

That very practical combination of responsibility with intellectual humility may be the closest we can come to the truth.

NOTES

1 Rosen writes similarly of a young Islamic man of Marrakech:
   At no time does he say what he or anyone else thinks or feels: the dialogue ... focuses instead on what men say, what they do, and what social consequences result. The vocabulary of inner states is almost entirely absent. [This is] similar to the style of Homer ... everything is in the foreground, nothing is in the background. (Rosen 1984: 180)
2 This opposition was worked out in more detail in an unpublished paper: Greger, Sonia 1991 'Woman:Man::Peasant:Central Administration'.
3 Figure 9.1 is from Greger, 1985
4 Susanne Langer's distinction between discursive thought and the presentational forms of art and ritual is useful here.
5 Susanne Langer again:
   the power of symbols enables us not only to limit each other's actions, but to command them; not only to restrain one another but to *constrain*. That makes the weaker not merely the timid respecter of the strong, but his servant. It gives us duty, conscription and slavery. (Langer 1963: 186–7)
6 Susanne Langer again:
   Only as one culture supersedes another, every new insight is bought with an older certainty. The confusion of form and content which characterizes our worship of life symbols works to the frustration of well-ordered discursive reason. (Langer, 1963: 294)
7 I quote here from Nigel Blake's conference paper which forms Chapter 12 in this volume.
8 'Large-scale societies with specialization and division of labour ... have not yet developed a structure capable of maintaining social and economic order over long periods of time. The very flexibility and mobility ... may, however, provide better conditions for the emergence of existential communitas, even if only transient, than any previous forms of social order' (Turner 1969: 202).
9 While the exercise of irony can be a useful technique for taking theories with a practical pinch of salt, to focus exclusively on layerings of textual material seems to work in the opposite, anti-practical direction; so with its practical bias, this paper selects and rejects from postmodern fashion.

PART IV

Constructing Dialogues

TEN

The Arts, Postmodern Culture and the Politics of Aesthetic Education

Peter Abbs

Carnivals are fun, but carnivals without end are tedious. Treating all cognitive claims like masks and costumes at a permanent fiesta, optional and free of any factual or logical restraint, all allegedly in the name of inter-cultural equality, will not do.

(Ernest Gellner 1995)

THE INNER POLITICS OF ARTS EDUCATION

Václav Havel (1987) once wrote: 'the main instrument of society's self-knowledge is its culture.' I am sure that most arts teachers would endorse his proposition but, of course, it can quickly generate a number of negative questions. What, for example, if the dominant culture of any particular society tends to promote self-ignorance or self-indifference or self-indulgence or some form of self-alienation? And what if that culture, in one way or another, for whatever reason, conscious or unconscious, tends to withhold the cultural means for the continuous development of thinking, feeling and imagining? What then?

In this chapter I will examine what could be broadly termed the inner politics of arts education, the seminal politics of aesthetic and intellectual enquiry, at least, as it emerges in an educational context. What social values, what cultural virtues, are embedded in our work as we actively guide students into the making, performing and evaluating of artistic work and into the whole culture of the particular art form we represent? What are the dynamics of the activity released and what kind of image of the good society do they entail? And how do those dynamics and how does that image relate to the dominant international mass-culture, the consumer democracy of our times and the postmodernist thinking which so often accompanies it? These are difficult questions which need to be given a new edge and a further amplification – even a new reading. I want to consider the implications of this politics for the development of arts teaching in relationship to postmodern society – for the inner politics of arts teaching must have some bearing on the politics outside. To decide what that relationship is or should be, it is necessary to first define the set of social values and assumptions which shape the teaching of the arts.

ALEX'S STORY

I want to begin not with theory, but with a typical example of arts practice. The event I will describe took place in 1994 at the University of Sussex in England but, in principle, it could have taken place in any educational context anywhere in the world. I am not concerned to describe the event in detail, but rather to disclose the educational assumptions that inform it, to delineate the matrix of values and assumptions which make such work possible.

On a Tuesday, then, in the Autumn term three MA students[1] – arrive to make short autobiographical presentations in any expressive medium of their choice. One of them is a Russian student, Alex, and she has chosen to make her presentation in the form of a fairy story in what she calls 'the violent tradition of Russian fairy tales.' The group of students sit informally round the table. After a brief introduction, she begins the reading of her story:

> Once upon a time there was a woman neither beautiful nor plain, neither clever nor stupid, neither kind nor cruel. One day she gave birth to twins. So beautiful were the twins that she loved them more than her own life. The twins opened their eyes, looked upon their mother and cried, and the woman was frightened: what if the children should see the beauty of the world and should find something more wonderful than their mother and will not love her. And she decided: 'Better all my life I shall be their guide than let them love anyone more that me,' and she cut out their eyes. Some time had passed and the children learned to walk, and in spite of their blindness they began to stray away from their mother. Again she was frightened: what if the children should run too fast and too far for her to keep up with them. And she decided: 'Better all my life I shall carry them on my back than let them abandon me,' and she cut off their legs.
>
> Some more time passed and the children learned to speak, and they began to ask their mother questions about their eyes and legs. Again the woman was frightened: what if the children should accuse her of cruelty? And she decided: 'Better they never sing a single song than I should hear a word of reproach from them,' and she cut their tongues out.[2]

It is a shocking story; elemental, violent, inexorable. In the story, the mother buries herself and one of her crippled children alive rather than allow him freedom. The second cripple, however, escapes. Hidden away in a valley, he slowly regains the use of his limbs, his eyes and his tongue. Yet, even so, the story ends on a tormenting note of injustice – for the newly restored tongue can only utter a sense of outrage:

> And in his despair he remembered his brother with whom he shared his mother's womb and the loneliness of his childhood and he cried; 'Who and why and how and by what right, has deprived me and my brother of the world, of the love and of life itself?'

The story ends as tragedy, but in the introductory note which Alex read at the beginning she observed: 'the life's record is up to date and leaves the tale ending on a very sad and morbid note. The writer may only hope that the future will provide a concluding part to his story in which he might be transformed from a pathetic victim of circumstances into a triumphant hero and might live happily ever after.'

What is going on here in this act of art-making and art-performing? Well, at the level of factual description, it seems simple enough. A fairy story is being told to a group of students who, because of the particular conditions set for the work, are responding to it both as a fairy story and an allegory for the life of the person reading it. Such an event – a presentation of a piece of art-work, complete or nearly complete, to a group of students who, in turn, have just presented or are about to – is an absolutely essential part of good arts education. It is the central drama at the heart of our work, often providing the highest moments of absorbed attention and fulfilment. Yet the psychological and symbolic processes involved in these moments are extremely complex, densely interwoven and all but defy adequate formulation. I have in recent writing concentrated on the formal and aesthetic elements in such work; I want now to concentrate on the social and educational expectations which make it possible and give it a particular kind of collective and democratic dynamic.

I will first consider *the individual presentation* and, then, *the context* which has elicited it.

In creating the fairy story, Alex has found an artistic form for her own experience. She has found in her own Russian culture a way of transposing what she sees as the essential drama of her life into an allegorical narrative. While the story is compelling in its own right, it carries at the same time the painful burden of her life. It is not her life, of course. It is a representation of it and, therefore, in principle, open to all kinds of editing and re-description. Through working on a popular genre, Alex has made herself an object of her own contemplation. She has created a symbolic world which allows her to shape and re-shape, revise and re-vision, her own hidden and subjective life. She has become a creative agent within the life of culture, a maker of stories and a potential remaker of herself.

The sense of hope accompanying the project is very tangible, not only in Alex's remark, couched in the exact idiom of fairy stories – that she may one day become a triumphant hero and live happily ever after – but also in the fact (revealed in the discussion after her reading) that she has sent the story to her brother challenging him to continue it. The desire not only for representation but also for a positive and collaborative redescription is obvious. The literal past is always over but the symbolic retelling – and the elaboration of its personal meaning – remains the compelling task of the present and the future, and requires not only memory but also imagination. In this case the genre chosen supports the inner hope – for most fairy stories *do* have happy resolutions. The next chapter remains to be written.

However, the story has been also created for her fellow-students who sit and listen. The fairy tale is her formal introduction to the group. This is what she has chosen to bring to it. And here we can locate a crucial element in the transaction. The group – the first most intimate audience to the art-work – are being asked to witness the truth of the art – and to recognize its intimate relationship to her actual life. This would seem to involve a second vital distancing and placing. Already an object, standing free from the creator, the art now enters the collective arena. The simple performance – in this case, the reading out of the story – brings the work unequivocally into the collective imagination. This involves acts of cognition and recognition which may well be essential to any further development of the student as well as to the group. Here we are at the very heart of the dynamic which both holds the group together and, simultaneously, generates much of the vital symbolic material for subsequent artistic elaboration and reflection.

So the rhythm of Alex's work has moved from the act of making, to the act of presenting, to the act of witnessing by the group. And all of this, I want to suggest, not only contributes to the life of consciousness but, more immediately, *is* the life of consciousness as through the sequence of events it seeks ever more form, clarification and integration. I want to suggest that what we have here, as in so many similar art courses in our schools and colleges, is a minute, germinating, democratic culture moving, in an uncertain and fluid way, to self-knowledge. The small room in which the event is happening is, at best, a kind of cultural polis, a public arena in which the individuals in the group interact to recognize each other, challenge and extend each other's understanding, both of art and life. It is a Community of Recognition, through the arts.

However, the work is not coming out of the blue. It is not a 'happening'. It is not a chance event. It is not a natural eruption from the unconscious; it is more like a ritual and a cultural drama. The presentation has been invited as part of an educational programme grounded on a number of principles. These principles may never be fully formulated in the actual work – they may lie tacit and work at the level of guiding assumptions – yet they remain axiomatic to it. They form a paradigm at the base of the work. I would like to outline three of the key principles which, seen in reciprocal interaction, may further illuminate the encompassing context in which Alex is working and take us closer to the inner politics of arts education.

THE THREE PRINCIPLES OF EDUCATIONAL ACTIVITY

Education is existential in nature

That is the first principle. Put in a negative form, it means that education cannot take place against the intentions of the student or without his or her active participation. It is true that existence has become an unfashionable category, but it remains a primary one. The word existential derives from the Latin *existere* and means literally *to stand out*. Its original sense of *standing out* developed through the idea of *emerging* and *being visible* to that of *existing*. The verb indicates that as individuals we have to step out of the background of our lives into the foreground, that the mere fact of being alive is nothing. To exist is to make ourselves visible, to declare ourselves, to confess ourselves, to become the free and willing agents of our own actions and understanding. Just as no one can be ethically good for us or aesthetically experience for us, so no one can educationally learn for us. Learning may be released by a teacher but it can never be conferred – for it is not an object so much as a particular cast of mind, a creative and critical orientation towards experience. The student has to learn to become the protagonist of his or her own learning. This means that in the teaching of any intellectual or artistic discipline there must be open structures – gaps for the unknown, gaps for reflection, gaps for revision, gaps for contemplation, gaps for questions, gaps for the imagination, gaps for the Socratic *elenchus*[3] – gaps which constantly invite, provoke, and support the deep self-involvement of the student.

For this reason in my own teaching I always ask students who they are and what they wish to learn. I often invite the students to begin with autobiographical work – with the drama and the narrative of the self, with the fairy story by Alex. I begin with the individual having to stand out, having to shape something personal about themselves which cannot be taken out of the text-books nor relayed by anyone else in the group. If, as the novelist Milan Kundera has remarked, existence is being perpetually overlooked, then it is for the teacher to bring it back and make it the fine inner core of activity again.

According to the first principle, the teacher is a releaser, a midwife, aiming to give birth to existential acts of learning in the student.

Education is essentially a collaborative activity

This is the second principle; and it brings us at once to an obvious paradox. The individual to develop needs a community. In fact, the individual is inconceivable without the notion of others and of relationship with others. If the I exists it is because the we exists or in the rather more eloquent Swahili version: *I am because we are*. In Western culture the educational implications of this truth were first elaborated by Socrates and recorded in the philosophical plays of his student, Plato. For Socrates, the existential act of enquiry arises not in cultivated isolation, but in animated dialogue, in the disciplined narrative of conversation, in the careful exploration of opposed conceptions as uttered by various individuals engaged in the common pursuit of understanding. Learning becomes a philosophical drama between people who do not necessarily agree, but who wish to find out. Indeed, Socrates claimed that he could only think effectively when there was someone there offering a counter view.

Without a conversation to participate in, without the shock of difference, he regarded himself as intellectually sterile, a philosopher without an idea in his head. In the Socratic method the notion of truth is often confined to the logical development of concepts – this is one of its major critical limitations – but the principle of learning being an engagement not *in* but *between* people is seminal and one of the obvious foundations of the performing arts – for the performing arts are inherently collaborative in nature.

Such collaboration depends on trust that the collective pursuit is committed to the unknown outcome of the intellectual or artistic activity – concerned, that is to say, not with what is clearly partisan or narrowly ideological, but with the specific truth of what appears to be emerging in the creation of *this* argument or *this* particular piece of art-work or the contemplation of *this* fairy story, as it is being read by this student to this group, as it is happening between us *now*. The teacher must struggle to ensure that the activity is open, at least in principle, to all relevant perspectives, is always open to revision and is expressive of all those seriously engaged in it. This educational process is the very antithesis of a private activity. In the case of Socrates even his death – his death, most of all – provided both an existential opportunity and an absolute inner drama for collaborative enquiry.

The second principle, then, establishes the teacher as co-ordinator, conductor and democrat.

Education is always a cultural activity which has to be continuously deepened and extended

This is the third principle. It calls for a progressive initiation of the student into the culture of the discipline which extends and deepens the existential and collaborative process. The richer the cultural material, the greater the possible development. If, as Roger Scruton (1990) has argued, 'the immediacy of subjective awareness is an index of its emptiness' then to depend entirely on what has been existentially proffered or collaboratively worked on could easily result in an unremitting superficiality.

What has to be grasped is the intimate connection between symbol and consciousness. The more extensive and subtle the symbolism the greater the possibilities for the articulate flowering of consciousness. According to this third principle education exists to set up a conversation down the ages and across the cultures, across both time and space, so that students are challenged by other ways of understanding and, at the same time, acquire ever new materials – metaphors, models, ideas, images, narratives – for shaping and reshaping and testing their own lives. The third principle calls for endless acts of cultural re-incarnation – acts which enable students to see with new eyes, and to speak with new tongues. This merely extends the growing collaboration between the group to the whole of historic culture and brings the existential quest into relationship with all other such quests down the ages. Alex's work because it has chosen the genre of the fairy tale already operates inside the field of all other fairy-stories. It is already inside a cultural tradition. The task of teaching is to make the connections. Without this third principle, arts education could easily become a kind of free-wheeling Californian encounter group, limited to its own resources and its immediate assumptions and without any alternative wisdom or perspectives to draw on – and yet blissfully ignorant of its impoverishment.

Our third principle casts the teacher in the role of cultural guardian and initiator into the symbolic life, as connector and water-diviner.

The three principles acting together create the field of educational activity or so I believe. It is these principles which, though largely unformulated, have invisibly shaped the context in which Alex presents her work to the group for response and recognition. What, then, are the politics of the activity? They are the politics of education. The group regulates itself in a public space. It comes to its conclusions through the tangible presentation of art and the working through of arguments relating to its fitting interpretation. It makes its decisions openly and freely. The work involves acts of making, witnessing, and evaluating; it involves a dialectic of asking questions and examining answers. It also includes a serious engagement with some of the best answers given in the cultural inheritance – whether in the form of art or theory. And whatever is discovered remains always provisional, always open, at least, in principle to further experimentation or argument.

ARTS EDUCATION, MASS-CULTURE AND POSTMODERNISM

The Community of Recognition is, at its best and as a model, a small cultural democracy dedicated to art and enquiry. It is built on freedom, on personal engagement, on social collaboration, on cultural connection and the deep desire for transpersonal recognition. This, then, I would like to suggest is the politics of arts education and the social values intrinsic to its *modus operandi*. But what is the relationship of these politics to the mass-culture 'outside', to the dominant political reality and to the various claims made by the postmodernists? Is it possible to ground our educational politics in the wider social domain? And what are the implications for our teaching?

The prevailing democracy, in contrast to our Community of Recognition, would seem to be a rather abstract and over-centralized affair; its political life, except at the time of actual elections, is distant from the individual and most of its art seems to be slickly prefabricated in advance, requiring little personal response or recognition for its fulfilment. Most of mass-culture is manufactured purely to satisfy commercial ends and is as far removed from self-knowledge as an Amusement Arcade is from teaching philosophy. In the form of advertising much of it exists to indoctrinate while in the form of art much of it exists to anaesthetize, to arrest that active movement from diffuse self-consciousness to articulate self-awareness which is one of the principal aims of education to engender. It is characteristic of television and such video channels as MTV to be structured as seamless flows, endless streams of self-cancellation, with never a moment's gap to invite reflection or evaluation. Their very mode of presentation banishes the Socratic *elenchus*. In MTV an ever-dissolving sequence of images is hooked into a system of pre-critical sensations. Thus whatever enters the visual flow is immediately deprived of significance. As postmodernists have rightly observed this has led to a state where there is no meaning only simulacra – the problem with most postmodernists, however, is that they show us no way beyond this unprecedented crisis in representation. They elevate, rather than resolve it.

Most self-confessed postmodernists would seem to celebrate a free-wheeling cultural eclecticism with an ironic smile. The world is a carnival of changing images, sound-bites and endless quotations; it is a super-market of life-styles. Such a vision is regarded as the inevitable outcome of an advanced electronic age of communications: of the computer, of the word-processor, Internet, of television and video, where information generally floats free of its historic context and where art is presented as entertainment, often inseparable from advertising and general hype and where the two modes – of fact and fiction – all but co-exist. For the postmodernists all culture becomes a matter of style, display, appearance. Indeed, donning a glittering coat of irony some of them are quick to convert their own thinking into fashion and all of them would seem to espouse the relativism and eclecticism that informs the dominant consumer-culture.

The problem is that postmodernist thinking locks us even further into a mass-culture we need to be critical of. In essentially endorsing the status quo it deprives us of other ways of conceiving, imagining and desiring. If all cultural expressions are equal, if all differences are to be merged, if all classifications are to be de-classified, then we are robbed of a sense of significance and deprived, at once, of any real concept of education (such as defined earlier in my three axioms). For if all things are relative, there can be no leading out, no advance, no imaginative or intellectual accumulation. Yet this ignores the fact that we constantly make judgements and seek to validate them. Handling the arts in Higher Education we habitually define our responses in terms of structural form and human worth, of aesthetic and ethical significance, and find, again and again, a working consensus made vital by disagreement. It is precisely this critical activity which engenders a cast of mind which insists on discriminating, which establishes differences, which needs to classify. If all things are equal, nothing matters; and if nothing matters, the public space is quickly colonized by the most ruthless and the most rapacious, the thug and the quack. Inasmuch as postmodernism marks the end of a certain kind of modernism and the beginning of a sympathetic re-connection with the whole of historic culture, it is to be welcomed; but inasmuch as it marks a euphoric identification with mindless consumerism and a denial of transpersonal value and meaning it has to be severely questioned, even resisted.

Over ten years ago Neil Postman (1985) in his brilliant study *Amusing Ourselves To Death* took the city of Las Vegas as the icon of today's international culture, glossily alive with an endless stream of manipulated desire. What Postman saw rapidly emerging, through the shaping power of television, was a culture in which all public discourse had become a mode of entertainment, where all symbolic life was a variant of show business. 'Cosmetics', he wrote laconically, 'has replaced ideology';

and went on to point out that 'censorship is not a necessity when all political life takes the form of a jest' (Postman, 1985). The evidence of such a society is all around us. We have only to open our eyes to begin to chronicle it. What matters for us as arts teachers is a clear recognition of the nature of the loss.

Most of mass-culture is a surrogate culture. It robs its citizens of the materials they most need for the fulfilment of their freedom. It also tends to rob them of all the other cultural visions they need to keep their reflection bright and their minds expansive. In his Foreword to *Brave New World,* Aldous Huxley (1946) wrote: 'a really efficient totalitarian state would be one in which the all-powerful executive of political bosses and their army of managers control a population of slaves who do not have to be coerced, because they love their servitude'. Such a totalitarian society would not feel like one, of course. It would talk of, even parade, its freedom and its happiness.

Yet, at the same time, it would seem equally clear that the dominant democratic society *does* allow for freedom of thought and argument and *does* protect many individual rights. The strength of these legally encoded rights is that they protect the individual from abuse; but their weakness is that they invariably operate outside a positive conception of the good society. In their formulation they do not affirm the social and cultural conditions within which individual rights can be best realized. During the last two decades driven by vast technological and economic powers an international culture has emerged which is dedicated almost exclusively to the making of profits and the frenetic buying and selling of goods and services. While the 'pursuit of happiness' has become a private matter, the public spaces have become colonized by market forces. That space for the transpersonal – that arena where the personal and collective meet to animate each other – has closed in and virtually disappeared. In the emerging consumer-civilization, the old public spaces have been ravaged by market forces and are desperately occupied by the new dispossessed, and the private spaces, especially where they are opulent, are defended with iron spikes, grids, alarm systems, barking Alsatians and rented guards. We find not the drama of collaboration, but the drama of division; not a common community but a society riven by sub-cultures and carved up divisively by market managers into commercial niches. (This, as I implied earlier, is the economic condition for any cultural insights provided by the postmodernists).

In such a civilization the appeal to democratic values, while not exactly false, becomes deeply unconvincing. The liberal rhetoric fails to match the collective reality. It is as if from under the proclamation of human rights – partly articulated in the eighteenth century by educated gentlemen with the Greek *polis* in mind – there has grown a smooth over-arching managerial culture disseminated by global organizations, with a dramatically different set of symbols, values, relationships and expectations. This system does not deny the traditional democratic rights deriving from the Enlightenment, but under and over them spins a different kind of culture, based on leisure, consumption, services, life-style, display, appearance and the endless competition for markets. In the new society, there is a danger that freedom becomes largely confined to a choice between supermarkets, items and brand names; that happiness becomes reformulated as the need for fun (and the display of style) and the citizen is recast as consumer or customer.

THE POLITICS OF ARTS EDUCATION

Against the current erosions of meaning and value we can begin to see more clearly the seminal value of the politics of art teaching. The Community of Recognition provides a truer sense of democracy and a richer sense of participatory culture, a culture closer to the primary processes of making, presenting and evaluating and directed by the need for exploration and social confirmation. The teaching of the arts offers not only a democratic model but also a vivid apprenticeship into the making and sharing of embodied meaning and the making and sharing of collaborative relationships. Furthermore, it is not difficult to root this practice in a long tradition of thinking which has been concerned to place freedom within the embodied life of culture and community. This tradition has been represented by such educationists as Josiah Royce, John Dewey and Maxine Greene and by such thinkers as Hannah Arendt, Jürgen Habermas and Charles Taylor. It has one of its major sources in the philosophical writings of Hegel. For in Hegel's philosophy a primary significance is given to the place of recognition in the continuous making of culture – in the Hegelian myth the Slave discovers his repressed humanity and triumphs over his hedonistic Master through labour and the art of making, which releases the power of reflection and a growing sense of autonomy. Not only is there a right to private property and the free expression of opinion in Hegel but these rights are placed in a broader culture which seeks its own fullest realization. At the base there is the freedom for the market, but at the apex there is the freedom for the collaborative pursuit of meaning and the articulation of the spirit. It is the latter qualitative freedom (embodied in the life of a real culture, within a public space) that is so absent in postmodernist thinking and one of the proper functions of the community of learning should be to represent and reanimate it.

Hannah Arendt (1961) in *Between Past and Future* offered this description of politics:

> If, then, we understand the political in the sense of the polis, its end or raison d'être would be to establish and keep in existence a space where freedom as virtuosity can appear. This is the realm where freedom is a worldly reality, tangible in words which can be heard, in deeds which can be seen, and in events which are talked about, remembered, and turned into stories before they are finally incorporated into the great storybook of human history. Whatever occurs in this space of appearances is political by definition, even when it is not a direct product of action.

I want to suggest that Hannah Arendt's formulation illuminates both the democratic nature of the good society and also acts as an eloquent description of the Community of Recognition through the arts. There is, then, a broader political tradition in which our model of arts learning can be grounded and, if my brief description of today's society is at all accurate, its political value and cultural role must be only too clear.

Indeed, one could imagine a social experiment where Communities of Recognition might exist not only in our Universities and Colleges but, more freely, more daringly, in unexpected places – in empty factories, in unused warehouses, in corrugated huts, in disused or half-used churches and chapels and drawing in the dispossessed, the unemployed, the socially disaffected. Such communities in the making would draw on the skills of art-makers and set in motion new patterns of learning and creative expression.[4] They might re-activate in the heart of the social wilderness a sense of community and the deep satisfaction of culture-making.

But, more conventionally, within the curriculum of higher education we must work to see that the teaching of the arts is systematically grounded in aesthetic experience and in those universal conditions of open and collaborative enquiry which I have attempted to define and illustrate in this essay.

After writing and presenting her story about her own life with its suppression of freedom, Alex had declared: 'The writer may only hope that the future will provide a concluding part to his story in which he might be transformed from a pathetic victim of circumstances into a triumphant hero and might live happily ever after.' Such a hope and such a desire for freedom must also provide the political energy behind good arts teaching and take us beyond the fashionable but shallow claims of postmodernism.

NOTES

1 *Language, Arts and Education* , MA Course, The Institute of Education, University of Sussex, UK.
2 From Alex's unpublished fairy story written as the autobiographical presentation at the beginning of the course.
3 *Elenchus* is the concept used to characterize the system of cleansing the mind through the method of casting doubt on received opinion.
4 For a fuller understanding of the nature of the aesthetic in arts education see *The Falmer Press Library on Aesthetic Education* and also Peter Abbs, *The Educational Imperative: A Defence of Socratic and Aesthetic Learning*, London, Falmer Press, 1994.

ELEVEN

A New University Space: A Dialogue on Argument, Democracy and the University

George Myerson

INTRODUCTION

Democracy requires argument, and a good democracy requires good argument. But what makes a good argument? Participation is important, free and open access to discussion; but information is also important. Must good argument produce consensus? Must good argument be 'balanced' between different views? How does 'the better argument' emerge? The questions are theoretical, but the answers have practical consequences, because argument also requires *institutions*. Should the institutions of argument encourage compromise? Who should have access to the institutions of argument, and who must be excluded? How are experts to interact with lay participants? What relationship should exist between public argument and advanced research?

Argument is a controversial subject in contemporary thought. How much can be expected of argument, and where are the limits to argument? This chapter considers argument and democracy from the perspective of the university. Universities are institutions for arguing, among other things. But what kinds of argument should universities encourage? And where are the limits to influence over the argumentative processes within the university, processes central both to teaching and to the university's own organization? The university is a symbolic institution. Its future represents an idea, about reason and modern society (Barnett 1990). Universities are one embodiment of society's sense of reason, and of rational argument.

Many practical questions arise, about how universities teach argument (Andrews 1995: 138–47). In this chapter, I propose to stand back and consider the principles of argument and reason, and how they relate to conceptions of the university, the idealized university. I shall work by contrasts, between different theories. The aim is to construct a hypothetical dialogue (Myerson 1995). The form contains my general claim that only dialogue can adequately express the idea of the argumentative university. What is the point of general theory, and theory that issues in dialogue, not in a concrete proposal? The dialogue is intended to contribute, in its way, to resisting a process summarized critically by Barnett (1994: 61) as 'the substitution of technique for insight; of strategic reason for communicative reason; and of behaviour for wisdom.'

The dialogue has several voices. First, I shall interpret some ideas of Derrida, ideas which apply to argument and higher education. Derrida is famously, or notoriously, the proponent of 'deconstruction', which always makes him sound destructive. Indeed he is critical, sceptical, resistant to other people's solutions, whatever the subject. 'Deconstruction' is also commonly associated with literary theory and philosophy, the close analysis of how texts defeat their own ends. But Derrida has consistently explored the idea of the university, and he has a deep commitment to its past and future (Derrida 1980, 1983, 1992). Then I shall introduce Hilary Putnam, specifically as a critic of Derrida, a critic from an analytic tradition opposed to deconstruction. Putnam's work suggests another approach to argument and higher education, an approach contrary to Derrida. No 'common ground' appears. I shall not be reconciling the opposites! But I do not *need* deconstruction and analytical philosophy to agree: the aim is to advance a dialogue, not propose a resolution. To compound the dialogue, I shall also consider briefly the contrast between Derrida and Habermas, who is neither analytical nor deconstructive. Habermas presents a social theory of argumentative rationality and has his own objections to Derrida.

DERRIDA, ARGUMENT AND THE UNIVERSITY

> Contradiction: I do not wish to be independent; I do not wish to be what I am. ... This contradiction is unintelligible; its economy surpasses understanding; no formal logic can master or resolve it. (Derrida 1974: 18)

To all but enthusiasts, Derrida is frustrating. His style is both combative and opaque. He announces dead-ends as if they were advances. In the specimen above, we wonder how Derrida is assured that 'no formal logic' applies to his chosen contradiction. The sweep is grand, and grandly negative. Furthermore Derrida attracts commentaries that are equally frustrating: definitions of *his* definitions, celebrations of his dead-ends.

Why begin with Derrida then? He has a knack of awkward questions, including awkward questions about argument and the university. The questions are deconstructive in spirit. Derrida looks at how ideals undermine themselves, for instance the ideal of auton-omy in the passage above. He applies the same approach to the ideal university. The out-come is provocative, questioning: certainly, it is not 'constructive', but then Derrida shows repeatedly how people overvalue constructiveness. A dialogue needs a provocative start, and the dialogue on the argumentative university is no exception. Indeed a dialogue *about* argument is in particular need of an intellectual objector, and no objector is more conscientious than Derrida.

I am not proposing a 'Derridian' approach to universities and democracy, nor 'applying' Derrida's style of thought. I wish to extract a few questions from Derrida, and I take them as they stand, without trying to insert them into his larger scheme. The result is itself 'un-Derridian', but I think the questions are worth consideration. Then I shall look elsewhere for a constructive response to Derrida's dilemmas and warnings, and particu-larly to Hilary Putnam.

Given his oblique style, one might distrust Derrida's commitment to understanding and exchange. But he always looks to dialogue, however imperfect and difficult (Derrida 1983). Derrida is not 'against' communication. On the contrary, he celebrates dialogue and interaction. Derrida endorses human dialogue: dialogue is the basic impulse:

> the problem that I wish to raise. It concerns an irreducible experience of language, that which links it to the liaison, to commitment, to the command or to the promise; before and beyond all theoretico-constatives, opening, embracing, or including them, there is the affirmation of language. The 'I am addressing you'. (Derrida 1992: 60–1)

The tone is characteristic: he wishes to interrupt, to raise a problem, to insert a difficulty. But then he is definitive, almost ecstatic: 'an irreducible experience' is proclaimed. How is it 'irreducible'? How does he know what comes 'before and beyond' everything else in language? So the effect is frustrating in detail.

But there is also a challenge: consider language as if there were an original greeting, an act of address that preceded everything else, all content, all ideas, all description, all per-suasions or requests. The view is strangely romantic, 'I am addressing you' is a *feeling* at the heart of language. Derrida discerns a value in communication, in dialogue. However, for our current purposes, he denies that this dialogic value is identical with rational argu-ment or critical reasoning, or with any language dependent on 'theoretico-constatives', propositions, reasons and assertions. Dialogue affirms: 'I am addressing you'. The value of dialogue is deeper than discursive norms or rational standards. Address is present in the very beginning of language; ideas and arguments come later.

Argument depends on 'theoretico-constatives', 'this is how the world is', 'here are my reasons', 'this is the evidence', 'here are the facts'. Derrida believes these are secondary effects: 'before and beyond' them is address, 'I am addressing you'. Rational argument does not reach to the roots of language: the depths belong to other communicative forces and impulses present in dialogue, particularly the impulse to address the other person, and to be recognized in return. Yet Derrida also feels the allure of disputation, the idealized play of ideas which is one understanding of argument, for him the most appealing project of Europe, despite its flaws.

Derrida considers the university as a communicative enterprise. His starting-point is an ideal, almost a romantic ideal of contact and address. At the heart of language, the self reaches out to an addressee, the other person. Communication raises ethical questions: 'what is it "to respond"? To respond to? To be responsible for? To respond for? To respond, be responsible, before?' (Derrida 1992: 53).

Derrida sees that argument is definitive for the university, that it is always looking towards a principle of rational exchange (Derrida 1983). Derrida understands the hope of an argumentative university. If any phrase stands a chance of promoting the ideal of higher education, surely it is 'free and open discussion' (Derrida 1992: 43). But what makes an argument free? When is an argument fair? Derrida makes his 'deconstructive' turn. The ideal contains its own undoing:

> The best intentioned of European projects, those that are quite apparently and explicitly pluralistic, democratic, and tolerant, may try, in this lovely competition for the 'conquests of spirit(s)' to impose the homogeneity of a medium, of discursive norms and models. (Derrida 1992: 54)

For Derrida, free and fair argument *is* 'the best intentioned of European projects', both politically and culturally. He half-celebrates argument's 'lovely competition', for is not the conquest of spirits preferable to other kinds of conquest? Is higher education not the privileged space of this 'lovely competition'?

But Derrida is cautious. He senses a paradox in free and fair argument, a deconstructive tension. The ideal is attractive; its attractiveness is its undoing. For free debate justifies many measures of restraint and regulation. To be free and fair, rules are needed. But rules are potentially oppressive, particularly if they are rigid. Yet how could fair argument be guaranteed unless the rules by which it were conducted were rigid? Argument needs 'discursive norms', does it not. Arguers must take their turns; points must be relevant, tones reasonable. Or are these 'norms' too repressive?

Derrida does not deny that the 'competition' of ideas places limitations on the participants. The problem is: who decided the rules, and what side-effects will they have? Derrida sees universities as spaces for the lovely competition:

> For it is necessary that we learn to detect in order then to resist, new forms of cultural take-over. This can also happen through a new university space, and especially through a philosophical discourse. Under the pretext of pleadings for transparency (along with 'consensus', 'transparency' is one of the master words of the 'cultural' discourse I just mentioned), for the univocity of democratic discussion, for communication in public space, for 'communicative action', such a discourse tends to impose a model of language that is supposedly favourable to this communication. (Derrida 1992: 54–5)

One contentious phrase is 'cultural take-over'. How could free and fair argument result in 'cultural take-over'? Derrida suggests that a definition of argument might include 'transparency', which is clarity. There must also be the desire to communicate, but, more than that, arguers must be open. They must not conceal motives of meanings. In fair argument, the parties would be open about their points of view. The definition sounds persuasive. But, asks Derrida, can all perspectives be conveyed through transparent communication? Indeed *can* views be transparent? Derrida assumes an adversary who believes that a criterion for good argument might be the pursuit of consensus. But, he asks, whose consensus will it be? Will not the question of consensus remain part of the argument, not an end to arguing?

One problem is that Derrida is also arguing with Habermas, as proponent of 'communicative action'. Typically, he does not acknowledge the particular context, but alludes in passing. The 'debate' between Derrida and Habermas has generally been frustrating, with half-engagements of 'scandals' on either side. Habermas is well able to defend himself, of course, and I have chosen in this chapter to circumvent this contest, and look instead to other contexts. But I shall consider a 'Habermasian' perspective as part of my wider conclusion. However, it is already evident that Derrida is dismissing many possibilities rather easily. Could we really do without criteria like clarity or reasonableness in establishing democratic discussion and argument? Yet I think a question can be extracted, perhaps at odds with Derrida's spirit of provocative comprehensiveness.

The question is: can we be sure to apply criteria democratically in establishing the context of argumentative exchange? Transparency may be desirable, as far as possible: but how far it is possible may be the subject under discussion. Willingness to agree may also be desirable, but parties may differ about agreement, what counts as agreement. So I would translate Derrida's questions, and ask about the criteria for applying criteria to arguments. Derrida tries to demolish the first-order criteria of evaluating arguments; but instead we could ask: what are the second-order criteria, the standards for judging the application of rules?

A NEW UNIVERSITY SPACE

Derrida (1992: 54) posits 'a new university space' in Europe, across the EC and perhaps also in the former 'East'. His approach is again allusive and general, but his reference seems to be to what he perceives as new styles of administered education. I think Derrida is trying to articulate an anxiety, strike a chord, rather than to specify a problem. The university must change: that is the agenda under discussion (Gibbons *et al.* 1994; Barnett 1994). Some respond hopefully; others are more reserved. Derrida recognizes the hope, and speaks to the reservation.

Gibbons *et al.* (1994: 19) embody the hope: 'The production of knowledge is advancing into a new phase'. The ideal is a wider and wider discussion, 'Participation in the increasing flow of information' (Gibbons *et al.* 1994: 64). The claim is eloquent, a new university in a web of wider dialogues. Derrida voices fears and doubts. This university space will be regulated, he fears, in ways which repress the place of ideal. He is not talking about state censorship here. On the contrary, the regulation will be internal, and precisely in the name of free and fair debate, of transparent and constructive debate. Universities will try harder and harder to live up to the ideal, and the more they try, the less they will succeed. The paradox emerges: may not the very idea of argument be used to rule out of court many viewpoints, since they are views which cannot express themselves in the acceptable terms?

I do not find the view convincing as a description of current realities: no one is imposing rules of proper argument either on teaching or on organizational discussion. But, typically, Derrida catches a recognizable anxiety, over-emphatically. One can imagine the scenario. Under pressure for efficiency and cost effectiveness, pressure from what Galbraith (1992: 11) calls 'the dynamic of bureaucracy', an attempt is made to codify intellectual practice, so that it may be economical and rational, value for money. In good faith, codes of argument are drawn up. They will make sure that universities are functioning networks of thought: 'managing the national innovation system is essentially about developing human resources' (Gibbons *et al.* 1994: 64).

No one is proposing detailed 'argument regulations'. Derrida is referring to a more diffuse process of adjustment, under the sign of modernization, being up-to-date, competitive in the knowledge market. There may emerge a kind of moral agenda designed to balance a shift towards economic agendas. Derrida is half-sympathetic to these needs, but he sees a danger. The more the argument is codified, the more the rules will determine which views are represented. In an attempt to underwrite a fair hearing, the code may exclude views which fail the basic tests of argumentation, say tests of transparency or willingness to reach agreement ('reasonableness').

In an atmosphere of codification, argument is subject to regulation, and the regulations close the space they were meant to open. Philosophically, 'transparency' and 'reasonableness' are defensible criteria, as Habermas and others maintain. I do not find Derrida's general scepticism compelling. But I think his specific doubts about institutions are worth pondering. In a context of other processes of rationalization, would reasonableness be defined in a sufficiently open-ended way? How are we to design the second-order criteria, such that argument is as diverse and wide-ranging as possible? We must, according to Derrida (1992: 55), begin by acknowledging that fair exchange may, ironically, be imposed by 'certain institutional powers'. Yet he knows about 'nationalistic tensions' (1992: 58), voices that do not wish simply to debate, but to end the debate by force. As Derrida asks (1992: 53): 'What is it "to respond"? To respond to'?: particularly in the face of threat, there is no easy answer. And that is the point: we must not be tempted to formalize the insoluble, to substitute rules for dilemmas.

Derrida thinks universities are important. He is critical of the university's past, and he is sceptical about the future; but he is an insider, and anxious participant. Derrida asks if the university can even be discussed coherently:

Could we understand ourselves, so as to debate about the responsibility proper to the university? I am not asking myself whether we could produce or simply spell out a consensus on this subject. I am asking myself beforehand if we could say we and debate together, in a common language, about the general forms of responsibility in this area. Of this I am not sure, and herein lies a being-ill doubtless more grave than a malady or a crisis. (Derrida 1980: 7)

Who will discuss the university? What language applies to the topic? The passage is characteristic: spontaneous and gloomy! But Derrida is committed to the university, and he wants to discuss it, although he is sceptical about the discussion.

Again, I think we can translate the question into more constructive terms. There need be no insurmountable barrier to advancing the debate, as Derrida seems to imply. The issue again is the second-order, the standards for assessing the argumentative criteria themselves, the way the argument is conducted. It will not be enough to measure cases for transparency and reasonableness. A more holistic ethic is implied. The second-order may also concern expertise and information: is the debate open to the appropriate kinds of expertise and is there space for criticism? I want now to consider alternative approaches to argument and reason, and how they might influence institutional arrangements for a democratic university space. My theme follows from the dialogue with Derrida: how to conceive a second-order assessment of standards used in regulating debate.

PUTNAM AND ARGUMENT

I begin with a glimpse into the complex philosophy of Hilary Putnam, a philosophy emerging from an American analytic tradition. Putnam imagines a dispute about reason. The parties are Cardinal Newman and Rudolf Carnap. The disagreement is drastic, because they disagree about arguing itself:

> The conception of rationality of a John Cardinal Newman is obviously quite different from that of a Rudolph Carnap. It is highly unlikely that either could have convinced the other, had they lived at the same time and been able to meet. (Putnam 1981: 136)

When people disagree about rationality, they differ about rational argument. No one can offer them a neutral definition of rationality:

> The question: which *is the rational conception of rationality itself* is difficult in *exactly* the way that the justification of an ethical system is difficult. There is no *neutral* conception of rationality to which the appeal.

For my present argument, they key word is 'difficult'. Decisions are not impossible: he believes that we can often judge. But when parties disagree about reason itself, the judgement is difficult. *Above all, we must not pretend our judgement is 'neutral'.* We endorse one or other side, or neither: we are not above the dispute.

Someone mediates between the parties. Perhaps a third party defines their positions:

> One might attempt various conventionalist moves here, for example saying that 'justified/Carnap' is one 'property' and 'justified/Newman' is a different 'property', and that a 'subjective value judgement' is involved in the decision to mean 'justified/Carnap' or 'justified/Newman' by the word 'justified' but that no value judgement is involved in stating the fact that a given statement S is justified/Carnap or justified/Newman. (Putnam 1981: 136)

An outsider describes what each party means by 'justified'. However Putnam believes that no one can describe neutrally the conflict about reason: 'But from whose standpoint is the word "fact" being used'?, he demands (ibid.). Neutrality is impossible, even a neutral description.

Is Putnam saying that disagreements cannot be judged? No: they cannot be judged *neutrally*. We apply criteria, which he calls 'cognitive values', values like 'coherence'. Cognitive values are part of 'human flourishing': alone, they make no sense. Putnam (1981: 148) advocates his own 'ideal of human flourishing'. We must 'reject (some) ideals of human flourishing as wrong, as infantile, as sick, as one-sided'. For Putnam human flourishing includes human dialogue:

> We are not trapped in individual solipsistic hells, but invited to engage in a truly human dialogue; one which combines collectivity with individual responsibility. (Putnam 1981: 216)

By whom are we 'invited' to converse? The invitation is complex. People invite each other into a discussion. But the issues themselves are inviting, they demand dialogue.

'Human flourishing' eludes statement. Although Putnam does believe in rules, including rules of rationality the rules cannot be rigid or fixed. Putnam argues that people *make* rules, and rule-making is a process:

> The central purpose of Kant's ethical writing, in fact, is not to issue detailed rules at all but to give us a normative picture of the activity of arriving at such rules (Putnam 1990: 197)

To codify argument removes a major subject of arguing: the rules of discussion. The ideal is powerful. Invite people into the discussion, and include the rules as a subject. Some rules already exist, and we should use them to stimulate dialogue. The more important the rule, the more urgent the discussion about how to express it, when to apply it, whether to qualify it. Rules are dialogic:

> Rules (from the Decalogue to the ERA) are important because they are the main mechanisms we have for challenging (and, if we are successful, shaping) one another's consciences. (Putnam 1990: 195; ERA = Equal Rights Amendment)

Through dialogue, we take rules seriously: rules should not be beyond our arguments, but within them.

Putnam shows how difficult it will be to develop second-order criteria of argument, criteria for assessing the assessment of a debate. He believed that there are standards, but that these standards are entwined together with other values. Therefore, the second-order is part of the whole cultural context. There are no technical solutions, no expert standards of assessment which are distinct from general values and visions.

A THEORETICAL CONVERSATION

Now consider the impact between Putnam and Derrida. Putnam passionately disagrees with Derrida about the problems of argument affecting education and intellectual practice. Putnam addresses Derrida:

> In the opinion of most analytic philosophers, trying to criticize Derrida is like trying to have a fistfight with a fog. Indeed, although Derrida does not disdain argument, some of his followers seem to scorn it. The very habit of arguing in a close analytic fashion is seen by many deconstructionists as a sign that one is 'out of it'. (Putnam 1992: 109).

Putnam fears that by casting doubt on argumentative procedures, Derrida encourages his 'followers' to despise arguing. From the educational point of view, the next point made by Putnam is crucial:

> These followers interpret Derrida as teaching that logic and standards of rightness are themselves repressive. ... In certain ways, one can understand the reasons for this inter-pretation. Traditional beliefs include much that is repressive (think of traditional beliefs about various races, about women, about workers, about gays). Our 'standards' require not only rational reconstruction but criticism. But criticism requires argument, not the abandonment of argument. (Putnam 1992: 130)

Putnam senses in Derrida a recoil from 'logic and standards of rightness', at least the po-tential for such a recoil. We saw that Derrida is indeed suspicious of criteria such as 'transparency' and 'consensus' in argument, though these terms are more subtle than the term 'logic' and 'rightness' attributed to him by Putnam. Putnam concedes that Derrida is subtle, but worries about his influence on others. For Putnam also believes argument is the vehicle of change and improvement. In the past, authority has often misappropriated the rational space and forged the outcomes of argument; but without argument, change is impossible. Therefore, for Putnam, to abandon faith in argument is to abandon hope of improvement.

Putnam pursues his case against Derrida's influence:

> The problem is that notwithstanding certain moments of argument, the thrust of Der-rida's writing is that notions of 'justification', 'good reason', 'warrant', and the like are primarily repressive gestures. (Putnam 1992: 132)

The key is 'primarily': Putnam concedes that argumentative standards *may* be repressive: but he denies that these standards are always repressive. Argument, says Putnam, is ra-tional and equitable at heart, though anything good can be distorted or misused. There are areas of overlap between Putnam and Derrida. Putnam does not urge 'transparency', so he is not directly in Derrida's line of fire. And Derrida is too subtle, as Putnam concedes, to fall into the trap of arguing while denying the value of argument. Nevertheless, they di-verge: Putnam advocates something close to 'discursive norms' of argument, flexible norms admittedly, and Derrida suspects that discursive norms repress dissent and difference.

Putnam's academy would be a place of free and fair argument. Guiding values support the exchange, values always open to discussion themselves. The second-order would be an open-ended agenda – there could be no fixed rules for assessing the standards applied to particular disputes. Putnam's academy is argument-centred, but his philosophy precludes a fixed code of argument. Putnam uses the 'search' as metaphor for intellectual practice:

> cognitive values are arbitrary considered as anything but a part of a holistic conception of human flourishing. Bereft of the old realist idea of truth as 'correspondence' and of the positivist idea of justification as fixed by public criteria, we are left with the necessity of seeing our search for better conceptions of rationality as an intentional human activity, which, like every activity that rises above habit and the mere following of inclination or obsession, is guided by our idea of the good. (Putnam 1981: 136)

Putnam recommends a holistic conception, not a set of procedures; he points towards our idea of the good, not a list of good practices. Arguments should be guided by arguable ideas, not by mechanisms, Putnam also argues against public criteria. They are self-refuting: no public criterion enforces public criteria. Putnam's work points towards argument, argument as a self-determining search, regulated from within.

ARGUMENT: A PROBLEM OF EVALUATION

Derrida warns that the fairest arguments are limited, and that when universities require fair argument, they may act oppressively. Putnam disagrees with Derrida about argument. Putnam does believe in fair argument: it is a necessary ideal. However, Putnam too suggests why arguing eludes easy regulation. Both deconstruction and analytical liberalism provide reasons not to regulate argument rigorously. Derrida and Putnam each suggest that there should be no code of argumentative practice, whatever other codes are necessary. Derrida and Putnam *are* antithetical. But both thinkers provide good grounds to resist the codifying of argument, to be sceptical about externally regulating the exchange of ideas. On other codes, Putnam and Derrida might often coincide, endorsing measures against racism and sexism. Neither writer's work suggests support for a bureaucratic code to govern argumentative practice.

The dialogue also invites a Habermasian perspective. Habermas's work requires fuller contextualization than is appropriate to a short speculation. But I do not think his contribution would promote the detailed regulation of argument by any fixed code. Quite the contrary. Habermas propounds a complex theory of language and communication. His theory grounds argument in the fundamental structures of communication:

> This concept of *communicative rationality* carries with it connotations based ultimately on the central experience of the unconstrained, unifying, consensus-bringing force of argumentative speech. (Habermas 1984: 10)

Habermas is not advocating external codes for regulating argument. The standards are implicit in the process of communication itself. We need to draw out these implicit standards, and to embody them constructively. But we do not need to invent regulations for the efficiency of arguing. In fact, Habermas is deeply critical of misplaced instrumental standards, more profoundly perhaps than Derrida. Habermas advocates a deep regard for the living process of arguing, and its organic contexts. One could disagree with Habermas's depiction of culture and communication:

> Certainly, some cultures have had more practice than others at distancing themselves from themselves. But all languages offer the possibility of distinguishing between what is true and what we hold to be true. The *supposition* of a common objective world is built into the pragmatics of every single linguistic usage. And the dialogue roles of every speech situation enforce a symmetry in participant perspectives. (Habermas 1992: 138)

But clearly Habermas sees standards as organic to the process of communication.

Habermas does seek criteria for assessing argument and its social contexts. He goes further than Putnam, certainly than Derrida: his 'unconstrained, unifying, consensus-bringing force' does translate into an evaluative programme. But the programme stops short of a set of rules. We might consider some questions; is the context constraining? Are the arguers seeking consensus, as far as possible? (Derrida would dissent.) But even for Habermas, we can only assess argument by developing a deep inwardness, a communicative practice attuned to different contexts. No one can just list the rules for ruling on argument, on what is a fair and good debate. Indeed Habermas's whole theory testifies to the difficulty of defining second order criteria for assessing the standards applied to debate in any given context. He adopts a systematic mode, but behind the system is an experience, 'the central experience of ... argumentative speech' (Myerson 1994). Habermas advocates *lived* standards, the very reverse of bureaucratic regulations.

The hypothetical dialogue does not issue in agreement between Derrida, Putnam and Habermas. Common ground is elusive, at most a shared concern with the futures of reason. But I think each thinker cautions us, in a different way, not to believe that it is easy to regulate an institution whose rationale is argument. I believe Derrida is too ready to dismiss the obvious requirements of good argument, but I also think he is right to ask sharp questions about the whole process of institutional regulation for an argumentative space. Putnam is more precise about why it is difficult to regulate the standards applied to argumentative differences. Habermas would supply a still more profound sense of how argumentative practice is intertwined in the developments of culture and communication.

My conclusion is that it is worthwhile to ponder the distinction between first-order standards of argument and the second-order assessment of how standards apply in an institution. The problem is most acute for universities, because of their symbolic significance, as a home of reasoned discourse. It is important to be patient with the difficulties in defining regulations for argument, particularly when in practice some standards do seem urgently required by universities. Two reactions are possible to difficulties in formulating the rules for democratic discourse and procedure: one would be a permissive, almost anarchic response to difficulty in legislating for universities as contexts for argument; and the other that of pre-emptive rigidity. A third reaction is dialogue. A 'new university space' demands continuing dialogue about the principles of argument. The dialogue will not resolve the dilemmas of argument, but it is the way to live with them.

TWELVE

Truth, Identity and Community in the University

Nigel Blake

POSTMODERN SUBVERSION OF THE MODERN UNIVERSITY

Modern foundations

The idea is around that we currently face a 'crisis in knowledge', provoked by new ideas and projects loosely associated with postmodernism; and that entails a crisis for higher education. 'Postmodernist' developments have prompted doubts on many fronts as to the status and even validity of our deepest assumptions about knowledge. And if knowledge is in question, so too must be the institutions which formulate, preserve and transmit it.

It is not obvious, though, why a supposed 'crisis in knowledge' should constitute a challenge to the universities. First, it is not clear whether the crisis really is a crisis. It is not as if we have discovered that academics do not actually know anything or can no longer distinguish between better and worse academic work. No 'crisis in knowledge' could ever be that deep. We take contemporary doubts seriously precisely because so many are well-argued and seemingly well-founded. They look like *contributions* to knowledge, as much as assaults upon it. *Pace* the deconstructionists, we do not face a complete failure of knowledge on all fronts.

None the less, such doubts as there are confront individual academics with serious challenges. For instance, feminism, post-structuralism and anti-foundationalist shifts in methodology and philosophy all have deep intellectual implications. But it is not obvious that they have institutional implications. Why should the social or political position of academics change, or their relations with each other and their students, or those of students with each other? Why might the syllabus need re-examination, or teaching methods? I want to broach these institutional questions here.

I suggest that at least three assumptions typically inform the institutional organization of universities, concerning disciplinarity, autonomy and authority. Notwithstanding openness to interdisciplinarity, the basic units of the university still tend to be its disciplinary groups. And the autonomy which disciplines typically claim for themselves is not just social and institutional, but epistemological autonomy. They claim their own domain of interest, methods and methodologies, concepts and theories. Thus, it is 'bad form' for a philosopher to take a sociologist to task and vice-versa, unless the other has strayed into her field.

The presumption of autonomy seemingly legitimizes the authority of an academic. Her expert understanding of the potential and the limits of her autonomous discipline wins for her institutional authority – a right to resist critique from outside the discipline. This same authority informs her academic relationship to students. Academics have diminished authority outside their own field.

However, the mutual independence of disciplines does have an important positive aspect. The full realm of knowledge can seemingly grow simultaneously, because the disciplines are mutually autonomous. Growth in one discipline does not impede or counteract growth in any other. Advances in all disciplines contribute to the growth of knowledge. They can therefore be conceived as cognate activities in one unified enterprise.

The consequences of these three assumptions for the internal organization of universities do not need labouring. Let us rather look in a different direction, to the conception of knowledge underlying these assumptions; knowledge as a representation of objective truth.

Richard Rorty has pointed to a potent metaphor informing this conception; the figure of 'the mind as the mirror of nature' (Rorty 1980; see Introduction and passim). Western culture since the pre-Socratics has been predicated on a split between subjects and objects: on the one hand, entities characterized, individuated and identified by their particular experiences, and on the other, entities which do not have experience but which are themselves experienced by subjects. Subjects are usually taken to maintain social relations with each other.

Knowledge is then thought of as representation; as an image of the objective or social world, in the mirror of a subject's consciousness. It is passive inasmuch as the world is what it is. A subject cannot control what images form in his metaphorical mirror. The challenge is for men to eradicate error by working on their failings as individual knowing subjects – 'getting more accurate representations by inspecting, repairing and polishing the mirror' (Rorty 1980: 12). Rorty suggests that modern (or

Cartesian) epistemology, from Descartes to the mid-twentieth century, simply tried to put philosophical flesh on these metaphorical bones.

If the mind is indeed a Cartesian mirror of nature, then (to switch metaphors) nature is the *foundation* of knowledge and the structure of knowledge will reflect the supposed objective structure of this foundation. And it has seemed, until recently, a given of the structure of knowledge that images in the mirror of nature cluster themselves into closely interrelated groups, the disciplines, which have little to do with images in other clusters. For instance, ethics is just a radically different formation of knowledge from mathematics, and it is pointless to try to explain this.

Now, if the disciplines really are 'givens', we can explain their autonomy. If knowledge mirrors reality and reality is in itself coherent, there can be no contradiction between true items of knowledge, regardless of their discipline. It follows that different disciplines must be compatible but independent, and thus autonomous. And their autonomy is properly enshrined in and protected by institutional arrangements within universities. Disciplinarity and autonomy help legitimate academic institutional authority; disciplinarity circumscribes that authority while autonomy partly explains it. Thus, Cartesian epistemologies have underpinned academic institutions.

The modern articulation of the image of the mirror of nature subtends two further essential ideas which define universities as characteristically modern institutions, those of history and of the growth of knowledge.

Following the anthropological observations of Max Weber, Jürgen Habermas has argued that the disciplines themselves fall naturally into three epistemic realms correlated with the three-way epistemological distinction between subjects, objects and social relations (Habermas 1981: 48–53). The various kinds of enquiry concerning objects of consciousness together constitute the cognitive realm of the sciences. We also have enquiries into the realm of subjectivity, particularly in relation to expressive activity and aesthetic experience, though our understanding of this affective realm is less secure. And since subjects enjoy social and moral relations, we also have discourse on a normative realm of ethics and law – though we sometimes doubt whether it constitutes knowledge. These three realms articulate the differential structures of the realm of knowledge; and they are intimately related to the basic concepts of the 'mirror' or foundationalist conception of knowledge – for all that, as we will later see, Habermas himself repudiates that conception.

Banal as this three-fold distinction may seem, none the less anthropologists tell us it is not observed within all cultures. Pre-historic tribes may mistake magico-religious *social* rituals for being effective on the *objective* physical world; whilst their accounts of that objective world are governed by *social* convention, rather than by *subjective* personal observation and insight. The distinctions between subjective, objective and social are thoroughly confused for them. It is a significant cultural achievement to separate them. And only in doing so does the 'mirror conception' of knowledge become available.

Further, the conceptualization of history only becomes possible once a social group has grasped these distinctions. In history, *social and individual* change is governed by subjective *personal agency*, yet limited by *objective physical constraints*.

Here we find the social, the subjective and the objective (respectively) intertwined. Thus there can be no history unless one can draw on all three kinds of knowledge – the normative, the affective and the cognitive. We who operate with these distinctions can conceive of ourselves as historic rather than pre-historic, as situated in history. We can call our condition 'modern', on the understanding that in this sense, Plato's Athens was modern too. It is a distinctively modern characteristic to keep the distinction between the cognitive, normative and affective clear and salient. And importantly, cleaving to this distinction makes possible and promotes the acquisition of a sense of history.

The ability to think historically made it possible for the modern mind to conceive of the growth of knowledge. In the seventeenth century, a heightened awareness of disciplinary difference and autonomy laid the foundation for a newly reflexive attitude to knowledge, crystallizing around the end of the eighteenth century. Descartes and the rationalists, Hume and other empiricists had sharpened academic appreciation of the differences between the empirical sciences and mathematics, and between both these and ethics and politics. Locke, Hume and Kant progressed to an internal or reflexive critique of the nature and potential of philosophy itself, and this reflexive understanding came to seem a model for other disciplines. Inasmuch as differences between them were perceived, it seemed worth pursuing a critical understanding of the internal logics of different forms of knowledge and their limits and limitations. This critique constitutes their rationalization. It fosters the growth of knowledge, the reappraisal of ethics and the refinement of taste. Such progress in the realms of the cognitive, normative and affective constitutes cultural progress, which in turn affects social progress. Thus rationalization constitutes cultural modernization and impinges upon social modernization. The agents of rationalization are rational subjects, socially interacting in intellectual discourse.

This is the story Weber tells and which Habermas has taken on and revised; the story of the Enlightenment Project. This project has been an advanced enterprise within the modern era. And if the university is the institution most devoted to reflection on the nature of knowledge and the pursuit of its growth, it must be accounted a paradigm institution of modernization; the heir of Cartesian epistemology and the Enlightenment project, and a motor of modern progress.

But herein lies our true crisis. We have increasing difficulty conceiving knowledge as a mirror of nature. In postmodern quarters, the very distinctions between subjects, objects and social relations seem to be breaking down and Cartesian epistemology totters. Even the prospect of the growth of knowledge now looks sickly. The Enlightenment project has seemingly failed. Now progress may be off the agenda. Let us glance briefly at some of the philosophical reasons for these doubts.

Foundations undermined, rationality deconstructed

In the Enlightenment paradigm. it is the 'sovereign' individual subject operating in solitude, monologically, who attaches words to things, and so can represent them to herself. Thus knowledge becomes possible for her. But then a problem arises; how can knowledge be shared? How can we ensure that we all attach the same words to things, or even pick the same things to attach words to?

In a paradigm shift between the 1930s and the 1960s, a range of philosophers repudiated this problem; from Wittgenstein and Austin, to Gadamer and Heidegger, Saussure and Barthes. In fact, it is not a solitary subject who attaches words to things, but rather a social group who share the same language. Both words and their meanings exist only as social constructs, sustained and occasionally refashioned within rule-governed social intercourse or discourse. Creating relations of representation between words, consciousness and things is an ongoing *social* practice. Learning to talk about the world is learning to play language games – that is, to follow complex sets of rules for sharing words and concepts with others.

In this view, knowledge is necessarily shareable because language is social from the outset. Consequently, representations of the physical, social or mental worlds are also social constructs. They are not images in the mirror of consciousness and are not 'founded' in the natural world. Language is not a reflection of the world in itself.

Nowadays, then, for some philosophers it is communicative interaction within language communities rather than private subjectivity which concerns them. Habermas calls this a shift from a paradigm of consciousness to a paradigm of communication[1] (Habermas 1987; McCarthy 1981). It constitutes a major and irreversible gain in philosophy, dissolving many serious problems within the Cartesian paradigm and opening new perspectives.

But the priority of language games strains Cartesian epistemology. What we academics can learn is determined by the language games we play. But whatever realm of knowledge we are working in, the world does not oblige to us play any particular games rather than others. No language game is 'more true to the world' than another. This freedom calls in question the transhistoric validity of the established disciplines. Concomitantly, as Rorty (1989) suggests, the concept of truth begins to seem not so much empty as only secondarily important, compared with the question of which games to play. And all this undermines the Enlightenment project. The growth of knowledge through refinement and elaboration of established and valid disciplines begins to seem a chimera, and truth no lodestone to any such development.

In continental philosophy, on the other hand, the very concept of the rational subject, the agent of rationalization, has been under attack since Nietzsche, and the paradigm of communication has been implicated in the onslaught. The social dimension has come to seem ontologically prior to the concept of the subject. If it is in discourse that meaning is constituted, and discourse delimits how we can think and what we can know, then the role of the individual and rational subject seems at best marginalized and possibly a delusion. Discourse theorists such as Foucault have argued that the very dynamic of cultural change is located within the autonomous structures of discourses themselves, not within the intentions of individual subjects. Barthes and Foucault have argued that the concept of an agent who originates meaning is superfluous in explaining the meaning of a text (Barthes 1977; Foucault 1977) or the development of knowledge (Foucault 1972). And since Foucault argues that public discourse constitutes and structures our private subjectivity at even the supposedly intimate, bodily and irreducibly personal level of sexuality (Foucault 1979), then the subject seems to be a constructed entity rather than a fundamental given. Furthermore, if rationality is an intentional property of constructed subjects, not of discourses, then rationality itself begins to seem irrelevant to the autonomous development of discourses.

But if the concept of the subject begins to seem otiose, so too must its pair, the concept of the object. For deconstructionists, discourse has no place for either the subject or the object. For them, it came to seem that *'il n'y a pas de "hors texte"'* – that there is nothing outside discourse. But if there is no valid subject/object distinction, then there is no rational agency, and thus no true rationalization; nor therefore genuine Enlightenment nor valid modernization.

Thus contemporary philosophy undermines the self-assurance of the universities in a variety of ways. Post-foundationalism impugns the concept of a discipline, whilst post-structuralism (and deconstructionism) undermines the notion of rationality. Such recent developments in philosophy, in both Anglo-Saxon and continental modes, attack the epistemological bases of both modern rationalization and the growth of knowledge. Therefore they are typically characterized as 'postmodern'.

So we must ask: what would happen to the actual development of knowledge if it came to reflect these philosophical doubts – either consequently or coincidentally? How would we conceptualize its pattern, or lack of pattern? And what would be the salient characteristics of knowledge under those new conditions? The questions are urgent, because postmodern theorists believe that these philosophical innovations are indeed impinging now on the development of knowledge.

A REVOLT OF SUBCULTURES

Small narratives and local discourses

Jean-François Lyotard, in *The Postmodern Condition* (1984), attempts to trace the implications of postmodernism for the contemporary university. First, he points out that knowledge presupposes a set of social and individual competences. And it is a matter of consensus whether some disposition constitutes a genuine competence. For without some such consensus, no products of thought could count as knowledge, since all would be contested. This consensus, says Lyotard, constitutes the culture of a society. It is the relatively unchanging and stable foundation of knowledge.

In traditional societies, he suggests, such consensus is encapsulated in the form of narratives, such as popular stories or myths. They are concerned with what it takes for individuals to fit in as legitimate members of the society, defining criteria of competence for various activities and evaluating examples of action. Narratives gain authority simply from ritual repetition, and the value of the social bond which this repetition reinforces. They define what has the right to be said and done in the culture in question, and since they are themselves a part of that culture, they are legitimated by the simple fact that they do what they do. (Lyotard 1984: 23)

Traditional narratives govern societies not much concerned with the accumulation of knowledge but rather with the maintenance of orthodoxy. But narratives do not have to function this way, and since the Renaissance, says Lyotard, they have not done so. With the rise of science, narratives have taken on some new functions.

Scientists abjure ritual stories for observable facts and testable theories. Consequently, scientific knowledge does not have the ritual social function of narrative. But the rise of science has not obviated the need for narrative. For the validity of science itself is open to question and its place in society requires legitimization. In fact, post-scientific cultures have constructed new narratives whose function is to legitimate science. Thus science and narrative now sit side by side.

Modern narratives emphasize progress. Necessarily they have recourse to very general concepts which transcend a concern with science alone – truth itself, meaning, rationality, objectivity, consensus and so on. In view of their encompassing scope, Lyotard calls them 'Grand Narratives' or meta-narratives. In particular, the Enlightenment project has been underpinned by what Lyotard calls 'the narrative of emancipation' – a Grand Narrative legitimating the growth of knowledge through rationalization.

One purpose of legitimization is to discriminate *degrees* of legitimacy. Consequently, under any Grand Narrative, certain kinds of knowledge become marginalized. But Lyotard suggests that in recent decades, this marginalizing power of Grand Narratives has dramatically weakened. They no longer convince. He defines postmodernism as incredulity toward Grand Narratives.

Lyotard is avowedly vague as to why this has happened. But anyway, Grand Narratives legitimating intellectual critique have succumbed to critique. Repudiations of Cartesian epistemology have eroded the narrative of emancipation by undercutting faith in the growth of knowledge. And recent philosophical developments, as I have argued, have hastened the decline in their academic credibility. Academics now share incredulity toward Grand Narratives.

Our concern here is with the consequences of this incredulity for the conduct of academic life. Michel Foucault described some early episodes in the postmodern counter-revolution against Grand Narratives, and I think we can learn from his account.

In 1976, reviewing a decade of academic activity, Foucault perceived what he called 'an insurrection of subjugated knowledges' (Foucault 1980: 81). 'Subjugated knowledges' refers to two things. First, there is a mass of historical researches that never make it into the canon – interesting but marginal, eccentric perhaps or surplus to intellectual requirements. Second, there are bodies of popular knowledge, but not mere common-sense, which share this marginalized status; in Foucault's words, 'knowledges that have been disqualified as inadequate to their task or insufficiently elaborated: naive knowledges, located low down on the hierarchy' (Foucault 1980:

82). For instance, in the social history of health, he cites the knowledges 'of the psychiatric patient, of the ill person, of the nurse, of the doctor – parallel and marginal as they are to the knowledge of medicine' (Foucault 1980: 82).

These subjugated knowledges share two characteristics; a connection to questions of identity and an historic connection with discursive and interpersonal struggles. The connection of popular knowledge with social identity is obvious. As the knowledge of a particular group, it issues from a particular perspective. Others may understand it; but are unlikely to endorse it. And, says Foucault, it is typically harshly opposed. In his example, members of the medical establishment have the institutionally sanctioned power canonically to define and redefine medical situations, in ways that marginalize the minor knowledges of the inmate, the nurse, and so on. The records of these minor knowledges get forgotten or lost.

It is the same with the first kind of subjugated knowledge. The more peripheral the academic research, the less its apparent relevance to other areas, and the weaker its implications for the discipline, then the less the status of the researcher, and the further she is from seats of patronage and influence. But intellectual development within a discipline is a dynamic process which involves renegotiating the relative importance of familiar ideas. Academic life is essentially one of confrontation, struggle and shifting status and power. The academic rat race is not *wholly* extrinsic to the pursuit of knowledge.

I have just referred to work in the disciplines as 'forms of life'. Forms of life are constellations of practices, purposes, beliefs, dispositions and attitudes, and may be described and partially constituted in correlative discourses. Foucault's work on discourse theory attempts to theorize the description of the discursive products of certain circumscribed forms of life.[2] Arguably, these discursive products (books, reports, documentation of various kinds) are subjugated in their collision with Grand Narrative. They are not exactly jettisoned, but excluded from the canon. Grand Narrative provides little or no legitimacy for them. But in that case, do they have any other legitimacy?

Lyotard proposes the concept of little narratives (*petits recits*) (Lyotard 1984: 60), local narratives which describe the immanent 'logic' of specific forms of life and indicate what counts as progress within them. Little narratives need no validation by meta-narrative. They are their own sufficient justification. Like the narratives of traditional societies, they too 'are legitimated by the simple fact that they do what they do'.

If Lyotard is vague about reasons for the fall of Grand Narrative, he is clearer about the rise of little narratives. He espouses those recent views of the development of science, such as Kuhn's (1962, 1970), which emphasize not systematicity and accumulation of knowledge but rather radical leaps of imagination and disjunctions between old and new bodies of accepted knowledge. Many have abandoned the idea of a stable narrative of scientific development indicating the nature and trend of the growth of knowledge. But this was a core narrative component of the Enlightenment project. So if science can abandon Grand Narrative and survive, why not also those disciplines with even less investment in it?

But inasmuch as little narratives obviate legitimization by Grand Narratives, they are implicated in conflict between marginal and established groups, eccentric and canonic discourses. And inasmuch as they legitimate the practices and discourse of particular milieux, they are implicated in questions of identity. Thus, postmodern scepticism as to Grand Narrative brings to academia two concerns which the traditional academic sought to expunge from her concerns, identity and conflict. Her identity was always a predicament to transcend; conflict was a failure of disinterested rationality. Universities have always been pluralist in respect of disciplines. But we now see emerging a new kind of pluralism based on concepts of self and struggle. How, then, have identities and conflicts actually entered the academic arena? And what are the consequences?

Identities, conflicts and the fragmentation of knowledge

Consider the impact of feminism. In discipline upon discipline, we find ourselves in the midst of refurbishment or rejection of a male canon and scrutiny of methodology for gender bias. Sometimes, the very identity of a discipline itself is critiqued in terms of its place in patriarchy. Feminist scholars are embroiled in intellectual struggles which implicate questions of social identity. Similarly, issues of racial identity and sexual orientation are increasingly institutionalized in academic specialisms. Less obviously, the new enterprise of cultural studies also sometimes aligns itself with the experience and interests of particular social groups, when as so often it concentrates on various forms of popular culture, not just as alternatives to élite high culture but as formations more worthy of intellectual attention. The academic influence of all these developments is broad. Wherever there is an interest in the subjective or practical aspects of an intellectual pursuit, these issues inevitably become involved. And there are few areas now whose subjective and practical aspects still seem unimportant. Thus we even have, for instance, distinctively feminist histories of science. The political impact of these new studies can be profound, epitomized in demands for 'Political Correctness'. The catch is that much that has been accomplished by these new formations just cannot be dismissed. Feminism for example, has enriched the canon of the arts and offered valid critiques of methodology in social science. These are intellectual gains. But they also generate a problem.

This new salience of identities threatens a disintegration of the university community. To criticize academically the discourse and practice of some identity group is typically to mobilize some Grand Narrative. To some, this seems like domination; and Political Correctness is sometimes an attempt to resist it. But it seems that its *social* expression can become a kind of campus apartheid. Student society on some American campuses[3] seems to be splintering into isolated and introverted identity groups, each resistant to external critique. The academy seems to have achieved little in moulding a commitment to an academic community which transcends sectional interests. Postmodernism and Political Correctness seem eventually to undermine traditional academic values of open-mindedness and self-criticism; and even to militate against sharing values.

How do these social developments relate to the new philosophical ideas we looked at earlier? Recently, many philosophers have impugned a general and even transcendental concept of the subject; whilst simultaneously, academic groups such as those concerned with women's, black or gay studies have emphasized their specific identity, in *social* as much as subjective terms. It is not surprising, then, that the latter often find themselves drawn to post-structuralist and deconstructionist theories, which marginalize or repudiate the subject. Furthermore, they often claim for themselves their own distinctive forms of life and language games. And this aligns them with anti-foundationalists in denying that an objective world compels us to play some language games rather than others.

Predictably, then, they often espouse relativism. But relativism is not the *central* issue. Cultural pluralism, in itself, does not *entail* relativism. As Isaiah Berlin has pointed out (Berlin 1990: 10–12), we can recognize that some other cultural group operates with different norms of truth and rationality from our own, without inferring that this makes them incomprehensible to us or beyond our criticism. Arguably, in the postmodern context it is simply pluralism rather than relativism which is responsible for the threat of institutional disintegration. Why should this be?

The prospect of the growth of knowledge is undermined by any conflict between differing intellectual projects if this cannot be resolved by a neutral appeal to Grand Narrative. The loss of Grand Narrative involves a loss of shared aims and standards for evaluating the point and force of any criticism, and making progress accordingly. We may cease to be able to agree whether some response to criticism constitutes growth in knowledge or not. In such circumstances, the pursuit of the growth of knowledge may cease to be co-operative and come to be replaced by separatist enterprises, each pursuing only what counts as the growth of knowledge for them. There arises a plurality of paradigms of the growth of knowledge itself, each embodying different criteria.

But this threatens to stunt growth of *any* kind. In the past, it seemed essential to resolve conflicts between different projects in mutually acceptable terms, thus reconstituting their autonomy. Progress was made that way. For instance, resolution of the war between science and theology fostered the fruitful development of both. But intellectual separatism threatens a sterile stand-off, in which different projects respond only to criticisms generated within their own accepted terms and by their own committed adherents.

The dangers of this situation can be expressed in Kuhnian terms. It promises a proliferation of paradigms of the growth of knowledge, but with no prospect of a dominant paradigm. Where particular paradigms are aligned with particular social identities, and those identities fiercely defended and promoted, any new paradigm would have to be considered just an addition to the repertoire, aligned to some new identity. Thus, there would be no prospect of intellectual revolution through shift of a dominant paradigm.

Yet it is just this position of stasis which Kuhn himself thought characteristic of immature, pre-theoretical sciences. A science begins to progress once it learns to keep assumptions and expectations open to revision and rejection. It must be similar with the growth of knowledge more generally. Growth cannot be guaranteed if any assumptions about knowledge are barred from examination. Thus, even a paradigm of the growth of knowledge must be open to critique. But where there is no prospect of dominant paradigm shift, such critique is simply off the agenda.

So identity-based pluralism threatens much that the university has stood for. Its separatist implications undermine any guarantee of the growth of knowledge. Without commitment to some conception of that growth which transcends their own concerns, subject areas may cease to be fully critical enterprises which guarantee progress. They may cease, in effect, to be disciplines. Academic authority may edge closer to the authoritarianism of dogma. And it ceases to be clear why differing intellectual projects should locate themselves within the same institution. Disputes over intellectual territory and pedagogic propriety may begin to take a largely political form; whilst segments of the university may find their allegiances drawn rather to *external* groups than to mutual *academic* support.

So can the university still find values to bind it together and give it shape and form, whilst facing squarely the collapse of Grand Narrative? Pluralist as it was, though in a different and less dangerous context, the traditional university gained two things from the narratives informing the Enlightenment project: a commitment to resolving or avoiding conflicts between disciplines; and a recognition of the validity of higher-order study of each and every discipline, which secured their healthy openness to external critique. Thus disciplines could see themselves as cognate activities in the same intellectual enterprise, a communal rather than separatist pursuit of the growth of knowledge. Can we reconstitute this commitment under postmodern conditions? I shall look to an analysis of the ideas of truth and rationality to indicate how we might do so.

IDEAL CONSENSUS AND CRITICAL PRACTICE

Some recent writers have queried whether we need the ideas of truth and rationality at all. Habermas and Lyotard offer much the same reply to this. Those who are engaged in a discourse themselves care implicitly whether it is true. As Habermas says, it may be possible to query the notion of truth from the detached perspective of the theoretical observer, but 'From the perspective of the first person, the question of which beliefs are justified is a question of which beliefs are based on good reason' (Habermas 1985: 295).

Nobody doubts that there are real differences in the nature of truth and rationality between economic forecasting, legal advocacy or art criticism. But the goals of truth or validity remain operative within each of them. Relativists typically prevaricate between the perspectives of the first person and of the theoretical observer, claiming in theory what they betray in practice – an indifference to truth and validity. For even they are inclined to talk about their own truth or 'what's valid for them'.

It is arguable, then, that all academics are implicitly involved in the activity of making truth claims or, more generally, validity claims. I suggest that we can use

Habermas' analysis of this activity to identify some implicit common commitments in the academic community.

According to Habermas, whenever we make a statement, we imply that our judgement is capable of carrying a consensus – that any and every rational person who ever has lived or who will live, and who fully examined the validity of what we say would come to agree that we were right.

Now this seems a curious suggestion. This universal consensus is a purely theoretical idea, an unrealizable ideal. And besides, consensus surely has nothing to do with validity or truth in everyday life. People typically disagree about things. And when they do, there is no compulsion to bow to consensus: others may be wrong, and we right. And even where there is consensus, everyone may be wrong. Surely truth is determined by facts or experience, not by consensus?

This objection carries less weight than it might seem. Few now believe that the truth of a judgement lies in its correspondence to facts or experience. To propose that the criterion of truth is 'correspondence to fact' is to suppose that facts can be identified independently of the statements we make about them, then 'held against' our statements to judge their truth. But this is not possible. A fact is not something that can be dumbly pointed at. Words are needed to show what you wish to draw attention to. And 'facts' are nothing to us unless they can be understood; unless they can be compared, interrelated or reasoned from, for instance. All this requires their codification in statements. Therefore we cannot get 'behind' language to some bare and unmediated fact. It follows that facts are not the criteria of true statements. On the contrary, a fact is nothing other than what a true statement states; and the 'correspondence' of true statements with facts is nothing other than their simple identity with each other.

If 'facts' are not an independent guide, then ultimately there is nothing to guide us in seeking knowledge but reasoned argument. Truth and rationality are indissolubly connected. But reasoned argument is an irreducibly social and discursive pursuit. Nobody's opinion on a matter of fact should be dismissed without reasons for doing so. The reasons may be brutally simple, such as 'You weren't there, so you can't know'. But if we have no reasons, then by definition our dismissal of an opinion is irrational. And an irrational position is no adequate basis for judgements of truth.

But suppose there is complete consensus – no adverse opinions to meet; why then should we not take the consensus to be correct? The trouble is that consensus can be irrational. People's opinions may be vitiated by extraneous constraints; the effects of power, either physical or social, or psychological impediments – neurosis or the distortions of ideology. Only a purely rational consensus would be of interest.

Of course, it can be difficult in practice to recognize constraints on rationality or avoid them. But we can tell what a rational consensus would require: in particular, that *everyone* who wished to do so were able to contribute to the discourse; and that *all* new ideas were considered seriously. One could meaningfully aim for such conditions. They are appropriate for the pursuit of truth.

Now imagine something we can never know to exist; a rational consensus between all people living and all the testimony of the dead. Then we ourselves would have no reasons for dissent from it. *Ex hypothesi*, we would in fact be part of the consensus. But in such a case, could everyone still be wrong? It might at first seem so. After all, all judgements are fallible. But fallible is one thing, untrue another. Mere fallibility provides no substantive reason for doubting any particular consensus. In this ideal case, *ex hypothesi* no-one actually has any reason to doubt the consensus view. So we would not just *think* we were right; it would be irrational to doubt it. We would have to say that we *were* right.

This, then, is Habermas' basic thesis about truth claims; that in offering any truth claim, we imply that under ideal conditions, our view would be the consensus view. (Obviously, one can imagine various problems about truth and consensus, which I cannot pursue here. But I think the thesis is robust and can be further defended.) All possible people would agree with us after discussion, if there were no extraneous constraint on them, and nothing to distort their dialogue with us. And this position carries an important implication; that the pursuit of truth is intrinsically communal.

Now, there is no point in entering into a form of life under a little narrative unless to contribute to it in its own terms of rationality and truth. But now we see that this entails an obligation to be open to any potential contributions. Exponents of particular forms of life cannot rationally cut themselves off from external conversation, however critical. The consensus theory of truth does not preclude commitment to specific forms of life; but it does imply that all must be seen as open to critique.

It also implies the possibility of what Habermas calls 'the radicalisation of argument'. If any idea may be added to a discourse, so too any idea may be called in question. It follows that higher-order questions may always be raised within a discourse. Participants in a form of life may always discuss and debate the very nature of the rationality inherent in it. Thus, Habermas' position does not commit us to a universalistic notion of rationality, contrary to his conventional representation.[4] But it does imply that little narratives must themselves be held open to critique.

All this presents us with a very different picture of the postmodern condition. It need not issue in introverted and non-communicating interest groups. Even if knowledge is legitimated by little narratives which relate to identities and are formed in struggle, they cannot be anyone's private intellectual property. They are all necessarily open to discussion. Any exponent of any form of life should welcome openness and community in the academic world, providing only that it controls as far as possible the impositions of external and internal constraints on debate. The world of the Politically Correct academy is no such community.

The Habermasian university would be unfettered by the tyranny of Grand Narratives; but the social specificity and incommensurability of forms of life would be no barrier to their external critique. The social norms of such an institution would not be those of mutually hostile isolationism but those of an open, self-reflective and innovative community, whose members share these values. As Seyla Benhabib has argued (Benhabib 1992: esp. Part II), personal identities themselves could be liberated. They should come to be freely accepted, modified or rejected; not some prison without bars.

Where does this now leave our traditional academic concepts of disciplinarity, autonomy and authority and the prospect of the growth of knowledge?

The constitution of disciplines is put in question. If argumentation is radicalized, any form of life which we currently call a discipline may not actually be one. Some forms of life may need relocation in different disciplines, or removed from the academy altogether. Indeed, the very idea of a discipline must be open to critique. Second, claims to disciplinary autonomy lose their credibility. The growth of knowledge would now be secured rather by a radical opening of disciplines to possibilities of valid mutual critique (compare Midgely (1989) on overspecialization). Thus academic authority can no longer be grounded in disciplinary autonomy; while in the new picture, there is an obligation to take the sectional insights of students such as blacks and women more seriously. Authority now seems to inhere as much in duties to students as in obligations to particular traditions of knowledge.

The crisis we face does not have an epistemological cure. Beating back disturbing views may be legitimate but cannot be relied on, and is anyway itself contentious. The cure must lie with a revived commitment to community and democracy in academic life. The threat to any such resolution comes not from new epistemologies but from pressures which are fracturing the academic community. And the social pressures which are fracturing it from the inside are exacerbated by economic and political pressures from the outside – but that is another story.

NOTES

1 See in particular Habermas 1987, ch. XI and the Introduction by Thomas McCarthy. Also see McCarthy 1981: 91; 'the traditional analysis of the isolated consciousness, its acts and ideas, represented a peculiar abstraction from the intersubjectively valid "grammars" of (ordinary or ideal) languages ... [and] further radicalization of the critique of knowledge calls for reflection on the function of knowledge in the reproduction of social life and of the objective conditions under which the subject of knowledge is historically formed'.

2 The subjugated knowledges of medical and psychiatric practice are amongst those discussed in *The Archaeology of Knowledge* (Foucault 1972).

3 This seems actually not to apply to the most discussed case, that of Stanford and its revised foundation year programme. I am grateful to Professor Denis Phillips of Stanford University for information about the situation there; and more generally for helpful comments on this chapter.

4 It can be argued that some forms of rationality could become socially universalized through democratic discussion, which is a different matter altogether (Blake 1995).

PART V
Conclusion

THIRTEEN

A Knowledge Strategy for Universities

Ronald Barnett

SAFE IN THEIR HANDS?

Is there a knowledge crisis in higher education, after all? Even if there is, the academics are surely competent to sort it out; and doubly so. First, their stock-in-trade is knowledge: that is where, if anywhere, their competence lies. There might be general doubts and confusions about knowledge and understanding, modern society having become epistemologically uncertain in various ways. Even so, the academics, having been appointed for their substantive knowledge in particular areas, can be sure about their epistemological anchorage. They actually know some things and *that* competence is attested by their peer communities.

Second, even if there are substantive uncertainties in the academy and even if these are multiplying, again the academics can be relied on to iron things out. Their communicative processes, their peer review procedures, and their intellectual openness can take care of things. The academics not only know things substantively; they also understand how to engage productively with each other so as to advance our knowledge. Our knowledge and understanding of the world *is* advancing; it does not recede. The journals proliferate; the topics under discussion grow; the technologies of communication widen, the Internet being but the latest medium. This is an expanding universe of knowledge. Disputes there may be but they do not get out of hand.

Academe offers, then, a robust but infinitely flexible communication system or, rather, sets of communication systems. Conversations of a kind do occur. The academics know how to talk to each other. So, substantively and communicatively, the academics can be left to get on with things. Knowledge is safe in their hands; or is it?

However, as the contributors to this book imply, in relation to knowledge, safety is not the issue. The academics might know things and might have evolved procedures for sorting out disputes, and even may have sufficiently adaptable communicative systems which allow the rules of communication to bend and change over time. In that sense, they can be relied on to keep their own house in order. This is a mansion which can grow and grow with new rooms being added on, even if their relationship to the rest of the structure is haphazard. But the contemporary problem of knowledge resembles architecture in another way. Just as it makes sense to ask – in an age of postmodern architecture – 'what is to count as a house?' so we have to ask 'what is to count as knowledge?' The fundamental criteria are themselves in dispute.

The dispute is conducted *sotto voce*, so much so that it hardly appears as a dispute. The crisis, therefore, is far from apparent. War has not yet broken out: it is, at most, a tacit war. Polanyi, after all, spoke of tacit knowledge where we know more than we can tell (Polanyi 1966). Here, we have a war in which the combatants are unaware that they are at war. It may be that we are just witnessing the reconnaissance, even before the skirmishes begin. A war it is shaping up to be, none the less.

MULTIPLE CRISES

The contributions to this book indicate that we are in the presence of multiple crises. Problematic as the distinction is, it may be helpful to classify the crises according to whether they are generated within or externally to the academy.

Within the academy, a crisis could be said to be developing over the purposes, status and criteria of what passes for knowledge. According to many of the contributors to this volume, we are witnessing a loss of confidence in the set of beliefs that have underpinned the university, beliefs which have clustered around ideas of reason, knowledge, progress, universality and enlightenment. In this sense, postmodernism is to be read as a symptom of this disenchantment rather than its cause; and other recent varieties – such as relativism, post-structuralism, radical philosophy of science (as with Feyerabend) and the attack on 'scientism' – are only its progenitors. All of these intellectual movements have been mounted largely within the academy and purport to offer a debunking of academic thought. These are all Trojan horses in the grand style; an assault on the citadel of knowledge from within it.

Postmodernism is merely the latest in this particular line. It is a little local difficulty in a double sense. First, it celebrates the local as against the universal: Lyotard's sense of postmodernism as an incredulity towards meta-narratives is an apt summary. Second, it is local in the sense of being intellectually to hand, so to speak. We are especially aware of it since it is of the moment. To say this is not to reduce its significance; but reminding ourselves that postmodernism is but the latest in a certain line of thought gives it a necessary placing. There are two ironies at work. On the one hand, postmodernism repudiates the universal but has become a kind of universal in itself. On the other hand, postmodernism is part of the reflexivity of modernism: it has not after all shaken off its modernist inheritance.

From outside the academy, three attacks on its intellectual foundations are identified in this volume. First, there is the marketization of higher education. In the UK especially, higher education has been subject to the marketization of the welfare state: literally, it has become subject to market forces, both externally and internally. Modularization creates an internal market as students become customers for courses now marketed as products. In turn, markets in an educational context have epistemological consequences.

Second, in addition to the propositional knowledge produced internally in the academy (Mode 1) has come knowledge-in-use in the wider world (Mode 2) (see Scott in this volume). In the process, the academy is having to adjust its conceptions of knowledge so that courses now include more action-based learning and policy studies. Third, state ideologies bear directly on the academy: the competency-based model of the NCVQ (see Usher in this volume) is but one of a number of state-sponsored conceptions of knowing which challenge the traditional conceptions held in the academy.

Certainly, this dual set of challenges on the knowing projects of the academy – internal and external – are not entirely separate. For example, Lyotard's sense of local languages being understood as forms of performativity is echoed in the NCVQ's notion of competence: in both, what counts is not what a person understands but what she can do. How might such a conjunction be explained? Is there a link between a philosophical account of knowledge in modern society and its practical and policy interpretations? A link can be glimpsed in that, in both texts, there is a repudiation of any overarching sense of what a valid encounter with the world looks like. All we have are our local encounters, and our ways of going on. This conjunction of the pragmatic and the eschewing of a project built around knowing and understanding that we find *both* in postmodernism and in a state-sponsored initiative built around 'competence' cannot be coincidence. And yet, the NCVQ conception of learning has to be understood as a form of strategic modernism: the taking of means to ends, the formation of a national strategy, and the framework itself, with its sense of progression through the 'levels' of competence, are all signs of modernity.

A full teasing out of this relationship between postmodernism and the state-sponsored celebration of 'competence' cannot be undertaken here. At one level, it suggests that Lyotard was right. Performativity is a codeword of the modern age, whether we call it postmodern or not. It stands for the repudiation of a human project, in which through the identification of the rules and the methods of right reason, enlightenment, emancipation and improvement will follow. At another level, the take-up of this 'postmodern' attitude as part of a state-sponsored strategy indicates that the category of the postmodern – if it is at all useful – has to be deployed with considerable circumspection, as others in this volume have shown (for example Soper; Seller).

The knowledge crises that the university faces, therefore, have both links and tensions between them. On the one hand, the university is faced with an opening up of valid forms of knowledge. And nor is this to open the door to 'anything goes' but it is to require of the university that it form a clearer view as to the rules by which participants engaged in enquiry will follow. On the other hand, the discourses available to the university bear unequal weight. The university is faced with discursive hegemony, a matter which Lyotard underplays but which was central to Foucault's offerings (Gordon 1980). Some discourses are saturated with power. And it is hardly surprising, therefore, if significant proportions of the academic 'community' have fallen in with alacrity in furthering the new modes of learning and reflecting the new dominant discourses of competence and skill.

The university is not free to determine the nature of the knowledge projects in which it is engaged. In both teaching and research, and indirectly through new evaluation systems, the knowledge projects are encouraged in the direction of competence in the most general sense. Likely effectiveness in a dual context of a global economy and of a problematic welfare state (Scott 1995) are the order of the day rather than a contribution to human understanding. Knowledge becomes reduced to information; wisdom (a now archaic term) becomes reduced and altered into mere competence.

The internal crises encourage the external crises and give them support. The disavowal of an overarching knowledge project leaves the door open to an outflanking attack on the intellectual life, an outflanking attack by modernism itself. Despite the apparent identity between Lyotard's performativity and a national initiative such as the NCVQ's competence approach, despite their both celebrating performance, the former is undone by the latter. Lyotard's performativity denies discursive supremacy to any of the discourses: competence can here be demonstrated in any local form of life. This competence has no particular home; it is domicile-neutral, so to speak. The NCVQ's competence, on the other hand, is a nice example of discursive hegemony (see Usher in this volume). It is its own version of competence, a competence of operationalism. The terms – competence, operationalism, performativity – seem to apply equally to postmodernism and to the NCVQ; but this is a mirage. It cannot be the case. The one is playful, egalitarian, disavowing general principles; and the other is stern, domineering, hierarchical, and contains its own prescriptions as principles having general application.

The knowledge crises, therefore, of the modern university seem to take in each other's washing. Internal and external crises: they appear almost to be variants of the same discourse. But these are traps for the unwary. Their similarities are more apparent than real.

But if there are fundamental differences here, if we are in the presence of genuinely disparate crises, how is the academy to respond? The argument I want to make is this: that neither sets of conceptions of knowledge and learning offer a constructive way forward. In a situation of unequal power, the generosity of postmodernism in celebrating the local becomes naive. On the other hand, new versions of competence may sound up-to-date but impose technological reason on the academy. A third way is both possible and necessary. It has two elements. The first is that of reworking the university as a genuine forum for debate (see Blake and Myerson in this volume). But this, while necessary, cannot be sufficient. A second element is required, that of the university vigorously engaging with the wider world in providing accounts of the world. Academics, I shall argue, have to become practical epistemologists.

Even faced with postmodernism on the one hand and state-sponsored operationalism on the other, it remains possible to conceive of and to develop practices in the academy which would sustain its role as a forum for debate. Such a role is all the more necessary in the face of the two challenges, those of Postmodernism and of state-sponsored operationalism. Both would render that role – the university as a forum for debate (and, therefore, for critical debate) – impossible. The one would reduce the academy, if it would be honest, to an anarchic babble, without discursive rules; the other would reduce the academy to an instrument of technique and so deny not only the role of the university as a means of sustaining open debate but of reducing, therefore, the possibility for discursive openness in society.

But argument within the academy cannot be sufficient to withstand the *external* knowledge crises which threaten separately both to marginalize the academy and to overrun it (despite the contradictory nature of these claims). Knowing projects in the modern world have to be understood through and through as a form of radical action. The role of the university has, therefore, to incorporate an active dimension: truth claims have to be won, combated or repudiated as a form of societal action.

Before developing that argument, we should do more justice to the knowledge crises, for up to now they have been unduly corralled together under an over-simple postmodernism/operationalism disjuncture.

'THE NEW PRODUCTION OF KNOWLEDGE'

What it is to know has become problematic in the modern world. Michael Gibbons and his associates talk of a shift from Mode 1 to Mode 2 knowledge (Gibbons *et al.* 1994). Mode 1 is the traditional forms of knowledge favoured by the academy, built around propositional knowledge. Mode 2, the new form, is knowledge in use, arising out of and addressed to problems in the world. In essence, this is a shift – to use terms different from Gibbons – from contemplative to operational knowledge.

Coupled with this shift is a shift in power. No longer are the academics in the position of near-monopoly that they have long held (for the past 100 years) in defining what is to count as worthwhile knowledge. Now, industrial corporations, finance houses, consultancies and professional bodies are all involved in quite formal ways in producing knowledge and in defining the key problems.

The two shifts, in the distribution of knowledge and in its definition, go together. In a changing world, corporate life (I use the expression generically) needs to anchor

its practices on a secure base; so knowledge is important. But the formal propositional knowledge produced by the academy and which appears in the journals, often
two years or more after the related research or scholarship, is felt to be inappropriate.
Applied knowledge, knowledge-in-action, professional knowledge based on firm
professional principles, problem-solving, focused inquiry, and action learning: these
ideas, when taken together, indicate at least a shift in our definitions of knowledge.
Even the term 'research' takes on a narrower meaning, to convey a sense of the assembly of data and information relevant to an already defined problem.

Problems are messy in the real world and so the requisite knowledge and human
capacities for solving them are also less straightforward. Interdisciplinary teams, often short-lived, come into play to address particular issues, in which there are practical, policy or resourcing issues. The capacity not just to engage with multiple discourses and modes of interaction but to engage in meaningful and productive dialogue in interdisciplinary teams becomes important, but it is also problematic since
by definition, such teams lack a mutual language and set of shared values and assumptions of the kind on which much research in a traditional university setting is
founded (see McNair in this volume). The messiness is compounded because what
counts is increasingly coloured by what seems to work in the world. And even effects in the world – economic, social, technological – are subject to considerations of
cost, efficiency, political fall-out and organizational impact.

In this epistemological order, definitions of knowledge change from contemplative to more operational and instrumental definitions; but definitions of truth also
change. In the past, the academy has mainly built its truth claims around either a correspondence theory (does this proposition match the state of affairs in the world
which it purports to describe?) or a coherence theory (does this theory seem to carry
meaning in relation to our current understandings of the world?). Now, the underlying theory of truth takes on a pragmatic edge: does this idea inform our practices in
the world? Does this proposed set of practices, systems or technologies actually
work? Is this finding usable? The pragmatic mode of thought works in subtle ways.
It is not just that questions of this kind are increasingly raised, such that findings,
ideas and intellectual products are assessed, are considered valid, only insofar as they
come up to muster on pragmatic considerations. It is a much more circular state of
affairs in which relevant issues for inquiry are set by emerging problems in the
world, in which the techniques and strategies are geared towards the presenting
problems, and in which the validity criteria of the findings are those of effectiveness,
which is itself subject to ideological, political and organizational presuppositions.

It will be said that there is no crisis here. All this is just the idea of applied
knowledge with which the academy has been familiar for some time. But the notion
of applied knowledge cannot begin to address the changes at work which are at issue
here. Applied knowledge retains the sense of knowledge which is produced and validated in traditional ways in the academy, albeit with an orientation to the wider
world. It is knowledge-in-application. What is being posited here, however, is the
idea that knowledge is now being produced in the wider world and validated in the
wider world according to criteria of the wider world. Notions of action learning, re-

flective practice, knowing and knowledge-in-use reflect this widening sense of what is to count as knowledge. These notions speak to a sense that genuine knowledge can be and is created in practice. This is an echo of the Greek idea of practical wisdom; that a genuine hold on the world is possible not just through the creation of theoretical ideas which are then exerted on the world but can also be obtained through engaging with the world.

Things are messier than a simple addition of knowing-how to knowing-that, however. As the academy comes to be more of an actor in the world rather than just analysing and commenting on it, hybrid forms of knowledge and understanding are to be found both in the academy and in the world of action. In the academy, we see the proliferation of fields, such as transport studies, business studies, management studies, tourism studies, and accountancy, which are neither disciplines (or even collections of disciplines) nor are they pure forms of knowing-how. These, I would term *problem nets*. They are clusterings of inquiry and reflection which are engaged with a loosely defined territory of action and issues in the world and which seek to offer a way of corralling a messy area of practice and imparting principles of action.

Problem nets betoken an organized effort to net a number of like activities in the world and to identify the problems that those activities are posing. In turn, the resources that might be harnessed to offer solutions to those problems are varied: they may include concepts and theories from the disciplines (and many disciplines might be called upon) but they are also likely to include prescriptions informed by practice deemed to be good, judgements of value and effectiveness as well as of efficiency and economy, and the capacity to see issues and problems in the widest perspective.

THE MARKETING OF KNOWLEDGE

Higher education in the UK has departed from the European model in that, in the British shift to a mass system, the market has come into play. It is a matter of educational policy at both national and institutional levels; and we are seeing, through policy moves at both levels, the generation of markets which are both external to universities and are internal within universities. The modularization of UK higher education is the key instance here, being a carrier of all four kinds of marketization (which the combination of national/institutional and external/internal produces). For example, in modularization, we are witnessing a *national* attempt to create *internal* markets within individual universities; and we are also seeing institutional attempts to generate more of an *external* market for a university's teaching services.

In the marketization of higher education, what counts as knowing changes. There are epistemological qualities to these systemic changes. Markets bring about a transformation in the realization of knowledge. They do so because the pedagogical relationship necessarily changes. The pedagogical exchange in a market situation is that of supplier to consumer; and the pedagogical transaction becomes one of consumption. Both terms – supplier and consumer – are significant.

Suppliers do not have to be producers; they can obtain their knowledge goods from elsewhere (using information technology software created elsewhere, for instance; or even teach modules designed on a national basis over which the individual has had little or no input). Knowledge is coming, therefore, to be pre-packaged, the opportunities for knowledge creation in the context of the pedagogical situation being severely reduced. *Consumers*, in turn, receive – for a price which they, as students, increasingly meet themselves – the knowledge goods. The goods are inert; there is no transformation on the part of the consumer: what counts is whether the goods are of reliable quality, are of relatively uniform character, and meet prescribed quality standards. The sources of validity lie outside the consumer. Consumers do not feel that they have a responsibility for the quality and character of the services and goods that are supplied.

The marketization of higher education, then, has epistemological consequences. With knowledge products and services now becoming economic activities, two things happen. First, an economic relationship is a non-tuistic relationship (Downie 1990). That is, the supplier does not take into account the particular interests of the consumer. There may be a generalized taking into account of the interests of the consumer as one of a number of potential consumers: course leaders become sensitive to (anonymous) student feedback and to the market situation of their course. But the supplier of goods and services in an economic relationship feels no duty to take into account the particular position of the consumer.

Second, with knowledge goods and services having become commodities, exchanged for a price, it is the commodities that move in this pedagogical relationship (from supplier to consumer). The consumer, especially in a unitized modular programme, is not fundamentally transformed but, instead, rakes up the credits for each unit which are then banked. Commodification means inertness: personal transformation is precluded. The student no longer gives of herself but expects that the commodity will already be of high quality; its assimilation can then safely be banked. In this economy, credits are given for safe banking, not for daring reinvention on the part of the student.

Third, in this educational economy, what counts as knowledge changes. Knowledge is reduced to mere information (Hague 1991; Edgley 1989). Being understood as mere information, knowledge becomes inert. As a result, deriving efficiency savings through national course design and deliverables becomes a logical option. There are certain things to be known: very well. Let us identify them, package them as well as we can, and so ensure that students in the total system have access to high quality products. This produces a further knowledge crisis in higher education, even if it is unnoticed.

The Western university has been developed around an epistemology of openness. This marketization produces closure at two levels. First, there is a closure at the level of knowledge itself. The openendedness and contestability of knowledge, both its knowledge claims and more importantly, the frameworks in which those claims are secured, tend to close. Frameworks are not up for scrutiny in a market situation. Second, there is a closure of mind. The notion of understanding drops out of the lexicon to be replaced by notions of competence and mastery over knowledge 'content'. This epistemology converts the learner into a recipient rather than one who engages actively, developing her interpretations of her epistemological encounters.

Markets are sites of power. In an open pedagogical encounter, where what counts as knowledge and students' realization of it are both genuinely open, unequal power is reduced. The student, indeed, is offered power over the framing of her educational experience. In this market situation, by contrast, the power of the producer and the supplier over the consumer are reinforced. This, of course, is a paradox since the rhetoric of the marketization of higher education is precisely that it gives power to the consumer. Nothing could be further from the truth for this is a managed market. But, in the closure of knowledge that it heralds, we are also seeing the power of the academics themselves reduced to mere suppliers of educational products produced by others.

INCLUSION OR TRANSFER?

What counts as knowledge is undergoing subtle changes. Crisis may be too bold a term in the sense that individuals are not by and large holding their heads in angst over the epistemological foundations for their work, whether professional or academic. Epistemologies are social in character, as Gellner insisted (1991); and being social, they will shift over time. Academics take on new epistemological identities. Nevertheless, as the contributors to this volume have indicated, the current age is perhaps especially challenging. There are more runners in the epistemological stakes and they seem to be going in different directions.

It is not just that our definitions of knowledge are moving from the largely contemplative to encompass the more operational, from knowing that things are the case to knowing how to do things. If that were all that was at stake, far from a sense of crisis, an appropriate response would be much more one of relief that we were becoming more tolerant epistemologically. We may not have reached the position of 'anything goes' to which Feyerabend aspired (1978); but at least much more goes, so to speak. However, the issue *is* both more complicated and more serious than this.

The key issue is one of inclusion or substitution: are our views about legitimate ways in which we can get a hold on the world shifting from one kind to another, quite different, kind; or are they widening to embrace the alternative forms? Is knowledge as a form of theorizing about the world giving way wholesale to knowledge as a form of intervention in the world or is the former being supplemented by the latter? If we are in the presence of substitution rather than inclusion, then we *can* justifiably talk of a crisis. That would be tantamount to a fundamental shift in the ways in which we construe the world and in the criteria which inform what we take to be legitimate claims about the world.

It will be said that things are neither one thing nor the other; that for two thousand years, Western culture has lived with this tension between contemplative and interventionist orientations to the world. That is so, but the issue in front of us, in an age of globalization, of new levels of economic competitiveness, of instantaneous change (aided by information technology), and of systemic social and environmental change much of which is brought about unwittingly but as a result of human knowledge and technologies, is whether we are not now seeing a new and arguably distorted configuration of our efforts to know the world. Here-and-now action suddenly takes on a new priority: if we do not act now, events will overtake us, others will have passed us by, and our wider environment will be out of rational control.

We can, therefore, justifiably talk of a crisis arising out of a new ordering of our epistemological priorities. It is not that we are giving up in any absolute sense a serious wish to understand the world disinterestedly. But it is that that wish is now accompanied by more performative claims on the world; and it is somewhat displaced as a result. The crisis goes further for, in a fast-moving world, where one just has to keep up with the game, performance is becoming severed from understanding. Science always had – at least, since its modern development in the Enlightenment – an instrumental quality. Not far beneath the disinterested inquiry lay 'a knowledge-constitutive interest' in prediction and control (Habermas 1968). But there were protocols which ensured that the wish to know the world remained immune, to some degree, from its underpinning interests. Now, the boot is on the other foot. An interest in intervening in the world takes priority and, therefore, knowledge of a contemplative kind only comes into play where it appears necessary to support action.

It will be said that all this is exaggeration. We are in the presence only of tendencies, not yet of wholesale changes. The tendencies, though, have powerful backers in the state and in the economy; and they reach deeply into higher education itself. The National Council for Vocational Qualifications, with its insistence on competences seen as performance in pre-defined settings; the endorsement given by the Enterprise in Higher Education initiative to 'transferable skills'; the encouragement given by the government to the creation of a national credit accumulation and transfer system together with modularization: all these shift what counts as higher education.

To say all this is not to express nostalgia for a golden age; still less to hanker after a time when we knew what the idea of higher education amounted to. In the modern age – whether one of late modernity or of postmodernism – there cannot be a single essence of higher education of any straightforward kind. Mass higher education repudiates any such simplifications. But it may be that the knowledge crises facing higher education can and should prompt thinking about what we might term the 'knowledge constitution' of higher education in the current age.

A KNOWLEDGE STRATEGY FOR HIGHER EDUCATION

I suggested earlier that there are two elements in working out a new knowledge constitution for the modern university, one procedural hinging on communication within the academy; the other practical, looking to the university to engage with the wider world in its knowing activities. Both are necessary and both have to be pursued together. Simply attaining a genuine (Habermasian) forum for debate within the university would still leave the dominant epistemological voices in place in the wider society. But equally, engaging with those dominant voices in the wider society without subjecting them to the critical dialogue of the academic forum is liable to lead to academics becoming dupes of technological reason. A knowledge strategy for the university has to be pursued, therefore, both internally and externally simultaneously. Despite the obvious difficulties, I shall develop this argument by attending separately to its two components.

Talking it through

There are two messages coming through this volume. First, the world is inherently unknowable in the sense that there are *no* supreme frameworks for yielding a firm grip on the world. Second, there are forces at work which threaten to *reduce* the knowability of the world, even if there are also forces which offer the promise of expanding our understanding of it. The first is an epistemological undermining of the knowledge project of higher education and is the internal one of postmodernism. The second is a social undermining of that knowledge project, and is the external one of state intervention, of marketization and of the rise of performativity. The strategy, the possibility of a coherent response to these knowledge crises that emerges in the final section of the volume, is one which takes seriously the notion of the university as a forum for dialogue.

This strategy is to recapture and to do justice anew to the idea of the university as a *universitas*. By a universitas is meant not – as is sometimes assumed – a site of universal knowledge (although that was John Newman's strategy in his *Idea of the University*) but a collectivity in which all its members were equal (Cameron 1978). In that sense, it was a universal gathering: none of the voices present were excluded. Such a strategy, I want to suggest, offers necessary conceptual and practical resources to address both the epistemological and the social underminings identified in this volume; but they are not sufficient. And even in itself, as an internal strategy over which the academics are supposedly in control, it is fraught with difficulty.

First, the university has become an organization, with its own hierarchy of power, its declared mission identity (to which its members are supposedly signed up), and its bureaucratic modes of control. Constructing a Habermasian 'ideal speech situation' in *this* situation is not a serious option. However, perhaps something approximating to a democratic speech situation can be obtained by creating discursive spaces within the university. Genuinely critical and communicative reason can still find a place within the university. It is not just a set of closed discourses.

Second, the university is a site of epistemological contest among the academics. Are the contending voices even willing to listen to each other, to give way, let alone to engage collaboratively and to welcome other forms of knowing and to allow them a genuine hearing?

The university as an open forum for debate has, therefore, to be constructed; and nor can its absence be put solely or even mainly at the door of external forces. Sheer hard effort lies ahead, therefore, in constructing the university as a genuine forum for debate. Some of that effort will be theoretical, working out the meta-rules of this epistemological game. But most of it will be severely practical, in which the contending parties come together or are brought together in a non-threatening space and offered a genuine hearing. Even the managers do not have to define their roles purely in terms of instrumental reason: they can work to widen discursive modalities and opportunities within their university. But creating such discursive space is only a start, not an end-point.

Practical epistemology

The problem is that our knowing activities – however theoretical they may be – are practical activities, taking place in the world. And those taking place in formal institutions such as universities are subject to the dominant, albeit emerging, epistemologies of the age. Action-based knowing is overtaken by the ideology of performativity. In the process, the potential for inclusion is being undermined. Exclusionary forces are at work (see Usher in this volume). Certainly, we have to become more *theoretically* adept by working at – if not working through – the contesting knowing frameworks which are proliferating. This calls, I have been contending, for universities to institutionalize the idea of a genuine forum for critical and creative debate (see Myerson and Blake in this volume). But we also have to be practically adept.

Practical adeptness poses challenges to the academic life. Despite their origins in the élite professions and the development of higher education as professional education, the idea of the modern academic as a professional engaging with and in society has not taken root (except, perhaps, in the USA). The available models of the modern intellectual – such as Gramsci's organic intellectual or Mannheim's utopian intellectual, supposedly enjoying an independent vantage point – are inadequate models for the modern age, an age in which higher education has become incorporated into the projects of the wider society if not the state. In a situation in which the role of the academic, the nature of academic work, epistemologies, research and scholarly activities, educational practices and technologies and pedagogical transactions are all subject to influences not under academic control, being an academic is partly preconstructed. That there remain very real differences in the way the academic role is performed is testimony, however, to the very real epistemological and practical space in which the role can be interpreted.

For the modern academic, knowing the world becomes an achievement but doubly so. It is an epistemological achievement: it requires of us that we formulate our criteria for knowing the world and that we secure assent for our knowledge claims. But it is a practical achievement too. Our knowing about the world ultimately has to be won in the world, the world having to give its assent. What counts as knowledge has to be validated by the wider society (see McNair in this volume).

In a world in which everyone is a knower, academics can only secure a legitimacy by fully engaging with the world and by demonstrating their capacity to handle multiple knowing activities as such. Knowing has now to be seen as action, as engagement but also as meta-knowing. Even if the ivory tower ever was once a suitable metaphor for academic life, now, in a world of distributed knowledge (see McNair), the university has to secure anew its legitimacy as a special site of knowing, of knowing about knowing. It does this through integrating the three epistemological elements of openness, responsiveness and action in the world. It does not so much test out knowledge but test out the validity and practicality of knowledge frameworks. Academics' new competence has to lie in knowledge discourse as such *and* their deployment in the world.

In the end, the problem is one of engagement: given the knowledge crises, both intellectual and practical, how are academics to engage with the world? 'The world', of course, has to include both epistemological frameworks and the political, economic and social institutions. Knowledge crises present challenges and opportunities. But just how should the university engage with the wider world such that it becomes an independent player in the epistemological stakes of modern society and in such ways that it is likely to be effective? There can be no general answer.

As the wider society engages in its own knowing activities, producing both new sites and new definitions of knowledge, institutions wishing to live up to the title of university have to engage with these definitions or resign themselves to becoming mere recipients and reproducers of others' definitions. Such a truncation of the role would deprive the university of its historic role as an independent player. The implication is that academics have to become *practical epistemologists*. This injunction bites deeply. There can be no escape. Academics have to engage both internally within and externally outwith the academy in securing legitimacy for their knowledge projects.

Public controversies are often, at bottom, contests over readings of a situation; over knowledge frameworks. And the knowledge frameworks are sustained by differential sources of power. So the task, as I put it, of being a practical epistemologist has a political dimension. Public enlightenment calls for political adroitness. Securing one's professional identity in the domain of knowledge and understanding in the modern age calls for active engagement and intervention if the knowledge crises identified in this book are to be confronted and displaced. The academic life today has to be that of the practical epistemologist: knowing the world can no longer be conducted internally within the academy.

CONCLUSION

The knowledge crises are real but they can be deflected by the university reconceiving its knowledge role. The challenges of the local (proferred by postmodernism), of performativity (promoted by the State), of the ubiquitous creation of knowledge (produced by globalization) and of manufactured uncertainty (caused by the radical reflexivity of knowledge in a world which understands itself in evermore sophisticated ways): all of these can only be countered by the universities, and their academics, certainly by recalling their heritage as sites of openendedness and critical reason but also by situating themselves anew in the wider world. Academics rest their legitimacy on their knowing capacities. But now, those capacities have to be continually reasserted, secured and legitimated in and by the wider world. Academics are epistemologists; but the modern world requires that they be practical epistemologists.

Select Bibliography

(This Bibliography contains all the works cited in the text and notes, together with a small number of other key works.)

Abbs, P. (1994) *The Educational Imperative: A Defence of Socratic and Aesthetic Learning*. London: Falmer Press.

Andrews, R. (1995) *Teaching and Learning Argument*. London: Cassell.

Appleyard ,B. *Understanding the Present: Science and the Sole of Modern Man*. London: Picador.

Arendt, H. (1961) *Between Past and Future*. London: Faber and Faber.

Ashworth, P. (1992) 'Being competent and having "competencies"', *Journal of Further and Higher Education* **14** 3–25.

Atkins, P. (1992) Will science ever fail? *New Scientist*, 8 August, p. 32.

Atkins, P. (1995) *The Limitless Power of Science in Nature's Imagination*, ed. John Cornwell, Oxford: Oxford University Press.

Austin, J. L. (1962) *How to do things with Words*. Oxford: Clarendon Press.

Ayer, A. J. (1936) *Language, Truth and Logic*. London: Victor Gollancz.

Ball, S. (1992) *Politics and Policy Making in Education*. London: Routledge.

Barnett, R. (1990) *The Idea of Higher Education*. Buckingham: SRHE/Open University Press.

Barnett, R. (ed.) (1992) *Learning to Effect*. Buckingham: Open University Press.

Barnett, R. (1994) *Limits of Competence*. Buckingham: SRHE/Open University Press.

Barthes, R. (1977) 'The death of the author' in *Image, Music, Text*, trans Stephen Heath, London.

Battersby, C. (1989) *Gender and Genius: Towards a Feminist Ethics*. London: The Women's Press.

Beck, U. (1992) *Risk Society: Towards a New Modernity*. London: Sage.

Benhabib, S. (1992) *Situating the Self*. Oxford/Cambridge.

Berlin, I. (1990) *The Crooked Timber of Mankind*. London.

Billig, M. (1990) 'Rhetoric of social psychology', in I. Parker and J. Shotter (eds.) *Deconstructing Social Psychology*. London: Routledge.

Blake, Nigel (1995) 'The democracy we need: situation, post-foundationalism and enlightenment', *Journal of Philosophy of Education* **29** (2).

Bocock, J. and Scott, P. (1995) *Redrawing the Boundaries: Further/Higher Education Partnerships*. Leeds: Centre for Policy Studies in Education, University of Leeds.

Burbules, N. C. (1995) 'Reasonable doubt: towards a postmodern defence of reason as an educational aim', in Kohli (1995).

Cameron, J. M. (1978) *On the Idea of a University*. Toronto: University of Toronto Press.

Caraveli, A. 1986. 'The Bitter Wounding: The lament as social protest in rural Greece' in J. Dubisch (ed.) *Gender and Power in Rural Greece* Princeton: Princeton University Press.

Carr, W. (1995a) *For Education: towards critical educational inquiry*. Buckingham: Open University Press.

Carr, W. (1995b) 'Education and democracy: confronting the postmodernist challenge', *Journal of Philosophy of Education* **29** (1) 75–91.

Christian, B. (1993) *The Women's Review of Books* **X** (6).

Code, L. (1988) 'Experience, knowledge and responsibility', in Griffiths and Whitford, (1988) pp. 187–204.

Connor, S. (1993) 'The Necessity of Value', in J. Squires (ed.) *Principled Positions*. Lawrence and Wishart.

Daly, M. (1984) *Pure Lust*. London: The Women's Press.

Department for Education and Employment (1995) *Lifetime Learning*. London: DFEE.

Derrida, J. (1974/1986), *Glass* trans J. P. Leavey and R. Rand, Lincoln: University of Nebraska Press.

Derrida, J. (1976) *Of Grammatology*. Baltimore: Johns Hopkins University Press.

Derrida, J. (1980/1992) 'Mochlos; or the conflict of the faculties', trans R. Rand and A. Wygant in *Logomachia: The Conflict of the Faculties*, R. Rand (ed.) Lincoln: University of Nebraska Press, pp. 1–34. (Paper delivered at Columbia University in April 1980).

Derrida, J. (1983) 'The principle of reason: the university in the eyes of its pupils', trans C. Porter and E. P. Morris, *Diacritics* **13** (3) pp. 3–20.

Derrida, J. (1992) *The Other Heading: Reflections on Today's Europe*, trans P.-A. Brault and M. B. Naas, Bloomington: Indiana University Press.

Derrida, J. (1994) 'The deconstruction of actuality', *Radical Philosophy* **68** Autumn.

Dewey, J. (1916) *Democracy and Education*. New York: Free Press.

Downie, R. S. (1990) 'Professions and professionalism', *Journal of the Philosophy of Education* **24** (2) 147–60.

Ecclestone, K. (1994) 'Democratic values and purposes: The overlooked challenge of competence', *Educational Studies*, **20** (2) 155–166.

Edwards, R. and Usher, R. (1994) 'Disciplining the subject: The power of competence', *Studies in the Education of Adults* **26** (1) 1–14.

Edwards, R. (1993) 'A wail of a time: The sirens of "progressivism" in the education and training of adults', Centre of Youth and Adult Studies Occasional Papers, Milton Keynes: Open University.

Edwards, R. (1996) 'Troubled times? Personal identity, distance education and open learning', *Open Learning* forthcoming.

European Commission (1995) *Teaching and Learning: Towards a Learning Society*.

Featherstone, M. (1995) *Undoing Culture: Globalisation, Postmodernism and Identity*. London: Sage.

Feyerabend, P. (1978) *Against Method*. London: Verso.

Ford, H. (1923) *My Life and Work.* London: Heinemann.

Foucault, M. (1972) *Archaeology of Knowledge*, trans A. M. Sheridan Smith, London.

Foucault, M. (1977) 'What is an author?' in *Language, Counter-Memory, Practice*, Donald F. Bouchard (ed.), Cornell University Press.

Foucault, M. (1979) *History of Sexuality, Vol.1*, trans Robert Hurley, London: Allen Lane.

Foucault, M. (1980) *Power/Knowledge.* C. Gordon (ed.), trans Gordon, Matchall, Mepham and Soper, Sussex.

Galbraith, J. K. (1992), 'The university: reflections over the years', *Academe* **78** (5) 10–12.

Geertz, C. (1983) *Local Knowledge.* New York: Basic Books.

Gellner, E. (1991) *Plough, Sword and Book: The Structure of Human Hisstory.* London: Paladin.

Gellner, E. (1992) *Postmodernism, Reason and Religion.* London: Routledge.

Gellner, E. 91995) 'Anything goes', *Times Literary Supplement* 16 June, p. 8.

Gibbons, M., Limoges, C., Nowotny, H., Schwartzman, S., Scott, P. and Trow, M. (1994) *The New Production of Knowledge: The Dynamics of Science and Research in Contemporary Societies.* London: Sage.

Giddens, A. (1990) *The Consequences of Modernity.* Cambridge: Polity Press.

Gilligan, C. (1982) *In a Different Voice.* Cambridge, MA: Harvard University Press.

Gordon, C. (ed.) (1980) *Michel Foucault: Power/ Knowledge.* Hemel Hempstead.

Gray, J. (1996) 'If the Fez Fits' *Guardian* 8 January.

Greene, M. (1995) 'What counts as philosophy of education?' in Kohli (1995).

Greger, S. (1985) 'Village on the plateau', Ph.D. Thesis University of Manchester. Publ. 1988 Brewin Books.

Greger, S. (1991) 'Woman:Man::Peasant:Central Administration' unpublished paper.

Griffiths, M. (1995) *The Web of Identity: Feminisms and the Self.* London: Routledge.

Griffiths, M. and Whitford, M. (1988) *Feminist Perspectives in Philosophy.* Bloomington: Indiana University Press.

Habermas, J. (1978) *Knowledge and Human Interests.* London: Heinemann.

Habermas, J. (1981) *The Theory of Communicative Action, Vol.1, Reason and the Rationalization of Society.* Oxford/Cambridge.

Habermas, J. (1985) *'Questions and Counter-Questions', Habermas and Modernity*, R. J. Bernstein (ed.) Oxford/Cambridge,

Habermas, J. (1987) *The Philosophical Discourse of Modernity*, MIT and Oxford/Cambridge.

Habermas, J. (1992) *Postmetaphysical Thinking*, translated by W. M. Hohengarten, Cambridge: Polity Press.

Hague, D. (1991) *Beyond Universities: A New Republic of the Intellect.* London: IEA.

Hampden Turner, C. and Trompenaars, F. (1993) *The Seven Cultures of Capitalism: Value Items for Creating Wealth.* New York: Doubleday.

Harvey, D. (1992) *The Condition of Postmodernity.* Oxford: Blackwell.

Havel, V. (1987) *Living in Truth*, London: Faber and Faber.

Hesse, H. (1943) *The Glass Bead Game*. Publ. in English by Penguin (1978).

Hirschmann, N. (1992) *Rethinking Obligation*. Cornell University Press.

Hofstede, G. (1994) *Cultures and Organisations*. London: Harper Collins.

Huxley, A. (1994) *Brave New World*. London: Flamingo.

Hyland, T. (1993) 'Professional development and competence-based education', *Educational Studies* **19** 123–132.

Hyland, T. (1994) *Competence, Education and NVQs*. London: Cassell.

Jameson, F. (1990) *Late Marxism: Adorno, or the Persistence of the Dialectic*. London: Verso

Jenkins, D. (1995) *Trust 16*. SCM Press.

Jessup, G. (1991) *Outcomes: NVQs and the Emerging Model of Education*. London: Falmer Press.

Jones, L. and Moore, R. (1993) 'Education, competence and the control of expertise', *British Journal of the Sociology of Education* **14** (4) 385–397.

Kenway, J. with Bigum, C. and Fitzclarence, L. (1993) 'Marketing education in the postmodern age', *Journal of Educational Policy* **8** (2) 105–122.

Kohli, W. (ed.) (1995) *Critical Conversations in Philosophy of Education*. London and New York: Routledge.

Kuhn, T. S. (1970) 'Logic of discovery or psychology of research?' in *Criticism and the Gro of Knowledge*, I. Lakatos and A. Musgrave (eds.) Cambridge: Cambridge University Press.

Kuhn, T. S. (1970) *The Structure of Scientific Revolutions*. Chicago: University of Chicago Press.

Langer, S. K. (1963) *Philosophy in a New Key*. Cambridge MA: Harvard University Press.

Lash (1990) *Sociology of Postmodernism*. London: Routledge.

Lennon, K. and Whitford, M. (1994) *Knowing the Difference*. London: Routledge.

Lovibond, S. (1989) 'Feminism and postmodernism', *New Left Review* **178** 5–28.

Lyon, D. (1994) *Postmodernity*. Buckingham: Open University Press.

Lyotard, J.-F. (1984) *The Postmodern Condition*. Manchester: Manchester University Press.

McCarthy, T. (1981) *The Critical Theory of Jurgen Habermas*. London and MIT.

McNair, S. (1994) *An Adult Higher Education: A vision*. Leicester: NIACE.

Midgley, M. (1989) *Wisdom, Information and Wonder*. London.

Midgley, M. (1992) *Science as Salvation – A Modern Myth and its Meaning*. London: Routledge.

Musil, R. (1995) *A Man Without Qualities*. London: Picador.

Myerson, G. (1994), *Rhetoric, Reason and Society*. London: Sage.

Myerson, G. (1995) 'Hypothetical dialogue and intellectual history', *History of the Human Sciences* **8** (4) 1–17.

Newman, J. H. (1976) *The Idea of a University*. I. T. Kerr (ed.) Oxford: Oxford University Pres

Norris, C. (1994) *Truth and the Ethics of Criticism*. Manchester: Manchester University Press.

Norris, N. (1991) 'The trouble with competence', *Cambridge Journal of Education* **21** (3) 331–341.

Nowotny, H. (1994) *Time: The Modern and Postmodern Experience*. Cambridge: Polity Press.

Nussbaum, M. (1992) 'Human functioning and social justice: In defence of Aristotelian essentialism', *Political Theory* **20** (2).

OECD (1994) *Jobs Study*. Paris: OECD.

Office of Science and Technology (1995a) *Forward Look of Government-funded Science, Engineering and Technology*. London: HMSO.

Office of Science and Technology (1995b) *Leisure and Learning*. Report of the Technology Foresight exercise. London: HMSO.

Parsons, T. and Platt, G. (1973) *The American University*. Cambridge MA: Harvard University Press.

Plant, S. (1995) 'Crash course', *Wired*, March, 44–47.

Polanyi, M. (1966) *The Tacit Dimension*. New York: Doubleday.

Pole, D. (1958) *Philosophy of the Later Wittgenstein*.

Postman, N. (1985) *Amusing Ourselves to Death*. New York: Viking.

Proceedings of the National Institute of Science of India (1950) **17** 564.

Putnam, H. (1981) *Reason, Truth and History*. Cambridge: Cambridge University Press.

Putnam, H. (1990) *Realism with a Human Face*. J. Conant (ed.) Cambridge MA: Harvard University Press, pp. 108–33.

Putnam, H. (1992) 'Irrealism and deconstructions', in *Renewing Philosophy*. Cambridge MA: Harvard University Press.

Rawls, J. (forthcoming) 'The idea of public reason: further considerations'.

Rawls, J. (1993) *Political Liberalism*. New York: Columbia University Press.

Reich, R. B. (1993) *The Work of Nations: a blueprint for the future*. London: Simon & Schuster.

Robbins, Lord (1963) *Higher Education: Report of the Committee*. London: HMSO Cmnd 2154.

Rorty, R. (1980) *Philosophy and the Mirror of Nature*. Princeton: Princeton University Press/Oxford: Basil Blackwell.

Rorty, R. (1989) *Contingency, Irony and Solidarity*. Cambridge: Cambridge University Press.

Rose, N. (1991) *Governing the Soul*. London: Routledge.

Rosen, L. (1984) *Bargaining for Reality*. Chicago: University of Chicago Press.

Ryle, M. (1994) 'Long live literature? Englit, radical criticism and cultural studies', *Radical Philosophy* **67**.

Samuel, R. (1994) *Theatres of Memory*. London: Verso.

Schama, S. (1995) *Landscape and Memory*. London: Harper Collins.

Scott, P. (1995) *The Meanings of Mass Higher Education*. Buckingham: SRHE/Open University Press.

Scruton, R. (1990) *The Philosopher on Dover Beach*. Manchester: Carcanet.

Scruton, R. (1979) 'Freud, Marx and meaning', in *TheAesthetics of Architecture*. London: Methuen.

Senge, P. (1994) *The Fifth Discipline: the Art and the Practice of the Learning Organisation*. New York: Doubleday.

Siegel, H. (1995) '"Radical" pedagogy requires conservative epistemology', *Journal of Philosophy of Education* **29** (1) 33–46.

Skinner, B. F. (1973) *Beyond Freedom and Dignity*. Harmondsworth: Penguin.

Soper, K. (1990) 'Feminism, humanism and postmodernism', *Radical Philosophy* **55** 11–17.

Soper, K. (1993) 'Postmodernism, subjectivity and the question of value', in J. Squires (ed.) *Principled Positions: Postmodernism and the Rediscovery of Value*. London: Lawrence and Wishart.

Sorell, T. (1991) *Scientism, Philosophy and the Infatuation with Science*. London: Routledge.

Spivak, G. (1991) 'Remembering the limits: difference, identity and practice', in P. Osborne (ed.) *Socialism and the Limits of Liberalism*. London: Verso.

Squires, J. (ed.) (1993) *Principled Positions: Postmodernism and Rediscovery of Value*. London: Lawrence and Wishart.

Steiner, G. (1989) *Real Presences*. London: Faber.

Taylor, C. (1989) *Sources of the Self*. Cambridge: Cambridge University Press.

Thompson, E. (1993) *Witness Against the Beast: William Blake and the Moral Law*. Cambridge: Cambridge University Press.

Trollope, A. *Barchester Towers*, ch. XIX.

Turner, V. W. (1969) *The Ritual Process: Structure and Antistructure*. London: Routledge and Kegan Paul.

Usher, R. and Edwards, R. (1994) *Postmodernism and Education: Different Voices, Different Worlds*. London: Routledge.

Williams, G. and Fry, H. (1994) *Longer Term Prospects for British Higher Education: A Report for the CVCP*. London: London Institute of Education.

Index of names

Index of subjects